Understanding SPELLING

Anne Seaton

First published 2002 by **Learners Publishing Pte Ltd**
222 Tagore Lane, #03-01 TG Building, Singapore 787603

Reprinted 2003 (twice), 2004

Email: learnpub@learners.com.sg
Visit our website: http://www.learners.com.sg

ISBN 981 4107 11 5

Printed by B & Jo Enterprise Pte Ltd, Singapore

Associate Companies

RIC Learners International Limited
P.O. Box 332
Greenwood
Western Australia 6924

RIC Publications Limited (Asia)
5th floor, Gotanda Mikado Building
2-5-8 Hiratsuka
Shinagawa-ku Tokyo
JAPAN 142-0051
Tel: 03 3788 9201
Fax: 03 3788 9202
Email: elt@ricpublications.com
Website: www.ricpublications.com

Learners Educational Publishing Sdn Bhd
43A, Jalan 34/154, Taman Delima
56000 Cheras, Kuala Lumpur, Malaysia
Tel: 603-9100-1868
Fax: 603-9102-4730
Email: enquiry@learners.com.my

CONTENTS

Introduction

English spelling has a bad reputation, deservedly. It appears unruly. There seem to be too many ways of spelling a particular sound, and too many sounds attached to a particular spelling. As for the rules, they are complicated, and you no sooner learn one than you are presented with numerous exceptions.

The main problem with English is that it has evolved from a variety of rather incompatible linguistic sources, and embedded in it are, accordingly, an uncomfortable mixture of spelling conventions, which nobody has so far been brave enough to rationalize.

Nevertheless, there are patterns to notice, and it is the purpose of this book to bring out what rationality and predictability there is in English spelling by investigating it from a number of points of view.

Attention is first given to the range of sounds represented by individual letters and combinations of letters, followed by a note on some special spelling quirks.

Then come rules for adding grammatical word endings, with useful lists of words that behave in the same way. Vocabulary-building sections follow, designed on the same principle, demonstrating, for example, the spelling issues that are involved in adding endings such as **-able**, **-ize**, and **-ful**, and beginnings such as **in-** and **un-**.

Some of the mystery of English spelling lies in the foreign elements imported, mainly from Latin and Greek, as compounding forms. A list of common and less common components is given, along with an explanation of their meanings.

British-English spelling is treated as the norm in this book, but American variations are given throughout, and there is also a special section on American spelling. This is important, because even in areas where British English spelling is preferred, American spelling is often regarded as acceptable for scientific and technical purposes.

The letter **l** behaves differently from the other consonants, and a special section is devoted to it. The punctuation-oriented topics of abbreviations, apostrophes and hyphens also each have a section to themselves.

There is a comprehensive list of words that cause spelling problems, without which no spelling book would be complete. This is followed by a list of words that tend to get confused, with an analysis of their distinctions in use and meaning.

Finally, Do-it-Yourself spelling exercises are given at the end of each section. These help the user to revise the spelling points just outlined, and provide an enjoyable challenge.

It is hoped that this book, with its practical approach, will divest English spelling of some of its terrors, and be informative and diverting to use.

Anne Seaton
Edinburgh, 2001

PRONUNCIATION SCHEME
used in this book

CONSONANTS

phonetic	sound
p	p
t	t
k	k
b	b
d	d
g	g
m	m
n	n
ŋ	ng
θ	th unvoiced
ð	th voiced
f	f
v	v
s	s
z	z, or voiced s
ʃ	sh
ʒ	s as in plea**s**ure
tʃ	ch as in ar**ch**
dʒ	j or soft g as in **judge**
h	h
l	l
r	r
j	consonant y as in **y**et
w	w

VOWELS

phonetic	sound
SHORT VOWELS	
ɪ	i as in h**i**t
e	e as in b**e**d
a	a a as in h**a**t
ʌ	as in h**u**t
ɒ	o as in h**o**t
ʊ	u as in p**u**t or b**oo**k
ə	schwa as in **a**live, ac**re**
i	final y as in dirt**y**
LONG VOWELS	
iː	long e as in h**ea**t
ɑː	long a as in h**ar**m
ɔː	o as in f**a**ll, br**oa**d
uː	long u as in r**u**de, f**oo**d
ɜː	long schwa as in b**ir**d
DIPHTHONGS	
eɪ	long a as in h**a**te
aɪ	long i as in b**i**te
ɔɪ	oy as in b**oy**, p**oi**nt
aʊ	ow as in s**ow**, b**ou**t
oʊ	long o as in r**oa**d, n**o**te
ɪə	as in r**ea**l, p**ee**r
eə	as in **air**, p**ear**, sh**are**
ʊə	as in s**ure**, p**oor**

1 THE ALPHABET and ITS SOUNDS

Of the 26 letters in the English alphabet five are **vowels** and the rest are **consonants**.

VOWELS

The five vowels are:

a ***e*** ***i*** ***o*** ***u***

a, **o** and **u** are called the **broad vowels**.
e and **i** are called the **narrow vowels**.

The honorary vowel y

As well as the vowels shown above, the letter **y** is often used as a vowel. It counts as a narrow vowel and is sometimes long and sometimes short.

y has the long sound /aɪ/, for example in these words:

by	*cry*	*cycle*	*fly*	*my*	*shy*
sky	*sly*	*spy*	*try*	*why*	

y has the short sound /i/ in these words:

baby	*bicycle*	*carry*	*city*	*easy*	*lady*
lazy	*party*	*silly*	*story*	*teddy*	

This brings us to the subject of **short vowels** and **long vowels**

Short Vowels

A

short *a* /a/

a is short in the following words:

ant	*cat*	*hand*	*hat*	*man*
map	*pad*	*pal*	*tram*	*van*

E

short *e* /e/

e is short in the following words:

bed	*bell*	*hen*	*mess*	*nest*
net	*pen*	*pet*	*step*	*web*

But you can also get the sound /e/ with **ea**, for example in the following words:

bread	*dead*	*deaf*
head	*spread*	*sweat*

and with **ei** and **ie** in these words:

friend *heifer* *leisure*

and exceptionally with **a** in these words:

any *many*

I

short *i* /ɪ/

i is short in the following words:

bib	*fish*	*fist*	*hill*	*kilt*
lid	*milk*	*pig*	*pin*	*pip*

but you also get the sound /ɪ/ with **y** and **ui**, for example in the following words:

build	*hymn*	*guillotine*
guilt	*pyramid*	*tyranny*

and exceptionally with **u**, **e**, **ie** and **o** in these words:

busy *English* *sieve* *women*

But many unstressed syllables have the sound /ɪ/, for example the final syllables of these words:

foreign *masculine* *message* *mountain*

and the first syllable of these words:

enormous *enough*

O

short *o* /ɒ/

o is short in the following words:

box	*cot*	*dog*	*frog*	*knot*
lock	*log*	*mop*	*pond*	*pot*

but you also get the sound /ɒ/ with **a**, for example in many words beginning with **qu** and **w**:

quantity	*quarrel*	*wad*	*want*
was	*wash*	*wasp*	*watch*
watt	*what*	*yacht*	

and with **ou** in:

cough

U

short *u* /ʌ/

u is short with the sound /ʌ/ in the following words:

bug	*bun*	*bus*	*cup*	*duck*
mud	*nut*	*plum*	*sum*	*sun*

but you also get the sound /ʌ/ with **o**, **oo**, and **ou** in the following words:

come	*does*	*done*	*son*	*tongue*	*won*	*wonder*
blood	*flood*					
couple	*courage*	*rough*	*trouble*	*young*		

> **Handy Hints**
>
> **u** is often short with the sound /jʊ/ when in an unstressed position, as in:
>
> *adulation* *annual*
> *argument* *communism*
> *educate* *executor*
> *formula* *immunize*
> *regular* *reputation*
> *singular* *valuation*

short u /ʊ/

u is short with the sound /ʊ/ in the following words:

bull *bush* *cushion* *full*
pudding *pull* *push* *put*

But you can also get the sound /ʊ/ with **oo**, for example in the following words:

book *cook* *foot* *good*
hood *look* *wood* *wool*

and with **ou** in the following words:

could *would* *should*

schwa /ə/

It is important to mention that when vowels are unstressed, they lose their distinctive sound and they all sound rather the same. The sound they make is called an **obscure vowel**, or a **schwa**, and is represented by the sign /ə/. You get it, for example, in the final syllable of all these words:

acre *anger* *battle* *devil* *failure*
fortunate *maiden* *martyr* *mission* *nation*
neighbour *opera* *pressure* *tartan* *thorough*

and in the first syllable of these words:

above *alive* *anatomy* *observe* *oppose*

Long Vowels

A

a has two different long sounds.

long *a* /eɪ/

a is long with the sound /eɪ/ in the following words:

cage *cake* *cave* *crazy* *face*
gate *lake* *lane* *page* *plate*

but you can also get the sound /eɪ/ with **ai**, **ay** and sometimes with **ae**:

jail *pail* *rain* *rail* *straight* *train*
day *hay* *pay* *play*
Gaelic

and with **ea**, **ei**, and **ey** in the following words:

break *great* *steak*
eight *feign* *neighbour* *reign* *vein*
prey *they*

long *a* /ɑː/

a is long with the sound /ɑː/ in the following words:

can't *castle* *dance* *graph* *grass*
mask *pass* *past* *path* *plant*

but you also get the sound /ɑː/ with **ar**, for example in the following words:

bark *card* *cart* *farm* *garden*
mark *park* *partner* *tart* *yard*

and with **al** in these words:

half *calf* *calm* *palm*

and with **au** in these words:

aunt *laugh*

and with **ear** in:

heart *hearth*

and with **er** in:

clerk *sergeant*

E long *e* /iː/

e is long with the sound /iː/ in the following words:

cede *equal* *eve* *gene* *obese*
scheme *scene* *these*

Handy Hints

- When **r** follows long ***a*** or any of the vowels with the sound /eɪ/, you get the sound /eə/, as in:

  fare *pair* *aerial*
  prayer *pear* *their*

- And you get this sound also in:

  there *where*

> ## *Handy Hints*
>
> - When **r** follows long **e** or any of the vowels that have the sound /iː/, you get the sound /ɪə/, as in:
>
>   *appear* *fierce*
>   *here* *souvenir*
>   *weird*
>
> - The **ei** in **either** and **neither** can be pronounced /iː/ or /aɪ/.

but you also get the sound /iː/ with **ee**, **ea**, **ie**, **ei** and **ey**, for example in these words:

bee	*feet*	*see*	*sheep*	*tree*
bead	*leave*	*peace*	*seat*	*eat*
believe	*chief*	*field*	*siege*	*thief*
caffeine	*either*	*neither*	*protein*	*seize*
key				

and with **ae** and **oe** in these words:

aegis *aeon* *amoeba* *phoenix*

and with **i**, for example in the following words:

concertina *police* *tangerine*

and with **eo** in:

people

> ## *Handy Hints*
>
> - When **r** follows long **i**, or a vowel with the sound /aɪ/, you get the sound /aɪə/, as in:
>
>   *dire* *fire*
>   *hire* *spire*
>   *wire*
>   *byre* *lyre*
>
>   and you get the same sound in:
>
>   *buyer*
>   *choir* (/kwaɪə/)
>   *crier*
>   *higher*
>
> - The **ei** in **either** and **neither** can be pronounced /iː/ or /aɪ/.

I

long *i* /aɪ/

i is long with the sound /aɪ/ in the following words:

dice	*dive*	*hide*	*kite*	*mice*
nine	*pipe*	*ride*	*while*	*wife*

but you also get the sound /aɪ/ with **ie**, **y** and **igh**, for example in these words:

die	*lie*	*pie*	*tie*	
buy	*cry*	*fly*	*sky*	*spy*
fight	*high*	*light*	*might*	*sight*

and with **ei** in:

either *height* *neither*

O

long *o* /oʊ/

o is long with the sound /oʊ/ in the following words:

bone	*code*	*hole*	*home*
joke	*mole*	*no*	*nose*
note	*open*	*piano*	*rope*

but you also get the sound /oʊ/ with **ao**, **oe** and **ow**, for example in the following words:

boat	*coat*	*goat*	*road*	*toast*
doe	*foe*	*hoe*	*toe*	*woe*
bowl	*crow*	*mow*	*row*	

and with **ou** in these words:

dough *shoulder* *soul* *though*

and with **oo** in:

brooch

and with **ol** in:

folk *yolk*

and with **au** in:

mauve

and with **eau** in:

gateau

U

Long **u** has two different sounds.

long *u* /uː/

u is long with the sound /uː/ in the following words:

chute *flute* *plume* *rude* *rule*

but you also get the sound /uː/ with **oo**, **o**, **ew**, **ue**, **ui** and **ou**, for example in the following words:

boot	*cool*	*moon*	*pool*	*room*	*stool*
move	*prove*	*to*	*who*	*whose*	
blew	*chew*	*crew*	*drew*	*flew*	*grew*
blue	*clue*	*glue*	*true*		
fruit	*suit*	*suitable*			
group	*route*	*soup*	*through*	*youth*	*you*

Handy Hints

- When **r** follows long **u**, or a vowel with the sound /uː/, you get the sound /ʊə/ or /jʊə/, as in:

  cure during lure
  pure sure
  moor poor
  amour dour tour

  and you get the same sound in:

  fewer newer pursuer

- Many speakers of American English say the following words with the sound /uː/ rather than /juː/:

  tune, tube, dew, knew, new, newt, stew, due

long *u* /juː/

u, **ew** and **ue** often have the sound /juː/, for example in the following words:

cute huge tube tune use
dew ewe few knew new stew
argue cue due hue pursue rescue
statue value

Other Long Vowel Sounds

or has the sound /ɔː/, for example in the following words:

afford border born cork for
morning order sport sword thorn

But you also get the sound /ɔː/ with **oa** and **oar** in these words:

abroad broad board hoard oar roar

and with **ou** and **our** in these words:

bought sought wrought
court four pour your

and with **oor** in:

door floor

and with **a** (usually when followed by **l**), **au** and **aw**, for example in these words:

all ball call fall hall
tall paltry small walnut walk
water caught flaunt haughty taught
dawn lawn fawn pawn spawn

and with **ar**, especially after **qu** and **w**:

quarter quartz war ward warm warp

oy and **oi** have the sound /ɔɪ/, for example in the following words:

boy buoy enjoy joy oyster ploy
boil coin join noise point spoil

ow and **ou** can have the sound /aʊ/, for example in the following words:

brow	*cow*	*now*	*owl*
power	*sow*	*towel*	*vowel*
house	*loud*	*mountain*	*mouse*
ounce	*plough*	*sound*	*shout*

er usually has the sound/ɜː/, for example in the following words:

berth	*concern*	*fern*	*germ*	*herd*
nerve	*sterling*	*stern*	*term*	*verse*

but you also get the sound /ɜː/ with **ir**, **or** and **ur**, for example in the following words:

bird	*birth*	*dirty*	*girl*			
shirt	*swirl*	*twirl*	*whirl*			
word	*work*	*world*	*worm*	*worse*	*worth*	
burn	*curd*	*curl*	*hurl*	*hurt*	*spurn*	*turn*

and with **ear** and **our** in the following words:

earn	*learn*	*yearn*
courteous	*courtesy*	*journey*

Handy Hint

When **r** follows **ou**, you get the sound /aʊə/, as in:

flour *hour*
our *sour*

and you get the same sound in:

cower *power* *shower*

CONSONANTS

The other letters in the alphabet are called **consonants**. They are**:**

b c d f g h j k l
m n p q r s t v w
x y z

Some Consonantal Quirks

B /b/

b is sometimes silent, for example in:

bomb *debt* *doubt* *plumber*

and is sometimes followed by a 'silent' **u** before another vowel with no change to its sound, for example in:

buoy *build* *buy*

C

c has two sounds: /k/ or /s/

hard *c*

c has the hard sound /k/ before **a**, **o** or **u**, before another consonant, and at the end of a word:

cat	*cot*	*cut*	*scatter*	*focal*
class	*clone*	*club*	*crab*	*cry*
act	*duct*	*fact*	*sect*	*strict*
attic	*comic*	*lilac*	*magic*	*panic*

You can't hear it when it comes before another **c**, or a **k**, or a **q**, as in the following words:

account *acquire* *back*

and **c** is silent in:

indictment

soft *c*

c has the soft sound /s/ before **e**, **i** or **y**, for example in:

centre *space*
acid *city* *exciting*
cylinder

but you can't hear it if it follows an **s** before **e**, **i**, or **y**:

scent *fascinate* *scythe*

You sometimes get a hard **c** followed by a soft **c** /ks/, for example in:

accelerate *accent* *accept* *flaccid*

F /f/

f has the sound /v/ in:

of

You get the sound /f/ with **ph**, for example in the following words:

graph *photo* *physical*

and sometimes with **gh**, for example in:

cough *enough* *rough* *tough*

G

g has two sounds: /g/ or /dʒ/

hard *g*

g has the hard sound /g/ before **a**, **o** and **u**, before another consonant, and at the end of a word:

big *gas* *glide* *got*
green *gun* *leg* *magnet*

g is sometimes followed by a 'silent' **u** before another vowel, with no change to its sound, for example in:

guard *guarantee* *guest* *guide*
guillotine *guilt* *guy* *vague*

g is silent in:

deign *gnash* *gnat* *gnaw*
gnome *reign* *resign* *sign*

soft *g*

g often has the soft sound /dʒ/ before an **e**, **i** or **y**:

gem *germ* *giant* *giraffe* *gymnasium*

but **g** sometimes has the hard sound /g/ before **e** and **i**, for example in:

gear *geese* *get* *gift* *girl* *give*

H /h/

h is sometimes silent, for example in:

heir *heiress* *honest* *honour* *hour*

wh has the sound /h/ in:

who *whom* *whose*

J /dʒ/

You get the sound /dʒ/ with several letters or combinations apart from **j** itself, for example, **g**, **dg**, **gg**, **di**, **du**, in the following words:

age *gentle* *edge* *exaggerate* *soldier* *gradual*

K /k/

k is silent before **n**, for example in:

knack knee kneel knife knight
knit knob knock knot know

You quite often get the sound /k/ with **ch**, for example in the following words:

character charisma chasm chemist
chlorine choir chorus Christian
chronicle monarch school stomach

L /l/

l is sometimes silent, for example in the following words:

balm calm calf could folk half
palm qualm should talk walk would yolk

l is written immediately after a consonant in words like *battle* and *trouble*, though there is actually the vowel sound /ə/ before the **l**. Here are more examples:

bauble cackle chronicle example fiddle
giggle little muscle people trickle

N /n/

n is silent in:

column solemn

P /p/

p is silent in:

pneumatic pneumonia

Q

q is usually followed by **u**.
qu usually has the sound /kw/, for example in the following words:

quack queen question quick
quiet quirk quiz request

but has the sound /k/ in:

cheque *lacquer* *liquor*

R /r/

In British English, **r** is inclined to affect the sound of any vowel that it follows, and to be swallowed up by it, so that it is difficult to hear. The sounds you get with vowels that combine with a following **r** are dealt with in the vowels section above.

In British English, when **r** follows a vowel in an unstressed final syllable, you can only hear it if another vowel follows it. For example, the **r** at the end of **whether** can only be heard in a phrase like *whether or not.*

In British English, **r** is written immediately after a consonant in words like *centre* and *metre*. In these words, **re** has the vowel sound /ə/. Here are more examples:

calibre fibre *litre* *sabre* *theatre*

S

s has four sounds: /s/, /z/, /ʒ/ and /ʃ/

- **s** has the sound /z/ when forming plurals or the third person singular, except after an unvoiced consonant such as **f**, **k**, **p** or **t**. For example, final **s** has the sound /z/ in:

battles *cases* *clouds* *dogs* *feels* *flushes*
goes *has* *pieces* *runs* *skies* *was*

but the sound /s/ in:

books *carpets* *cats* *gossips*
makes *reaps* *visits* *works*

s often has the sound /z/ in the middle or at the end of a word; only a dictionary can help you with this. Some examples are:

advertise	*as*	*cheese*	*cosy*	*easy*
misery	*nasal*	*phase*	*scissors*	*wise*

- **s** followed by **i** or **u** often has the sound /ʒ/, for example in:

allusion	*confusion*	*decision*
derision	*illusion*	*vision*
casual	*leisure*	*pleasure*
treasure	*usual*	*visual*

- **s** and **ss** sometimes have the sound /ʃ/, for example in the following words:

pension *pressure* *session* *sugar* *sure*

T /t/

t is sometimes silent, for example in:

castle *fasten* *listen* *mustn't* *often* *soften*

W /w/

You get the sound /w/ in some words that have no **w**, for example:

choir /kwaɪə/ *once* /wʌns/ *one* /wʌn/ *quite*/kwaɪt/

w is silent in:

sword /sɔːd/

X /ks/

x has the sound /kʃ/ in:

luxury *luxurious*

Z /z/

z has the sound /ʒ/ in:

azure *seizure*

Some Double Consonants

ch /tʃ/

As well as with **ch** itself, you get the sound /tʃ/ with **tu**, **ti** and **te**, for example in:

adventure *eventually* *future* *habitual*
ritual *virtuous* *question* *righteous*

You get the sound /tʃ/ with **c** in some Italian words:

cello *vermicelli*

gh

gh has the sound /g/ in:

aghast *ghastly* *ghetto* *ghost*

but has the sound /f/ in:

cough *enough* *rough* *tough*

and is often silent, for example in:

bought *dough* *eight* *fight* *fought* *height*
high *light* *naughty* *night* *ought* *plough*

ph /f/

ph always has the sound /f/ (for example in *photo*, *phrase*, *physics*), except in words that are really compounds, such as:

Clapham /ˈklaphəm/ *shepherd* /ˈʃephəd/ *(= sheep - herd)*

sh /ʃ/

As well as with **sh** itself, you get the sound /ʃ/ with **ch**, for example in:

chivalry *chute* *machine*

and with **ci** and **ce,** for example in:

coercion *gracious* *special* *species* *ocean*

and with **s** in:

sugar *sure*

and with **si** and **ssi** and **ssu**, for example in:

aversion *pension* *tension* *aggression*
mission *passion* *pressure* *session*

and with **sci** in:

conscience *fascist*

and with **ti** in:

attention *condition* *creation*
nation *pretentious* *rational*

th

th has two sounds /θ/ or /ð/. You need a dictionary to tell you which words have which sound.
You get the unvoiced sound /θ/ for example in:

path *thanks* *theatre* *thick* *thief*
thin *think* *thirsty* *thorn* *thought*
thread *three* *thumb* *thunder*

You get the voiced sound /ð/ for example in:

another *other* *that* *the* *then*
there *these* *this* *those* *whether*

ng /ŋ/ or /ŋg/

You sometimes get the sound /g/ after /ŋ/, for example in:

anger *finger* *longer* *single* *strangle*

But there is no following /g/ sound for example in:

banger *hanger* *singer*

n has the sound /ŋ/ before a **k**, for example in:

bank *blink* *drink* *frank* *stunk* *think*

2 ENGLISH SPELLING DEVICES

The purpose of many of the spelling devices used in English is simply to make the previous vowel short or long.

There are two main principles:

- The silent **e** makes a short vowel long:

cub	*cube*	*man*	*mane*	*sit*	*site*
fat	*fate*	*pin*	*pine*	*wag*	*wage*
hug	*huge*	*pop*	*pope*	*wok*	*woke*

- A doubled consonant keeps a vowel short:

bog	*boggy*	*run*	*running*
fat	*fatter*	*wet*	*wettest*

But there are several other points to notice:

- **f**, **l**, **s** and **z** are doubled at the end of most one-syllable words with a single, usually short, vowel:

staff	*stiff*	*stuff*	*off*	*cliff*	*cuff*	*huff*	
fall	*fell*	*fill*	*full*	*doll*	*dull*		
wall	*well*	*all*	*spell*	*tell*	*tall*		
lass	*pass*	*cross*	*miss*	*boss*	*loss*	*fuss*	*less*
buzz	*fizz*	*fuzz*	*jazz*				

Handy Hint

But there are some words with a silent **e** that have short vowel, for example:

the verb ***come*** /kʌm/
the verb ***give*** /gɪv/
the past participle ***gone*** /gɒn/
the verb ***have*** /hav/
the verb ***live*** /lɪv/
the verb and noun ***love*** /lʌv/
the pronoun or determiner ***some*** /sʌm/

Handy Hints

- There are some exceptions to this, for example:

if	*of*	*chef*	*clef*
gel	*nil*	*pal*	*bus*
gas	*this*	*is*	*was*
quiz			

- The vowel is long in the following words:

staff	*all*	*fall*	*wall*
tall	*pass*		

Did You Know?

*One-syllable, short-vowel words that end in **k** only, are usually of foreign origin, for example :*

flak trek yak

Did You Know?

*Words where initial **k** is followed by **a**, **o** or **u** are usually of foreign origin, or, in the case of scientific terms, derived from Greek:*

kaiser	*kaleidoscope*
kamikaze	*kangaroo*
karate	*karaoke*
koala	*kookaburra*
kosher	*kowtow*

- Things to notice about **k**:

ck performs the duty of a doubled consonant at the end of one-syllable words with a short vowel:

clock	*stick*	*stuck*	*stock*
deck	*dock*	*duck*	*kick*
mock	*muck*	*peck*	*pick*
pack	*knock*	*back*	*black*
sack	*sick*	*sock*	*suck*

c is not needed before **k** where another consonant comes after a single vowel:

milk	*silk*	*talk*	*walk*
bank	*blink*	*thank*	*think*
desk	*husk*	*risk*	

k is used without **c** at the end of one-syllable words with a double vowel:

beak	*leak*	*speak*	*steak*
creek	*meek*	*peek*	*reek*
cloak	*oak*	*soak*	
book	*hook*	*look*	*nook*

The vowel following initial **k** is commonly **e** or **i**:

keen	*keep*	*key*	*kettle*	*kernel*
kick	*kill*	*kind*	*king*	*kiss*

- **t** is used before **ch** to keep a short vowel short:

batch	*bitch*	*blotch*	*catch*	*clutch*
ditch	*Dutch*	*fetch*	*hatch*	*hitch*
itch	*latch*	*match*	*patch*	*pitch*
scratch	*sketch*	*snatch*	*switch*	*thatch*
witch	*watch*	*wretch*	*wretched*	*kitchen*

But a few short-vowel words end in **ch** without **t**:

attach	*bachelor*	*detach*	*duchess*	*much*
ostrich	*rich*	*sandwich*	*spinach*	*such*

After a double vowel, you don't need **t** before **ch**:

beach	*bleach*	*breach*	*each*
peach	*preach*	*reach*	*teach*
breech	*leech*	*screech*	*speech*
broach	*coach*	*poach*	*roach*
brooch	*mooch*	*smooch*	
couch	*pouch*	*touch*	*vouch*

- **d** is used before a soft **g** (with the sound /dʒ/) to keep a short vowel short:

badge	*bridge*	*cadge*	*dodge*	*dredge*
drudge	*edge*	*fidget*	*fledge*	*fridge*
fudge	*gadget*	*hedge*	*judge*	*ledge*
lodge	*midge*	*midget*	*nudge*	*pledge*
ridge	*sedge*	*sledge*	*sludge*	*smudge*
stodge	*trudge*	*wedge*	*wodge*	

But a few short-vowel, soft-**g** words are spelt without **d** before **g**:

allege	*frigid*	*privilege*	*rigid*	*tragedy*

You don't need **d** before **g** after a long vowel or a double vowel:

cage	*doge*	*huge*	*page*
rage	*sage*	*stage*	*gauge*
stooge	*gouge*	*rouge*	
deluge	*oblige*	*refuge*	

- You always get a silent **e** after **s** or **z** at the end of a word:

amuse	*because*	*cause*	*cheese*	*choose*
confuse	*course*	*dose*	*ease*	*else*
exercise	*expanse*	*false*	*goose*	*grease*
horse	*hose*	*house*	*immense*	*lapse*
loose	*mouse*	*nose*	*nurse*	*phase*
pause	*please*	*praise*	*rouse*	*sense*
surprise	*tease*	*verse*	*wise*	*worse*

blaze	*bronze*	*craze*	*doze*	*gaze*
idolize	*prize*	*realize*	*seize*	*size*
sneeze				

Handy Hint

Two exceptions are:

treble *triple*

■ Short-vowel words that end in **le** need a doubled consonant before **le**, to keep the vowel short:

apple *battle* *bottle* *bubble*
cattle *cuddle* *dazzle* *fiddle*
giggle *hassle* *kettle* *little*
meddle *middle* *muddle* *nibble*
piffle *puddle* *rubble* *ruffle*
saddle *sizzle* *struggle* *supple*
tattle *tussle* *waffle* *wriggle*

After a long vowel, or a double vowel, you only need a single consonant before **le**:

beetle *bible* *bridle* *bugle* *cable*
couple *cradle* *cycle* *doodle* *double*
eagle *feeble* *foible* *ladle* *needle*
noble *noodle* *people* *rifle* *scruple*
stable *stifle* *table* *title* *trifle*
trouble

But there are some exceptions, for example:

counterfeit *either*
neither *protein*
seize *seizure*
weird

■ **ie** and **ei**

When the sound is /iː/, **i** comes before **e**, except after **c**:

believe *brief* *chief* *field* *grief*
niece *piece* *relief* *shield* *siege*
thief *yield*

After **c**, when the sound is /iː/, you get **e** before **i**:

ceiling *conceit* *conceive* *deceit*
deceive *perceive* *receive* *receipt*

Handy Hints

- An exception is: *sieve*, which is pronounced /sɪv/
- The **ei** in ***either*** and ***neither*** can be pronounced /iː/ or /aɪ/.

When the sound is not /iː/, **e** always comes before **i**:

deign *eight* *either* *feign* *feint*
foreign *forfeit* *freight* *height* *inveigh*
leisure *neighbour* *neigh* *neither* *reign*
rein *reindeer* *sleight* *vein* *weigh*
weight

3 GRAMMATICAL WORD ENDINGS THAT AFFECT SPELLING

The *-ing* Form: the Present Participle or Verbal Noun

The regular way of forming the present participle or verbal noun is just to add -**ing** to the base form of the verb.

break	*breaking*	*buy*	*buying*
deny	*denying*	*despair*	*despairing*
fish	*fishing*	*grasp*	*grasping*
occupy	*occupying*	*play*	*playing*
regress	*regressing*	*sing*	*singing*
ski	*skiing*	*spell*	*spelling*
spoil	*spoiling*	*survey*	*surveying*
toy	*toying*	*walk*	*walking*

But verbs with one syllable, containing one short vowel, and ending with one consonant, have to double the final consonant before -**ing**, to keep the vowel short.

gas	*gassing*	*pat*	*patting*
step	*stepping*	*stop*	*stopping*
stun	*stunning*	*trek*	*trekking*
trim	*trimming*	*trip*	*tripping*

Handy Hint

If you are using **bus** as a verb, the **-ing** form can be **busing** or **bussing**.

Handy Hint

In American English the spellings **kidnapping** and **kidnaping** are both possible.

If a verb has two or more syllables and the last one has one short vowel and ends with one consonant, and is stressed (even if this is not the main stress) the final consonant is doubled.

admit	*admitting*	*equip*	*equipping*
forget	*forgetting*	*format*	*formatting*
handicap	*handicapping*	*incur*	*incurring*
kidnap	*kidnapping*	*nonplus*	*nonplussing*
program	*programming*	*rebut*	*rebutting*
refer	*referring*	*zigzag*	*zigzagging*

Handy Hint

An exception is:

worship *worshipping*

In American English **worshiping** is possible.

But if there is no stress on the final syllable, the final consonant is not doubled.

budget	*budgeting*	*edit*	*editing*
enter	*entering*	*focus*	*focusing*
gallop	*galloping*	*garden*	*gardening*
gossip	*gossiping*	*offer*	*offering*
pardon	*pardoning*	*target*	*targeting*

Handy Hints

- An exception is:
  paralleling
- In American English the **l** is not usually doubled in an unstressed syllable:
  dial *dialing*
  equal *equaling*
  libel *libeling*
  travel *traveling*
- In British English the spelling **install** and **instal** are both possible.

But notice that if the final consonant is **l**, it always doubles after a single vowel, no matter where the stress comes.

cancel	*cancelling*	*control*	*controlling*
dial	*dialling*	*equal*	*equalling*
fulfil	*fulfilling*	*instal/install*	*installing*
libel	*libelling*	*marvel*	*marvelling*
pedal	*pedalling*	*pencil*	*pencilling*
rebel	*rebelling*	*repel*	*repelling*
rival	*rivalling*	*signal*	*signalling*
travel	*travelling*	*tunnel*	*tunnelling*

You don't double the final consonant after a double vowel.

avoid	*avoiding*	*break*	*breaking*
brief	*briefing*	*fail*	*failing*
feel	*feeling*	*float*	*floating*
flout	*flouting*	*fool*	*fooling*
meet	*meeting*	*pour*	*pouring*
roam	*roaming*	*seat*	*seating*
suit	*suiting*	*spoil*	*spoiling*
wait	*waiting*	*zoom*	*zooming*

Verbs that end in **c** add **k** before -**ing**.

bivouac	*bivouacking*	*frolic*	*frolicking*
mimic	*mimicking*	*panic*	*panicking*
picnic	*picnicking*	*traffic*	*trafficking*

You always remove silent **e** before -**ing**. The ending -**ing**, since it starts with a vowel, does the work of silent **e** in keeping a single vowel long.

aspire	*aspiring*	*believe*	*believing*
booze	*boozing*	*bulge*	*bulging*
burgle	*burgling*	*change*	*changing*
clone	*cloning*	*curve*	*curving*
dance	*dancing*	*divide*	*dividing*
dodge	*dodging*	*double*	*doubling*
force	*forcing*	*like*	*liking*
loathe	*loathing*	*move*	*moving*
nurse	*nursing*	*puzzle*	*puzzling*
quote	*quoting*	*realize*	*realizing*
receive	*receiving*	*reverse*	*reversing*
rhyme	*rhyming*	*rinse*	*rinsing*
rouse	*rousing*	*scheme*	*scheming*
seize	*seizing*	*shake*	*shaking*
sieve	*sieving*	*surge*	*surging*
surprise	*surprising*	*tease*	*teasing*
teethe	*teething*	*tickle*	*tickling*
tingle	*tingling*	*trace*	*tracing*
tune	*tuning*	*warble*	*warbling*

But the following verbs often or always keep the **e** before -**ing**:

age	*ageing* or *aging*
binge	*bingeing* or *binging*
singe	*singeing*
swinge	*swingeing*
whinge	*whingeing*

Verbs ending with **ue** lose the **e** before -**ing**.

accrue	*accruing*	*argue*	*arguing*
glue	*gluing*	*imbue*	*imbuing*
issue	*issuing*	*pursue*	*pursuing*
queue	*queuing*	*value*	*valuing*

Verbs ending with **oe** or **ye** keep the **e** before -**ing**.

canoe	*canoeing*	*hoe*	*hoeing*
shoe	*shoeing*	*tiptoe*	*tiptoeing*
dye	*dyeing*	*eye*	*eyeing*

But verbs that end with **ie** change **ie** to **y** before -**ing**.

die	*dying*	*lie*	*lying*
tie	*tying*	*vie*	*vying*

Verbs that end with **ee** keep **ee** before -**ing**.

agree	*agreeing*	*decree*	*decreeing*
flee	*fleeing*	*free*	*freeing*
guarantee	*guaranteeing*	*see*	*seeing*

DO IT YOURSELF

Fill in the correct *-ing* form in the following sentences.

1 All teenagers go through a stage of __________ their parents. (**defy**)

2 A criminal is a person who has been convicted of __________ a crime. (**commit**)

3 Anorexia has been called the __________ disease. (**slim**)

4 Allan's knee trouble kept __________. (**recur**)

5 It's time Meg started __________ on her career. (**focus**)

6 They had given up hope of __________ the trapped men. (**rescue**)

7 The texts are identical, __________ only in font size. (**differ**)

8 Soap and water are not necessarily the best thing for __________ the skin. (**cleanse**)

9 Do stop __________ and cheer up. (**whinge**)

10 I'm thinking of __________ as a full member. (**enrol**)

11 Teachers are too keen on __________ children good, bad, clever, stupid, etc. (**label**)

12 __________ your problems is the first step towards __________ them. (**face, tackle**)

13 __________ is __________. (**see, believe**)

14 They all had their own reasons for __________ the female candidate. (**prefer**)

15 I can't face the boredom of __________ for hours to get tickets. (**queue**)

16 Some people are afraid of __________, but more are afraid of __________. (**live, die**)

17 They say that __________ your problems is a sure way of __________ them. (**share, halve**)

18 Parrots are good at __________ the human voice. (**mimic**)

The *-ed* Form: the Simple Past Tense and Past Participle

You usually form the simple past tense and past participle by adding -**ed** to the base form of the verb.

cross	*crossed*	*despair*	*despaired*
fish	*fished*	*grasp*	*grasped*
jump	*jumped*	*laugh*	*laughed*
lift	*lifted*	*look*	*looked*
open	*opened*	*paint*	*painted*
return	*returned*	*walk*	*walked*

Grammar Help

- Verbs that just add **-ed** for the simple past tense and the past participle are called **weak verbs** or **regular verbs.**
- A quick reminder about the terms **simple past tense** and **past participle**:
  The **simple past** is **active** and says what happened in the past:
  *I **returned** to Taiwan in 1998.*
- The past participle is the form used in the **perfect** tenses and in **passive** verbs:
  *They have **painted** the walls purple.*
  *I had never **experienced** such rudeness before.*
  *Weren't you **promoted** last year?*
  *The letter had not been **opened**.*
- The past participle of a weak verb is the same as the simple past tense.

As with adding -**ing** to form the present participle, you double the final consonant of verbs that have one syllable, one short vowel, and end with one consonant, before you add -**ed**.

gas	*gassed*	*pat*	*patted*
step	*stepped*	*stop*	*stopped*
stun	*stunned*	*trek*	*trekked*
trim	*trimmed*	*trip*	*tripped*

Handy Hint

If you are using **bus** as a verb, the past tense and past participle can be **bused** or **bussed**.

If a verb has two or more syllables and the last one has one short vowel and ends with one consonant, and is stressed (even if this is not the main stress) the final consonant is doubled before -**ed**.

admit	*admitted*	*equip*	*equipped*
format	*formatted*	*handicap*	*handicapped*
incur	*incurred*	*kidnap*	*kidnapped*
nonplus	*nonplussed*	*program*	*programmed*
rebut	*rebutted*	*refer*	*referred*
zigzag	*zigzagged*		

But if there is no stress on the final syllable, the final consonant is not doubled:

bias	*biased*	*edit*	*edited*
enter	*entered*	*focus*	*focused*
garden	*gardened*	*gossip*	*gossiped*
offer	*offered*	*pardon*	*pardoned*
reckon	*reckoned*	*target*	*targeted*

But notice that if the final consonant is **l**, it always doubles after a single vowel, no matter where the stress comes.

cancel	*cancelled*	*control*	*controlled*
dial	*dialled*	*equal*	*equalled*
fulfil	*fulfilled*	*instal/install*	*installed*
libel	*libelled*	*marvel*	*marvelled*
pedal	*pedalled*	*pencil*	*pencilled*
rebel	*rebelled*	*repel*	*repelled*
rival	*rivalled*	*signal*	*signalled*
travel	*travelled*	*tunnel*	*tunnelled*

You don't double the final consonant after a double vowel.

avoid	*avoided*	*brief*	*briefed*
fail	*failed*	*float*	*floated*
flout	*flouted*	*fool*	*fooled*
greet	*greeted*	*pour*	*poured*
roam	*roamed*	*seat*	*seated*
suit	*suited*	*wait*	*waited*

Handy Hint

In American English, the spellings **kidnapped** and **kidnaped** are both possible.

Handy Hint

An exception is:

worship *worshipped*

In American English the spelling **worshiped** is possible

Handy Hints

- An exception is:
  paralleled
- In American English, the **l** is not usually doubled in an unstressed syllable:
  dial *dialed*
  equal *equaled*
  libel *libeled*
  travel *traveled*
- In British English the spellings **install** and **instal** are both possible

Verbs that end in **c** add **k** before -**ed**.

bivouac	*bivouacked*	*frolic*	*frolicked*
mimic	*mimicked*	*panic*	*panicked*
picnic	*picnicked*	*traffic*	*trafficked*

For verbs that end with silent **e**, or with **-le**, or with another vowel before **e**, you just add -**d** for the past tense and past participle.

age	*aged*	*aspire*	*aspired*
clone	*cloned*	*divide*	*divided*
like	*liked*	*move*	*moved*
quote	*quoted*	*realize*	*realized*
rhyme	*rhymed*	*tune*	*tuned*
surprise	*surprised*	*trace*	*traced*
believe	*believed*	*booze*	*boozed*
loathe	*loathed*	*receive*	*received*
rouse	*roused*	*seize*	*seized*
sieve	*sieved*	*tease*	*teased*
bulge	*bulged*	*change*	*changed*
curve	*curved*	*dance*	*danced*
dodge	*dodged*	*force*	*forced*
nurse	*nursed*	*reverse*	*reversed*
rinse	*rinsed*	*surge*	*surged*
burgle	*burgled*	*double*	*doubled*
puzzle	*puzzled*	*tickle*	*tickled*
tingle	*tingled*	*warble*	*warbled*
wobble	*wobbled*		
accrue	*accrued*	*argue*	*argued*
glue	*glued*	*imbue*	*imbued*
issue	*issued*	*pursue*	*pursued*
queue	*queued*	*value*	*valued*
canoe	*canoed*	*hoe*	*hoed*
shoe	*shoed*	*tiptoe*	*tiptoed*
die	*died*	*lie*	*lied*
tie	*tied*	*vie*	*vied*
agree	*agreed*	*decree*	*decreed*
free	*freed*		
dye	*dyed*	*eye*	*eyed*

Some one-syllable verbs ending with **l**, **m**, **n** or **p** have either -**t** or -**ed** as the past-tense and past-participle ending.

smell	*smelt* /smelt/ or *smelled* /smeld/
spell	*spelt* /spelt/ or *spelled* /speld/
spoil	*spoilt* /spɔɪlt/ or *spoiled* /spɔɪld/
dream	*dreamt* /dremt/ or *dreamed* /driːmd/
burn	*burnt* /bɜːnt/ or *burned* /bɜːnd/
lean	*leant* /lent/ or *leaned* /liːnd/
learn	*learnt* /lɜːnt/ or *learned* /lɜːnd/
leap	*leapt* /lept/ or *leaped* /liːpt/

Verbs that end with **y** change **y** to **i** before -**ed**.

carry	*carried*	*cry*	*cried*
deny	*denied*	*dirty*	*dirtied*
occupy	*occupied*	*rally*	*rallied*
spy	*spied*	*try*	*tried*

But if there is a vowel before the **y**, you keep the **y** before -**ed**:

buoy	*buoyed*	*convoy*	*convoyed*
fray	*frayed*	*journey*	*journeyed*
play	*played*	*stay*	*stayed*
survey	*surveyed*	*sway*	*swayed*

But the following are exceptions:

lay	*laid* /leɪd/
pay	*paid* /peɪd/
say	*said* /sed/

There are many verbs in English that do not add -**ed** to form the simple past and past participle. Instead, the base form of the verb changes, and often the past participle is different from the simple past.

Here are some common examples:

buy	*bought*	*have bought*	*fight*	*fought*	*have fought*
come	*came*	*have come*	*see*	*saw*	*have seen*
hide	*hid*	*have hidden*	*know*	*knew*	*have known*
lead	*led*	*have led*	*rise*	*rose*	*have risen*
run	*ran*	*have run*	*sing*	*sang*	*have sung*
swim	*swam*	*have swum*	*win*	*won*	*have won*

Handy Hints

- These verbs have only a **-t** form in the past tense and past participle:

build	*built*
creep	*crept*
deal	*dealt* /delt/
feel	*felt*
keep	*kept*
kneel	*knelt*
leave	*left*
lend	*lent*
send	*sent*
sleep	*slept*
spend	*spent*
weep	*wept*

- The adjective **learned**, meaning 'full of knowledge' has two syllables: /ˈlɜːnɪd/.

Handy Hints

- Verbs like these are called **strong verbs** or **irregular verbs**.
- You will find a full table of irregular verbs at the end of the book.

DO IT YOURSELF

Fill in the correct past tense or past participle in the following sentences.

1 We ___________ Britain last summer. (**visit**)

2 Harry ___________ his childhood in Japan. (**spend**)

3 I like ___________ eggs for breakfast. (**fry**)

4 Have you ___________ before? (**ski**)

5 Anna ___________ for her purchase and ___________ the shop. (**pay, leave**)

6 I ___________ for two hours and ___________ two tickets for the show. (**queue, buy**)

7 The taxi ___________ us to the station in good time. (**convey**)

8 I ___________ English at school, but I haven't ___________ very much. (**learn, remember**)

9 I ___________ quite ___________ after my meal. (**feel, satisfy**)

10 The match has been ___________ and ___________ till next week. (**cancel, postpone**)

11 Have you ___________ in your password? Are you sure you've ___________ it correctly? (**key, spell**)

12 The prisoner ___________ the charge, was ___________ innocent, and ___________. (**deny, judge, free**)

13 Helen ___________ the table and ___________ dinner. (**lay, serve**)

14 Mike ___________ off the pavement and ___________ across the road. (**step, hurry**)

15 We ___________ that the meeting should be ___________ till more was ___________. (**agree, defer, know**)

16 The horse ___________ over the fence and ___________ down the road. (**leap, gallop**)

17 Then it ___________ down and ___________ back home quietly. (**slow, trot**)

18 I greatly ___________ having ___________ the post I had been ___________. (**regret, refuse, offer**)

The *-s* Form in Verbs: the Third Person Singular, Present Tense

In the present tense, the third person singular of a verb adds an **s**.

I run	*he runs*
you sing	*Billy sings*
we jump	*she jumps*
they break	*it breaks*

There are a few points to remember.

Verbs that end with **y** change **y** to **ie** before -**s**.

carry	*carries*	*cry*	*cries*
defy	*defies*	*fry*	*fries*
reply	*replies*	*try*	*tries*

But if there is a vowel before the **y**, you keep the **y** before -**s**.

betray	*betrays*	*buy*	*buys*
destroy	*destroys*	*obey*	*obeys*
stay	*stays*	*survey*	*surveys*

Verbs that end in **s**, **ch**, **sh**, **x** or **z**, add -**es**.

kiss	*kisses*	*pass*	*passes*
reach	*reaches*	*dash*	*dashes*
fix	*fixes*	*fizz*	*fizzes*

Verbs that end in silent **e** just add -**s**.

bite	*bites*	*hate*	*hates*
hide	*hides*	*rule*	*rules*
scheme	*schemes*	*vote*	*votes*

Handy Hint

If you use **gas** or **bus** as verbs, the third person singular for **gas** is **gases**, and for **bus** is **buses** or **busses**.

Verbs that end in **o** add -**es**, but those that end in **oo** just add -**s**.

do	*does*	*echo*	*echoes*
go	*goes*	*lasso*	*lassoes*
tango	*tangoes*	*torpedo*	*torpedoes*
veto	*vetoes*	*zero*	*zeroes*
boo	*boos*	*coo*	*coos*
moo	*moos*	*shampoo*	*shampoos*
tattoo	*tattoos*		

Grammar Help

- Sometimes you meet a third-person-present-singular form without an **s**. This is in cases where the **subjunctive mood** is being used.
- In the subjunctive you use the **base** or **infinitive** form of the verb for all persons. You sometimes get subjunctives after a verb like *suggest* or *insist*, or after *whether.* For example:

  I suggest he ***apply*** *immediately.*
  They insist that she ***have*** *a full medical examination.*
  It is important to obtain a visa, whether it ***be*** *for a long or short stay.*

DO IT YOURSELF

Fill in the correct third-person-singular form in the following sentences.

1. My husband ___________ on me to get him up in time for work. (**rely**)
2. Traditionally a man ___________ a woman rather than the other way round. (**woo**)
3. She usually ___________ by having a hot bath. (**relax**)
4. Jeff ___________ in a primary school. (**teach**)
5. The advertisement ___________ that candidates must be over 21. (**specify**)
6. The factory ___________ hundreds of people in this area. (**employ**)
7. Every morning she ___________ the position of her yacht to her sponsors. (**radio**)
8. He ___________ too much about his image. (**worry**)
9. Freda ___________ with her friends in Austria every winter. (**ski**)
10. Dad usually ___________ to work by bus. (**travel**)

The *-s* Form in Nouns: Plurals

You just add -**s** to form most plurals.

an alibi	*alibis*	*a camel*	*camels*
a monkey	*monkeys*	*a novel*	*novels*
a pie	*pies*	*a ski*	*skis*

For nouns that end with silent **e**, you just add -**s**.

bone	*bones*	*cake*	*cakes*
face	*faces*	*house*	*houses*
nose	*noses*	*piece*	*pieces*
pirate	*pirates*	*sponge*	*sponges*

For nouns that end in **s**, **x**, **z**, **ch** or **sh**, you have to add -**es**.

bus	*buses*	*cactus*	*cactuses*
circus	*circuses*	*class*	*classes*
cross	*crosses*	*dress*	*dresses*
gas	*gases*	*virus*	*viruses*
yes	*yeses*	*box*	*boxes*
fax	*faxes*	*suffix*	*suffixes*
buzz	*buzzes*	*waltz*	*waltzes*
arch	*arches*	*branch*	*branches*
sandwich	*sandwiches*	*brush*	*brushes*
marsh	*marshes*	*radish*	*radishes*

Nouns that end with **o** usually just add -**s**.

avocado	*avocados*	*cello*	*cellos*
dado	*dados*	*embryo*	*embryos*
fiasco	*fiascos*	*hippo*	*hippos*
kilo	*kilos*	*kimono*	*kimonos*
manifesto	*manifestos*	*radio*	*radios*
studio	*studios*	*video*	*videos*
yoyo	*yoyos*		

Handy Hints

- Notice that for the plural of nouns ending in **ful**, you put the **s** after **ful**:

  cupful *cupfuls*
  (not *cupsful*)
  pocketful *pocketfuls*
  spoonful *spoonfuls*

- For the plural of your in-laws, add **s** to the 'relation' word:

  daughters-in-law
  mothers-in-law
  brothers-in-law

Handy Hints

- The following -**z** word doubles its **z** for the plural:

  quiz *quizzes*

- Some -**ch** words have the sound /k/, not /tʃ/, so they just add **s**:

  monarch *monarchs*
  stomach *stomachs*

But some -**o** nouns that have been used a long time in English add -**es**:

cargo	*cargoes*	*dingo*	*dingoes*
domino	*dominoes*	*echo*	*echoes*
embargo	*embargoes*	*flamingo*	*flamingoes*
go	*goes*	*hero*	*heroes*
Negro	*Negroes*	*no*	*noes*
potato	*potatoes*	*tomato*	*tomatoes*
tornado	*tornadoes*	*veto*	*vetoes*
volcano	*volcanoes*		

You have a choice with other -**o** nouns.

archipelago	*archipelagos* or *archipelagoes*
banjo	*banjos* or *banjoes*
buffalo	*buffalos* or *buffaloes*
desperado	*desperados* or *desperadoes*
ghetto	*ghettos* or *ghettoes*
grotto	*grottos* or *grottoes*
halo	*halos* or *haloes*
innuendo	*innuendos* or *innuendoes*
lasso	*lassos* or *lassoes*
lingo	*lingos* or *lingoes*
mango	*mangos* or *mangoes*
memento	*mementos* or *mementoes*
mosquito	*mosquitos* or *mosquitoes*
motto	*mottos* or *mottoes*
portico	*porticos* or *porticoes*
torpedo	*torpedos* or *torpedoes*
virago	*viragos* or *viragoes*
zero	*zeros* or *zeroes*

Handy Hint

The plural of **do** is spelt **do's**, as in ***do's and don'ts***.

Nouns that end in **oo** just add -**s**.

cockatoo	*cockatoos*	*cuckoo*	*cuckoos*
kangaroo	*kangaroos*	*shampoo*	*shampoos*
tattoo	*tattoos*	*zoo*	*zoos*

> **Handy Hint**
>
> In American English a **storey** of a house is sometimes spelt **story**, with the plural **stories**.

Nouns that end in **y** change **y** to **ie** before -**s**.

ally	*allies*	*baby*	*babies*
dynasty	*dynasties*	*family*	*families*
fairy	*fairies*	*fly*	*flies*
library	*libraries*	*mystery*	*mysteries*
quality	*qualities*	*spy*	*spies*
story	*stories*	*trophy*	*trophies*

But if there is a vowel before the **y**, the **y** is kept before -**s**:

bay	*bays*	*buoy*	*buoys*
chimney	*chimneys*	*donkey*	*donkeys*
jersey	*jerseys*	*key*	*keys*
monkey	*monkeys*	*storey*	*storeys*
toy	*toys*	*trolley*	*trolleys*
turkey	*turkeys*	*valley*	*valleys*

Nouns that end in **f** change **f** to **v** and add -**es**.

calf	*calves*	*elf*	*elves*
half	*halves*	*leaf*	*leaves*
loaf	*loaves*	*self*	*selves*
sheaf	*sheaves*	*shelf*	*shelves*
thief	*thieves*	*wolf*	*wolves*

But some keep **f** before -**s**:

belief	*beliefs*	*brief*	*briefs*
chef	*chefs*	*chief*	*chiefs*
clef	*clefs*	*grief*	*griefs*
gulf	*gulfs*	*massif*	*massifs*
proof	*proofs*	*reef*	*reefs*
relief	*reliefs*	*roof*	*roofs*
serif	*serifs*	*spoof*	*spoofs*

Some can have a plural in -**fs** or -**ves**.

behalf	*behalfs* or *behalves*
dwarf	*dwarfs* or *dwarves*
hoof	*hoofs* or *hooves*
scarf	*scarfs* or *scarves*
turf	*turfs* or *turves*
wharf	*wharfs* or *wharves*

These words ending in **fe** have the plural -**ves**.

knife	*knives*	*life*	*lives*
midwife	*midwives*	*wife*	*wives*

But other nouns ending in **fe** just add -**s**:

carafe	*carafes*	*fife*	*fifes*
safe	*safes*		

Nouns that end in **ff** or **ffe** just add -**s**.

bailiff	*bailiffs*	*cliff*	*cliffs*
cuff	*cuffs*	*mastiff*	*mastiffs*
midriff	*midriffs*	*sheriff*	*sheriffs*
rebuff	*rebuffs*	*staff*	*staffs*
tariff	*tariffs*		
gaffe	*gaffes*	*giraffe*	*giraffes*
pouffe	*pouffes*		

Some of the commonest nouns have irregular plurals, without -**s**. Of these, some change the vowel to form the plural.

child	*children*
foot	*feet*
goose	*geese*
louse	*lice*
man	*men*
mouse	*mice*
ox	*oxen*
woman	*women*
tooth	*teeth*

Did You Know?

A computer mouse can have the plural **mice** or **mouses**.

Handy Hint

café is usually spelt with an acute accent on the **e**, pronounced /ˈkafeɪ/, and has the plural **cafés** /ˈkafeɪz/.

Handy Hints

- **staff**, meaning a group of employees, has the plural **staffs**.
- **staff**, meaning a stick or rod (an old word), has the plural **staves**.
- **staff**, meaning the set of lines used for writing music, has the plural **staves**.

  But the singular **stave** is also possible for the meanings 'stick' and 'set of musical lines'.

Did You Know?

The nouns in the list on the left come from Old English. **Human** is not related to **man**; it comes from the Latin adjective *humanus*, so it has the regular plural **humans**.

Some words that come via Latin from Greek have the ending -**sis**, and change the **i** to **e** for the plural, with the pronunciation /si:z/.

analysis	*analyses* /əˈnalɪsi:z/
axis	*axes* / ˈaksi:z/
basis	*bases* / ˈbeɪsi:z/
crisis	*crises* /kraɪsi:z/
emphasis	*emphases* / ˈemfəsi:z/
oasis	*oases* /oʊˈeɪsi:z/
parenthesis	*parentheses* /pəˈrenθəsi:z/

Handy Hints

- ***appendix****, meaning a section added at the end of a book, can have the plural* ***appendices****.*
- ***index*** *in its mathematical and other technical meanings has the plural* ***indices****.*
- ***species*** */ˈspi:ʃi:z/ and* ***series*** */ˈsɪəri:z/ have the same spelling and pronunciation for the singular and the plural.*

Some nouns of French origin end in a silent **s**. The plural is spelt the same, but the **s** is pronounced.

chassis / ˈʃasi:/	*chassis*/ ˈʃasi:z/
corps /kɔ:/	*corps* /kɔ:z/
fracas / ˈfrakɑ:/	*fracas* / ˈfrakɑ:z/
rendezvous / ˈrondeɪvu:/	*rendezvous* / ˈrondeɪvu:z/

Some words from Latin keep their Latin plurals, especially if they are used technically.

antenna	*antennae* /-ni:/ or *antennas*
formula	*formulae* /-li:/ or *formulas*
vertebra	*vertebrae* /-bri:/
alumnus	*alumni* /-naɪ:/
cactus	*cacti* /-taɪ/ or *cactuses*
fungus	*fungi* /-gaɪ/ or /-dʒaɪ/ or *funguses*
atrium	*atria* /-trɪə/ or *atriums*
phylum	*phyla* /-lə/
corpus	*corpora* /-pərə/
genus	*genera* /-ərə/
stigma	*stigmata* /-mətə/

Handy Hint

Most dictionaries show Latin plurals where appropriate.

Some nouns, especially types of animals, fish or birds, have the same form for both singular and plural.

a bison	*a herd of bison*
a carp	*a tankful of carp*
a deer	*hundreds of deer*
a fish	*not many fish*
a sheep	*a few sheep*
a salmon	*five salmon*
a swine	*a herd of swine*
a trout	*a riverful of trout*

With many other types of creature there is a choice, which dictionaries usually indicate:

several buffaloes (or buffalos) or *buffalo*
a flight of herons or *heron*
hundreds of herrings or *herring*

Handy Hints

- The plural **fishes** is often used when it is a question of different kinds of fish:

  *all the **fishes** of the Indian Ocean.*

- Notice also:

  an aircraft *several aircraft*
  an innings *three innings*

The number words **hundred**, **thousand, million**, **billion**, **dozen** and **score** do not add **s** when preceded by a number.

three hundred people
ten thousand sufferers
two billion dollars
two dozen bread rolls
three score years

But you say:

hundreds of people
thousands of sufferers
billions of dollars
dozens of examples
scores of occasions

Things that come in pairs are usually plural nouns already.

binoculars	*boots*	*braces*	*glasses*
jeans	*pants*	*scissors*	*socks*
stockings	*tights*	*trainers*	*trousers*

Handy Hint

You use ***a pair** of* or ***pairs of*** when you want to turn plurals like these into count nouns:

a pair of bermudas
a pair of scissors
a pair of pliers
two pairs of eyes
three pairs of pyjamas
eight pairs of chopsticks

DO IT YOURSELF

Fill in the correct plural form in the following sentences.

1 Some university __________ are livelier than others. (**campus**)

2 They heard __________ coming from the river. (**cry**)

3 The Presidency has weathered quite a few __________ recently. (**crisis**)

4 I spent the weekend putting up __________. (**bookshelf**)

5 We spent an evening going round the __________ of Las Vegas. (**casino**)

6 How many __________ of bread would you like this morning? (**loaf**)

7 His back was covered with __________. (**tattoo**)

8 Do you think __________ should be paid for the work they do? (**housewife**)

9 Certain illnesses may cause damage to the __________. (**kidney**)

10 Where do you keep your __________ during the summer? (**ski**)

11 Helen can tell you the __________ and __________ of most of these plants.(**genus, species**)

12 My hair was coming out in __________ .(**handful**)

13 We had a holiday diving among the coral __________. (**reef**)

14 There was a herd of at least two __________ __________ grazing on the slopes. (**hundred, reindeer**)

15 Dormant __________ may show signs of becoming active again. (**volcano**)

16 How many __________ did Shakespeare write? (**comedy**)

17 It is important to respect other people's religious __________. (**belief**)

18 There were several __________ at the end of the volume. (**appendix**)

19 All the suspects appeared to have watertight __________. (**alibi**)

20 We know that this country can rely on her __________ in a crisis. (**ally**)

21 One of the __________ was injured in the race. (**jockey**)

22 In punctuation, __________ are used for the same purpose as __________ .(**dash, parenthesis**)

-er and *-est* in Adjectives: forming the Comparative and Superlative

Most adjectives of one syllable have a comparative in -**er** and a superlative in -**est**.

POSITIVE	COMPARATIVE	SUPERLATIVE
clean	*cleaner*	*cleanest*
dark	*darker*	*darkest*
deep	*deeper*	*deepest*
firm	*firmer*	*firmest*
low	*lower*	*lowest*
old	*older*	*oldest*
warm	*warmer*	*warmest*

For adjectives ending in silent **e**, you just add -**r** and -**st**:

POSITIVE	COMPARATIVE	SUPERLATIVE
close	*closer*	*closest*
fine	*finer*	*finest*
large	*larger*	*largest*
rude	*ruder*	*rudest*
safe	*safer*	*safest*
wide	*wider*	*widest*

One-syllable adjectives that have one short vowel and end with one consonant, double the consonant before -**er** and -**est**.

POSITIVE	COMPARATIVE	SUPERLATIVE
big	*bigger*	*biggest*
fat	*fatter*	*fattest*
fit	*fitter*	*fittest*
hot	*hotter*	*hottest*
thin	*thinner*	*thinnest*

Handy Hint

One-syllable adjectives ending in **y** don't usually change **y** to **i** before **-er** and **-est**, whether or not there is a vowel before the **y**; but **dry** is an exception:

coy	*coyer*	*coyest*
dry	*drier*	*driest*
gay	*gayer*	*gayest*
grey	*greyer*	*greyest*
(gray)	*(grayer)*	*(grayest)*
shy	*shyer*	*shyest*
sly	*slyer*	*slyest*
spry	*spryer*	*spryest*
wry	*wryer*	*wryest*

Adjectives of two or more syllables

For two-syllable adjectives that end in **y**, change **y** to **i** and add -**er** or -**est**.

POSITIVE	COMPARATIVE	SUPERLATIVE
busy	*busier*	*busiest*
dirty	*dirtier*	*dirtiest*
easy	*easier*	*easiest*
funny	*funnier*	*funniest*
happy	*happier*	*happiest*
lovely	*lovelier*	*loveliest*

Some -**y** adjectives formed from nouns ending in silent **e** can be spelt -**ey**. But the comparative and superlative are always spelt -**ier** and -**iest**.

	POSITIVE	COMPARATIVE	SUPERLATIVE
cage	*cagy* or *cagey*	*cagier*	*cagiest*
dice	*dicey*	*dicier*	*diciest*
mate	*maty* or *matey*	*matier*	*matiest*
price	*pricy* or *pricey*	*pricier*	*priciest*
stage	*stagy* or *stagey*	*stagier*	*stagiest*

Several two-syllable adjectives ending with **le**, preceded by one or more consonants, add -**r** and -**st** for the comparative and superlative.

POSITIVE	COMPARATIVE	SUPERLATIVE
able	*abler*	*ablest*
ample	*ampler*	*amplest*
gentle	*gentler*	*gentlest*
humble	*humbler*	*humblest*
idle	*idler*	*idlest*
nimble	*nimbler*	*nimblest*
noble	*nobler*	*noblest*
simple	*simpler*	*simplest*
stable	*stabler*	*stablest*
supple	*suppler*	*supplest*

For some other two-syllable adjectives, there are -**er** and -**est** forms for the comparative and superlative.

POSITIVE	COMPARATIVE	SUPERLATIVE
clever	*cleverer*	*cleverest*
common	*commoner*	*commonest*
cruel	*crueller*	*cruellest*
handsome	*handsomer*	*handsomest*
narrow	*narrower*	*narrowest*
pleasant	*pleasanter*	*pleasantest*
polite	*politer*	*politest*
quiet	*quieter*	*quietest*
remote	*remoter*	*remotest*
shallow	*shallower*	*shallowest*
stupid	*stupider*	*stupidest*

Are you clear about how to count syllables? In case you are not sure, here is a table of words with two syllables, with three syllables, and with more than three syllables, as a model.

TWO SYLLABLES	THREE SYLLABLES
clev-er	*beau-ti-ful*
com-mon	*ca-pa-ble*
nar-row	*con-fi-dent*
pleas-ant	*de-li-cious*
po-lite	*ex-pen-sive*
qui-et	*for-tu-nate*
sil-ly	*gen-e-rous*
sim-ple	*pow-er-ful*
stu-pid	*un-hap-py*

MORE THAN THREE SYLLABLES

com-for-ta-ble
com-pet-i-tive
dis-ap-point-ed
em-bar-ras-sing
het-e-ro-ge-ne-ous
i-ma-gi-na-tive
in-con-ve-ni-ent
prob-le-mat-i-cal
un-so-phis-ti-ca-ted

Generally speaking, for adjectives of two syllables or more, you form the comparative and superlative using **more** and **most**; and you can be certain that most adjectives ending in -**able** (or -**ible** or -**uble**), -**al**, -**ant**, -**ate**, -**ed**, -**ent**, -**ful**, -**ic**, -**ing**, -**ish**, -**ive**, -**less** and -**ous**, form their comparatives using **more** and **most**.

POSITIVE	COMPARATIVE	SUPERLATIVE
active	*more active*	*most active*
brutal	*more brutal*	*most brutal*
careless	*more careless*	*most careless*
charming	*more charming*	*most charming*
cheerful	*more cheerful*	*most cheerful*
famous	*more famous*	*most famous*
foolish	*more foolish*	*most foolish*
fortunate	*more fortunate*	*most fortunate*
gallant	*more gallant*	*most gallant*
obedient	*more obedient*	*most obedient*
poetic	*more poetic*	*most poetic*
precious	*more precious*	*most precious*
reasonable	*more reasonable*	*most reasonable*
satisfied	*more satisfied*	*most satisfied*
soluble	*more soluble*	*most soluble*
terrible	*more terrible*	*most terrible*
valuable	*more valuable*	*most valuable*

Handy Hint

Farther and **farthest** are used to talk about distance.

Further and **furthest** can be used to talk about distance too, but are regularly the forms used when the meaning is **'more'** or **'additional'**:

*Which planet is **farthest** from the sun?*

*The earth is **further** away from the sun than Venus is.*

***Further** information will be sent when available.*

There are some irregular comparatives and superlatives that you have to learn.

POSITIVE	COMPARATIVE	SUPERLATIVE
bad	*worse*	*worst*
far	*farther* or *further*	*farthest* or *furthest*
good	*better*	*best*
little	*less*	*least*
many	*more*	*most*
much	*more*	*most*

DO IT YOURSELF

Decide whether the *comparative* or *superlative* is appropriate in each of the following sentences, and fill in the correct comparative or superlative form:

1. Susan was looking a good deal ________ than when I had last seen her. (**slim**)
2. That's the ________ idea I ever heard. (**stupid**)
3. The conference is to be ________ in the year than last time. (**early**)
4. George is ________ at maths than I am. (**good**)
5. We await ________ instructions. (**far**)
6. This loaf is ________ than that one. (**stale**)
7. The doctors are ________ about his condition than they were yesterday. (**hopeful**)
8. His failure has made him a lot ________ than he used to be. (**humble**)
9. The ________ person in the group was actually the ________(**elderly, lively**)
10. Is iron ________ than lead? (**heavy**)
11. The ________ thing about her death is that she never lived to see her grandchild. (**sad**)
12. This is the ________ September we've had for years. (**sunny**)
13. The ________ verbs in English are the irregular ones. (**common**)
14. The international situation is getting ________. (**bad**)
15. Never make the mistake of thinking you're ________ than other people. (**clever**)
16. My son is ________ than I was at his age. (**big**)

Adding *-ly*: formation of Adverbs

You just add -**ly** to most adjectives to form adverbs.

bad	*badly*	*bitter*	*bitterly*
foolish	*foolishly*	*free*	*freely*
neat	*neatly*	*patient*	*patiently*
quick	*quickly*	*quiet*	*quietly*
surprising	*surprisingly*	*triumphant*	*triumphantly*

Handy Hint

These adjectives drop **e** before -**ly**:

due	*duly*
eerie	*eerily*
true	*truly*
whole	*wholly*

Adjectives ending in silent **e** just add -**ly**.

attentive	*attentively*	*brave*	*bravely*
fierce	*fiercely*	*futile*	*futilely*
nice	*nicely*	*mature*	*maturely*
polite	*politely*	*servile*	*servilely*
sole	*solely*	*vile*	*vilely*

Handy Hint

But notice that these adjectives ending in **ll** drop one **l** before -**ly**:

dull	*dully* / ˈdʌlli/
full	*fully* / ˈfʊli/

Adjectives ending in **l** add -**ly**, so you get **ll**.

beautiful	*beautifully*	*cool*	*coolly*
cruel	*cruelly*	*equal*	*equally*
evil	*evilly*	*foul*	*foully*
level	*levelly*	*loyal*	*loyally*
oral	*orally*	*real*	*really*
social	*socially*	*special*	*specially*
typical	*typically*	*usual*	*usually*

Adjectives ending in **y** change **y** to **i** before -**ly**.

angry	*angrily*	*clumsy*	*clumsily*
easy	*easily*	*gloomy*	*gloomily*
happy	*happily*	*merry*	*merrily*
noisy	*noisily*	*ordinary*	*ordinarily*
primary	*primarily*	*sleepy*	*sleepily*
temporary	*temporarily*	*tidy*	*tidily*

Handy Hints

- Quite a few adjectives already end in **-ly**. In theory you could change the **y** to **i** and add **-ly**, but in practice this is rarely done, because the resulting adverbs are difficult to pronounce, and sound rather odd. So people are more likely to use an expression such as *in a silly manner* or *in a friendly way*, than to say or write *sillily* or *friendlily*.

  Here are some adjectives that come into this category:

beastly	*courtly*	*deadly*	*friendly*
ghastly	*ghostly*	*grisly*	*holy*
jolly	*likely*	*lively*	*lordly*
manly	*miserly*	*orderly*	*silly*
surly	*unruly*	*womanly*	*worldly*

- But notice that some **-ly** words can be both adjectives and adverbs:

daily	*early*	*hourly*	*kindly*	
monthly	*nightly*	*only*	*weekly*	*yearly*

One-syllable adjectives ending with -**y** behave in a variety of ways before -**ly**.

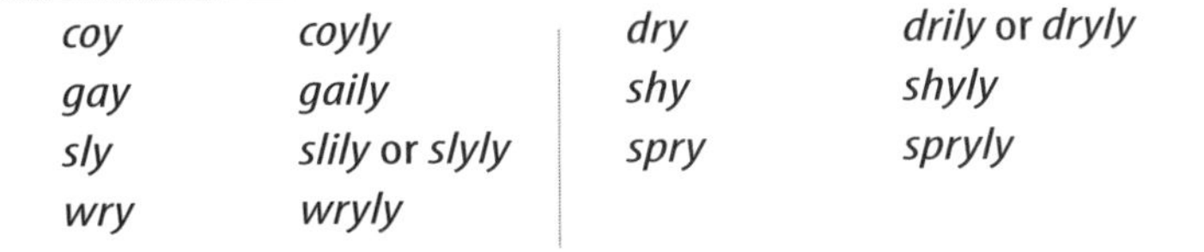

coy	*coyly*	*dry*	*drily* or *dryly*
gay	*gaily*	*shy*	*shyly*
sly	*slily* or *slyly*	*spry*	*spryly*
wry	*wryly*		

Notice also the spelling of **daily** from **day**.

Some adjectives formed from nouns ending in silent **e** can be spelt -**ey**. But the adverb is always spelt -**ily**.

cage	*cagy* or *cagey*	*cagily*
dice	*dicey*	*dicily*
mate	*maty* or *matey*	*matily*
price	*pricy* or *pricey*	*pricily*
stage	*stagy* or *stagey*	*stagily*

Handy Hint

Notice also:

phoney *phonily*

Adjectives that end in **le**, preceded by one or more consonants, just change **e** to **y**:

able	*ably*	*ample*	*amply*
comfortable	*comfortably*	*humble*	*humbly*
idle	*idly*	*noble*	*nobly*
simple	*simply*	*single*	*singly*
subtle	*subtly*		

Handy Hints

- The famous exception is:

  public *publicly*

- But the adjective ***politic***, meaning 'shrewd' or 'tactful', as distinct from the adjective ***political***, has the adverb ***politicly***:

  *I **politicly** pretended not to hear.*

Adjectives that end with **ic** add **al** before -**ly**:

basic	*basically*	*comic*	*comically*
economic	*economically*	*emphatic*	*emphatically*
heroic	*heroically*	*historic*	*historically*
idiotic	*idiotically*	*magic*	*magically*
majestic	*majestically*	*neurotic*	*neurotically*
romantic	*romantically*	*tragic*	*tragically*

There are several adverbs that do not end in **ly**, for example:

far	*fast*	*fine*	*hard*	*just*	*late*
little	*long*	*much*	*near*	*soon*	*well*

Did You Know?

Some non -**ly** adverbs have -**ly** forms with a different meaning:

*work **hard***	*I can **hardly** hear you.*
*I've **just** arrived.*	*He was treated **justly**.*
*I got up **late**.*	*Have you seen her **lately**?*
*You're doing **fine**.*	*Chop the onions **finely**.*
*The bus drew **near**.*	*I **nearly** forgot.*

Grammar Help

COMPARISON OF ADVERBS

Adverbs that end in **ly** form their comparative and superlative with **more** and **most**:

ably	*more ably*	*most ably*
quickly	*more quickly*	*most quickly*
economically	*more economically*	*most economically*

Adverbs that don't end in **ly** form their comparative and superlative with **-er** and **-est**:

fast	*faster*	*fastest*
hard	*harder*	*hardest*
late	*later*	*latest*
long	*longer*	*longest*
soon	*sooner*	*soonest*

Some adverbs have irregular comparatives and superlatives, which have to be learnt:

badly	*worse*	*worst*
far	*farther* or *further*	*farthest* or *furthest*
little	*less*	*least*
much	*more*	*most*
well	*better*	*best*

DO IT YOURSELF

Fill in the correct adverb in the following sentences.

1. The children were __________ thin and ragged. (**pathetic**)
2. The participants __________ assembled at the time arranged. (**due**)
3. Several people were __________ injured in the bus crash. (**grave**)
4. __________ enough, nobody recognized me. (**funny**)
5. She smiled __________ and opened the door __________ for us. (**shy, polite**)
6. Meetings are held __________ in the Town Hall. (**month**)
7. We can eat __________ in the cafeteria or more __________ at the local hotel. (**economical, pricey**)
8. He jumped __________ out of he car. (**nimble**)
9. __________ the ambulance got here __________ __________. (**lucky, amazing, quick**)
10. The room was __________ but __________ furnished. (**simple, expensive**)
11. She was careful not to reveal __________ what she felt __________. (**public, private**)
12. I'm not __________ convinced by that story. (**whole**)
13. I won't stand __________ by and watch animals being __________ treated. (**idle, cruel**)
14. He __________ admitted that he had __________ passed his test at the third attempt. (**wry, final**)
15. Throughout history, Malta has been __________ and __________ important.

    (**military, strategic**)
16. He was __________ caught off his guard. (**momentary**)
17. She returned to Frankfurt __________ for the job interview. (**sole**)
18. I __________ ignored her remark and __________ changed the subject. (**tactful, hasty**)
19. Those two suggestions are __________ silly and __________ forgotten. (**equal, best**)
20. Polio vaccine is __________ administered __________ (**normal, oral**)

4 OTHER WORD ENDINGS
Lists and Spelling Points

This section deals in alphabetical order with some of the common **suffixes** (word endings) in English that cause spelling problems.

Some general rules about adding suffixes:

> When you add a suffix beginning with a **consonant**, you usually keep silent **e**.

spite	*spiteful*	*state*	*statement*
nice	*niceness*	*hope*	*hopeless*

and usually change final **y** to **i**.

happy	*happiness*	*pity*	*pitiless*
weary	*wearisome*		

> When you add a suffix beginning with a **vowel**, you usually drop silent **e**.

style	*stylish*	*guide*	*guidance*
distribute	*distributor*	*extreme*	*extremism*
dispose	*disposal*	*adventure*	*adventurous*

and final **y** usually changes to **i**.

deny	*undeniable*	*copy*	*potocopier*
vary	*various*		

You sometimes have to double the final consonant of a one-syllable word, or a final stressed syllable, with one short vowel, ending with one consonant.

jog	*jogger*	*scab*	*scabby*
man	*mannish*	*remit*	*remittance*

-able or -ible?

These are adjective-forming endings, typically attached to verbs. Their meaning is generally 'that you can do a certain thing to', as in, for example, *washable*, *convertible*. But in some older words the meaning has developed along different lines, as with *comfortable*, *fashionable*, *probable*, *sensible*.

Another thing to notice is that the base word may be a noun rather than a verb, as with *peaceable*, *knowledgeable*.

The two endings **-able** and **-ible** are pronounced the same, so it is difficult to know from the sound whether **-able** or **-ible** is the correct spelling. It depends in many cases on whether the Latin verb from which the adjective comes has the infinitive form *-are* (giving -**able**), or *-ere* or *-ire* (giving **-ible**), and this kind of analysis is not possible for those unfamiliar with Latin.

-able adjectives

-able is by far the commoner ending. The main reason for this is that it is a 'living' suffix. People use it to create new adjectives from English verbs. So you can usually be sure that if you can recognize the first part of the adjective as an English verb, the ending is **-able**, especially in the case of new verbs or processes.

book	*bookable*	*break*	*breakable*
count	*countable*	*crush*	*uncrushable*
drink	*drinkable*	*eat*	*eatable*
microwave	*microwavable*	*stretch*	*stretchable*

Here are some other points about **-able**.

- If there is a hard **c** /k/ or a hard **g** /g/ before the suffix, the suffix has to be **-able**, not **-ible**:

amicable	*applicable*	*despicable*	*educable*
impeccable	*implacable*	*inexplicable*	*inextricable*
indefatigable	*irrigable*	*navigable*	*practicable*

- If the letter before the suffix is **i**, the suffix has to be **-able**, not **-ible**, because there are no words ending in **-iible**:

amiable	*appreciable*	*insatiable*	*liable*
negotiable	*pliable*	*sociable*	*viable*

- Verbs ending in silent **e** drop the **e** before **-able**:

adore	*adorable*	*cure*	*curable*
date	*datable*	*debate*	*debatable*
define	*definable*	*excuse*	*excusable*
grade	*gradable*	*note*	*notable*
quote	*quotable*	*repute*	*reputable*
use	*usable*	*value*	*valuable*

Handy Hints

The words above follow the rule that silent **e** is dropped before a suffix beginning with a vowel. But notice these points:

- If the base word ends with **ee**, the second **e** is kept before **-able**:

  agree *agreeable* *disagree* *disagreeable* *foresee* *foreseeable*

- Silent **e** is not dropped before **-able** if it is needed to keep **c** /s/ or **g** /dʒ/ soft:

change	*changeable*	*enforce*	*enforceable*	*knowledge*	*knowledgeable*
manage	*manageable*	*notice*	*noticeable*	*peace*	*peaceable*
replace	*replaceable*	*service*	*serviceable*	*trace*	*traceable*

- And there are other cases where silent **e** is often not dropped before **-able**:

blame	*blamable* or *blameable*	*like*	*likable* or *likeable*
live	*livable* or *liveable*	*love*	*lovable* or *loveable*
microwave	*microwavable* or *microwaveable*	*move*	*movable* or *moveable*
name	*namable* or *nameable*	*rate*	*ratable* or *rateable*
shake	*unshakable* or *unshakeable*	*size*	*sizable* or *sizeable*

- Notice the following spelling:

  recycle *recyclable*

- If the base verb ends in **y**, **y** changes to **i** before **-able**, unless a vowel comes before **y**:

classify	*classifiable*	*copy*	*copiable*
deny	*undeniable*	*duty*	*dutiable*
envy	*enviable*	*photocopy*	*photocopiable*
rely	*reliable*	*vary*	*variable*

But:

buy	*buyable*	*play*	*playable*
say	*sayable*		

- Verbs that double their last consonant when adding **-ing** also double it before **-able**:

club	*clubbable*	*hug*	*huggable*
regret	*regrettable*	*stop*	*stoppable*

Handy Hint

But verbs that end with **-fer** do not double the **r** before **-able**:

defer	*deferring*	but	*deferable*
infer	*inferring*	but	*inferable*
prefer	*preferring*	but	*preferable*
transfer	*transferring*	but	*transferable*

DO IT YOURSELF

Fill in the correct *-able* forms in the following sentences.

1 This __________ delay was surely __________. (**regret, avoid**)

2 Some of the refugees were in a __________ condition. (**pity**)

3 It's __________ that the earlier text is actually the more accurate. (**argue**)

4 Cases such as this are normally __________ to a higher court. (**refer**)

5 The fee is __________ to the company and __________ within 30 days. (**charge, pay**)

6 She totted up the figures in her head with __________ ease. (**envy**)

7 It's __________ to check those **un**__________ names before reading them out. (**advise, pronounce**)

8 Have you ever used __________ contact lenses? (**dispose**)

9 The two situations are not __________. (**compare**)

10 I'd do it at once if it were __________. (**do**)

11 We spent an **un**__________ evening sailing over the lake. (**forget**)

12 We witnessed scenes of **in**__________ suffering. (**describe**)

13 The ground is scarcely __________ in this frosty weather. (**dig**)

14 My kids are becoming **un**__________. (**manage**)

15 Most of the finds are __________ to about the mid fourth century BC. (**date**)

16 I don't think these vouchers are __________. (**transfer**)

17 This seems to me an **un**__________ use of the company's money. (**justify**)

18 What an __________ baby! (**adore**)

-ible adjectives

Here is a list of the commonest adjectives that end with **-ible**. It's a good idea to become familiar with them.

accessible	*admissible*	*audible*
coercible	*collapsible*	*compatible*
comprehensible	*compressible*	*contemptible*
contractible	*convertible*	*convincible*
corruptible	*credible*	*deducible*
defensible	*destructible*	*digestible*
discernible	*divisible*	*edible*
eligible	*fallible*	*feasible*
flexible	*forcible*	*gullible*
horrible	*illegible*	*imperceptible*
implausible	*impossible*	*inaccessible*
inadmissible	*inaudible*	*incombustible*
incompatible	*incomprehensible*	*incontrovertible*
incorrigible	*incorruptible*	*incredible*
indefensible	*indelible*	*indestructible*
indigestible	*indiscernible*	*indivisible*
inedible	*ineligible*	*inexhaustible*
inexpressible	*infallible*	*inflexible*
insensible	*intangible*	*intelligible*
invincible	*invisible*	*irascible*
irreducible	*irrepressible*	*irresistible*
irresponsible	*irreversible*	*legible*
miscible	*negligible*	*ostensible*
perceptible	*plausible*	*possible*
protractible	*reducible*	*reprehensible*
reproducible	*resistible*	*responsible*
reversible	*sensible*	*submersible*
suggestible	*susceptible*	*tangible*
terrible	*transmissible*	*unintelligible*
vendible	*visible*	

Handy Hints

- *It's fairly safe to assume that nearly all other adjectives ending with the sound /əbəl/ will be spelt* ***-able****.*
- *But apart from the* ***-ible*** *and* ***-able*** *adjectives there is a tiny group of adjectives ending with* ***-uble*** */jʊbəl/:*

soluble	*voluble*
indissoluble	*insoluble*

From **-able** adjectives you form nouns ending **-ability**, and adverbs ending **-ably**.

From **-ible** adjectives you form nouns ending **-ibility** and adverbs ending **-ibly**.

From **-uble** adjectives you form nouns ending **-ubility** and adverbs ending **-ubly**.

immutable	*immutability*	*immutably*
visible	*visibility*	*visibly*
voluble	*volubility*	*volubly*

-acy, -asy

These are both noun-forming endings with the sound /əsi/. Nouns formed this way have mostly abstract meanings such as the state, condition, or quality of something (for example, *literacy, obstinacy*), an office (for example, *papacy, magistracy*), or rule or dominance by something (for example, *democracy, bureaucracy*).

By far the biggest group are the **-acy** nouns.

Here are the commonest of them:

accuracy	*adequacy*	*advocacy*
aristocracy	*autocracy*	*bureaucracy*
candidacy	*celibacy*	*confederacy*
conspiracy	*delicacy*	*democracy*
diplomacy	*efficacy*	*episcopacy*
fallacy	*illegitimacy*	*illiteracy*
immediacy	*inaccuracy*	*inadequacy*
indelicacy	*innumeracy*	*intimacy*
intricacy	*legacy*	*legitimacy*
literacy	*lunacy*	*magistracy*
meritocracy	*numeracy*	*obstinacy*
papacy	*pharmacy*	*privacy*
profligacy	*supremacy*	*technocracy*

There are a very few nouns with the ending **-asy**.

Here are some examples**:**

apostasy *ecstasy* *fantasy* *idiosyncrasy*

-al

This is an adjective-forming and noun-forming ending.

Adjectives ending with **-al** usually have the meaning 'relating to something'.

abdominal	*adverbial*	*central*
coastal	*dental*	*digital*
emotional	*feudal*	*fictional*
fiscal	*floral*	*foetal*
fungal	*herbal*	*legal*
manual	*marginal*	*menstrual*
national	*optional*	*original*
personal	*pivotal*	*postal*
regional	*sexual*	*spiritual*
textual	*verbal*	*visual*

Nouns ending with **-al** usually have the meaning 'the process of something'.

avowal	*betrothal*	*dismissal*
rental	*ritual*	*withdrawal*

The ending **-al** is added in some cases to an English word (for example, *coastal, withdrawal*), but in many more cases to a Latin stem, so it is difficult to give rules for adding it.

But notice the following points:

- Silent **e** is dropped before **-al**:

adjective	*adjectival*	*approve*	*approval*
arrive	*arrival*	*base*	*basal*
bride	*bridal*	*culture*	*cultural*
doctrine	*doctrinal*	*globe*	*global*
hormone	*hormonal*	*medicine*	*medicinal*
recite	*recital*	*refuse*	*refusal*
remove	*removal*	*retire*	*retiral*
suicide	*suicidal*	*tide*	*tidal*

- The consonant is doubled at the end of a stressed syllable containing one short vowel and ending in one consonant:

acquit	*acquittal*	*commit*	*committal*
rebut	*rebuttal*	*refer*	*referral*

- Final **y** changes to **i** before **-al**, unless a vowel comes before **y**:

artery	*arterial*	*bury*	*burial*
colony	*colonial*	*custody*	*custodial*
deny	*denial*	*family*	*familial*
try	*trial*		

But there are some exceptions:

betray	*betrayal*	*portray*	*portrayal*

- Nouns ending in **-ce** change **e** to **i** before **-al**:

artifice	*artificial*	*commerce*	*commercial*
face	*facial*	*finance*	*financial*
prejudice	*prejudicial*	*province*	*provincial*
race	*racial*	*sacrifice*	*sacrificial*

-ance, -ence

These are noun-forming endings, with the sound /əns/. Nouns with these endings have largely abstract meanings, such as the state or the process of something.

Since the two endings **-ance** and **-ence** are pronounced the same, it is difficult to know from the sound which is the correct spelling. It depends in many cases on the Latin stems from which the nouns are derived and this kind of analysis is not possible for those unfamiliar with Latin. The easiest thing is to show the nouns in two separate lists, so that their appearance becomes familiar.

Here is a list of **-ance** nouns:

aberrance
accordance
allegiance
ambulance
appliance
assistance
avoidance
capacitance
clearance
complaisance
connivance
conveyance
deliverance
discordance
elegance
exorbitance
flamboyance
furtherance
guidance
ignorance
inductance
instance
intolerance
luxuriance
nonchalance
parlance
petulance
protuberance
radiance
recognizance
reluctance
remonstrance
resemblance
riddance
substance
sustenance
utterance
vigilance

abeyance
acquaintance
alliance
annoyance
appurtenance
assurance
balance
circumstance
cognisance
compliance
continuance
countenance
deviance
distance
encumbrance
extravagance
forbearance
governance
happenstance
imbalance
inheritance
insurance
irrelevance
maintenance
nuisance
performance
predominance
provenance
reassurance
reconnaissance
remembrance
repentance
resistance
semblance
sufferance
temperance
variance

acceptance
admittance
allowance
appearance
arrogance
attendance
brilliance
clairvoyance
come-uppance
concordance
contrivance
defiance
disappearance
dominance
endurance
exuberance
fragrance
grievance
hindrance
importance
insouciance
intemperance
luminance
misalliance
observance
perseverance
preponderance
pursuance
recalcitrance
relevance
remittance
repugnance
resonance
significance
surveillance
tolerance
vengeance

Handy Hints

- If there is a hard **c** /k/ or a hard **g** /g/ before the suffix, you know the suffix must be **-ance**, not **-ence**:

  arrogance
  elegance
  extravagance
  significance

- Silent **e** is dropped before **-ance**:

assure	*assurance*
contrive	*contrivance*
grieve	*grievance*
guide	*guidance*

- Verbs that double their last consonant before **-ing** also double it before **-ance**:

admit	*admittance*
rid	*riddance*
remit	*remittance*

- **y** changes to **i** before **-ance**:

ally	*alliance*
defy	*defiance*
rely	*reliance*

- The first part of **-ance** nouns is in many cases a recognizable English verb:

  appearance
  avoidance
  clearance
  performance

- Notice, however, that the **e** of the verb has dropped out before **r** in the following nouns:

  encumbrance
  hindrance
  remembrance

-ancy

This ending is used in preference to **-ance** for the following nouns:

ascendancy	*discrepancy*	*expectancy*
flagrancy	*hesitancy*	*inconstancy*
malignancy	*poignancy*	*redundancy*

Here is a list of **-ence** nouns:

abhorrence	*abstinence*	*accidence*
acquiescence	*adherence*	*adolescence*
affluence	*ambience*	*ambivalence*
audience	*belligerence*	*beneficence*
benevolence	*circumference*	*coherence*
coincidence	*competence*	*concupiscence*
concurrence	*condolence*	*conference*
confidence	*confluence*	*congruence*
conscience	*consequence*	*continence*
convalescence	*convenience*	*corpulence*
correspondence	*credence*	*decadence*
deference	*deliquescence*	*dependence*
difference	*diffidence*	*diligence*
disobedience	*dissidence*	*divergence*
ebullience	*effervescence*	*efflorescence*
effluence	*eloquence*	*emergence*
eminence	*equivalence*	*essence*
evanescence	*evidence*	*excellence*
excrescence	*existence*	*expedience*
experience	*flatulence*	*fluorescence*
fraudulence	*grandiloquence*	*imminence*
impatience	*impenitence*	*impermanence*
impertinence	*impotence*	*improvidence*
imprudence	*impudence*	*incandescence*
incidence	*incoherence*	*incompetence*
incontinence	*inconvenience*	*independence*
indifference	*indigence*	*indolence*
indulgence	*inexpedience*	*inexperience*
inference	*inflorescence*	*influence*
insistence	*insurgence*	*intelligence*
interference	*intransigence*	*iridescence*
irreverence	*jurisprudence*	*lenience*
licence	*luminescence*	*magnificence*
magniloquence	*malevolence*	*munificence*

Handy Hints

- *If there is a soft* **c** */s/ or a soft* **g** */dʒ/ before the suffix, you know the suffix must be* **-ence***, not* **-ance***.*
- *But notice the spelling of* ***allegiance*** *and* ***vengeance***.
- *Verbs that double their last consonant before* **-ing** *also double it before* **-ence***:*

excel	*excellence*

- *But with verbs that have a stressed final syllable ending with* **-r***, such as* **refer***,* **confer***,* **recur***,* **occur***,* **concur***, you only double the* **r** *before* **-ence** *if the syllable is stressed in the* **-ence** *noun, for example:*

confer	*conference*
defer	*deference*
refer	*reference*

But:

concur	*concurrence*
occur	*occurrence*
recur	*recurrence*

negligence
obedience
obsolescence
occurrence
omnipotence
omnipresence
omniscience
opalescence
opulence
patience
penitence
percipience
permanence
persistence
pertinence
pestilence
phosphorescence
precedence
preeminence
preference
prescience
presence
prevalence
prominence
providence
prudence
prurience
putrescence
quiescence
quintessence
recrudescence
recumbence
recurrence
reference
reminiscence
residence
resilience
resplendence
resurgence
reticence
reverence
salience
senescence
sentence
sequence
subservience
subsidence
subsistence
succulence
supereminence
transcendence
transference
transience
truculence
tumescence
turbulence
vehemence
violence
virulence

-ency

The ending **-ency** is used in preference to **-ence** for the following nouns:

complacency
consistency
contingency
deficiency
despondency
efficiency
frequency
inconsistency
insufficiency
proficiency
pungency
stridency
tendency
transparency
valency

-ant, -ent

Adjectives ending **-ant** correspond to nouns ending **-ance** or **-ancy**:

distance	*distant*
expectancy	*expectant*
nonchalance	*nonchalant*
poignancy	*poignant*
redundancy	*redundant*

Handy Hint

But **essence** does not follow this pattern:

essence *essential*
quintessence *quintessential*

Adjectives ending **-ent** correspond to nouns ending **-ence** or **-ency**:

frequency	*frequent*
intelligence	*intelligent*
subservience	*subservient*
transparency	*transparent*

Handy Hints

- Notice some common meanings of **-ary** nouns:
  - ➢ a person in a job or position (*secretary, missionary, beneficiary, plenipotentiary*)
  - ➢ a place (*sanctuary, aviary, mortuary, library*)
  - ➢ a collection or body of something (*constabulary, vocabulary, statuary, glossary*)
  - ➢ an activity (*plagiary, topiary, burglary*)
- The associated **-ar** nouns **burglar**, **bursar**, **nectar** and **seminar** help with the spelling of **burglary**, **bursary**, **nectary** and **seminary**. Notice also **beggar** and **beggary**.

-ary, -ery-, -ory

> These three endings are all pronounced /əri/, so it is difficult to distinguish between them from their sound.

The lists below will help you to become familiar with which words have which ending.

-ary

This is a noun-forming and adjective-forming ending.

Here is a list of **nouns** ending with **-ary**:

adversary	*anniversary*	*apiary*
apothecary	*aviary*	*beneficiary*
bestiary	*boundary*	*burglary*
bursary	*capillary*	*centenary*
commentary	*constabulary*	*corollary*
dictionary	*dignitary*	*dispensary*
dromedary	*emissary*	*estuary*
formulary	*functionary*	*glossary*
granary	*intermediary*	*itinerary*
judiciary	*justiciary*	*legionary*
library	*luminary*	*missionary*
mortuary	*nectary*	*notary*
obituary	*penitentiary*	*plagiary*
plenipotentiary	*quandary*	*rosary*
salary	*sanctuary*	*secretary*
seminary	*statuary*	*summary*
syllabary	*topiary*	*tributary*
vagary	*vocabulary*	*voluptuary*

Here is a list of adjectives ending with **-ary**:

alimentary
auxiliary
cautionary
contemporary
customary
dietary
documentary
epistolary
expeditionary
fragmentary
hereditary
incendiary
involuntary
mammary
momentary
numerary
parliamentary
planetary
preliminary
proprietary
reversionary
rudimentary
sanguinary
sedentary
stationary
sumptuary
temporary
tutelary
veterinary
ancillary
binary
complementary
contrary
deflationary
disciplinary
domiciliary
evolutionary
extemporary
funerary
honorary
inflationary
legendary
mercenary
monetary
ordinary
pecuniary
plenary
primary
pulmonary
revolutionary
salivary
sanitary
sedimentary
stipendiary
supernumerary
tertiary
unitary
visionary
arbitrary
budgetary
complimentary
culinary
devolutionary
discretionary
elementary
exemplary
extraordinary
geostationary
imaginary
insanitary
literary
military
necessary
paramilitary
pituitary
precautionary
probationary
reactionary
rotary
salutary
secondary
solitary
subsidiary
supplementary
testamentary
unnecessary
voluntary

Handy Hint

Adding **-y** to **sugar** and **vinegar** gives you two 'impostor' **-ary** adjectives, **sugary** and **vinegary**.

-ery

This is a noun-forming ending.

Here is a list of **nouns** ending with **-ery**:

adultery
bakery
brewery
cajolery
Chancery
creamery
delivery
archery
battery
buffoonery
cannery
chicanery
crockery
demagoguery
artery
bindery
butchery
celery
colliery
cutlery
discovery
artillery
bravery
buttery
cemetery
confectionery
debauchery
distillery

do-goodery	*drapery*	*drollery*	*drudgery*
dysentery	*eatery*	*effrontery*	*embroidery*
finery	*fishery*	*flattery*	*foolery*
foppery	*forgery*	*frippery*	*gallery*
greenery	*haberdashery*	*hatchery*	*hosiery*
housewifery	*imagery*	*ironmongery*	*jewellery*
jiggery-pokery	*joinery*	*knavery*	*lechery*
livery	*lottery*	*machinery*	*mastery*
midwifery	*millinery*	*misery*	*mockery*
monastery	*mystery*	*nunnery*	*nursery*
orangery	*perfumery*	*periphery*	*phylactery*
popery	*pottery*	*presbytery*	*prudery*
quackery	*raillery*	*recovery*	*rediscovery*
refinery	*robbery*	*rockery*	*savagery*
scenery	*scullery*	*shrubbery*	*slavery*
snobbery	*soldiery*	*stationery*	*surgery*
tannery	*thievery*	*thuggery*	*tomfoolery*
treachery	*trickery*	*trumpery*	*upholstery*
witchery			

Handy Hints

- Notice some of the common meanings of **-ery** nouns:
  - activity or behaviour, often of a dubious kind (*foolery, forgery, lechery, popery, prudery, quackery, robbery, savagery, treachery, trickery*)
  - an occupation or skill (*housewifery, midwifery, joinery, surgery*)
  - the product of a trade (*haberdashery, hosiery, jewellery, millinery, perfumery*)
  - a state (*misery, slavery*)
  - a place (*buttery, cemetery, nunnery, nursery, scullery, shrubbery*)
  - something regarded collectively (*finery, greenery, imagery, machinery, scenery*)
- Some **-ery** nouns are associated with a verb or noun ending with **-er**, for example:

verbs

embroider	*embroidery*	*flatter*	*flattery*
discover	*discovery*	*upholster*	*upholstery*

nouns

archer	*archery*	*baker*	*bakery*
confectioner	*confectionery*	*jeweller*	*jewellery*

The only genuine **-ery** adjective is:

slippery

But adding **-y** to verbs or nouns ending with **-er** gives you some 'impostor' **-ery** adjectives, for example:

verbs

bluster	*blustery*	*totter*	*tottery*
shiver	*shivery*	*slither*	*slithery*
waver	*wavery*		

nouns

feather	*feathery*	*flower*	*flowery*
ginger	*gingery*	*leather*	*leathery*
paper	*papery*	*pepper*	*peppery*
powder	*powdery*	*rubber*	*rubber*
spider	*spidery*	*thunder*	*thundery*
water	*watery*		

-ory

This is a noun-forming and adjective-forming ending.

Here is a list of **nouns** ending in **-ory**:

accessory	*allegory*	*armory*	*category*
chicory	*conservatory*	*depilatory*	*depository*
directory	*dormitory*	*factory*	*hickory*
history	*inventory*	*laboratory*	*lavatory*
memory	*observatory*	*offertory*	*oratory*
pillory	*priory*	*promontory*	*purgatory*
rectory	*refectory*	*reformatory*	*repository*
signatory	*suppository*	*territory*	*theory*
trajectory	*victory*		

Handy Hints

Notice some of the meanings of **-ory** nouns:

- a place with a special use (*conservatory, dormitory, laboratory, lavatory, observatory, refectory, reformatory*)
- a person in a certain capacity (*accessory, signatory*)

Here is a list of **adjectives** ending with **-ory**:

admonitory	*adulatory*	*advisory*
aleatory	*amatory*	*auditory*
circulatory	*commendatory*	*conciliatory*
condemnatory	*contradictory*	*contributory*
cursory	*declamatory*	*defamatory*
delusory	*deprecatory*	*derisory*
derogatory	*desultory*	*dilatory*

exclamatory	*excretory*	*expiatory*
explanatory	*exploratory*	*extrasensory*
gustatory	*hortatory*	*illusory*
inflammatory	*introductory*	*laudatory*
mandatory	*migratory*	*nugatory*
obligatory	*olfactory*	*peremptory*
perfunctory	*placatory*	*predatory*
prefatory	*premonitory*	*preparatory*
promissory	*refractory*	*repertory*
respiratory	*revelatory*	*satisfactory*
sensory	*statutory*	*supervisory*
transitory	*valedictory*	

Notice that several **-ory** nouns and adjectives are associated with a 'doer' noun ending with **-or**, for example:

depositor	*depository*	*director*	*directory*
orator	*oratory*	*predator*	*predatory*
supervisor	*supervisory*	*victor*	*victory*

-cede, -ceed, -sede

These three verb stems are all pronounced /siːd/. Although they are not verb-forming endings, it's useful to have a spelling note about them here.

The longest list contains the **-cede** verbs:

accede	*concede*	*intercede*
precede	*recede*	*secede*

There are three **-ceed** verbs:

exceed *proceed* *succeed*

And only one **-sede** verb:

supersede

-en

This is a verb-forming and adjective-forming ending.

As a verb-forming ending.

-en is typically added to adjectives to make verbs that mean 'to make or become something', for example *bright*, *weak*, *thick*, etc:

bright	*brighten*	*dark*	*darken*
deep	*deepen*	*fresh*	*freshen*
hard	*harden*	*less*	*lessen*
thick	*thicken*	*weak*	*weaken*

-en is also added to a few nouns to make verbs:

height	*heighten*	*length*	*lengthen*
strength	*strengthen*		

If the base word ends in silent **e**, you just add **-n**:

awake	*awaken*	*coarse*	*coarsen*
loose	*loosen*	*ripe*	*ripen*
wide	*widen*	*worse*	*worsen*

If the base word ends in one consonent after a one short vowel, the consonant is doubled:

fat	*fatten*	*mad*	*madden*
red	*redden*	*sad*	*sadden*

As an adjective-forming ending.

-en is added to some nouns that are names for materials, to make adjectives that mean 'made of or looking like, a certain material', for example:

gold	*golden*	*earth*	*earthen*
lead	*leaden*	*silk*	*silken*
wax	*waxen*	*wheat*	*wheaten*
wood	*wooden*	*wool*	*woollen*

Handy Hint

Notice that in British English the **l** of **wool** is doubled before **-en**, but in American English the spelling is **woolen**.

DO IT YOURSELF

A In the following sentences, fill in the correct *-ing* form of the appropriate *-en* verb.

For example: Peter was *sharpening* his pencil. (**sharp**)

1. Suddenly there was a __________ crash. (**deaf**)
2. The roadworks are causing __________ delays. (**mad**)
3. The international situation is __________ daily. (**worse**)
4. Ease the patient's breathing by __________ his collar. (**loose**)
5. Susan is __________ up after her journey. (**fresh**)
6. This pedal has the effect of __________ the sound of the note. (**soft**)
7. The grapes are __________ well this year. (**ripe**)
8. The farmers are __________ their cattle for the market. (**fat**)

B In the following sentences fill in the correct *-ed* form of the appropriate *-en* verb.

For example: The sky *brightened* towards the east. (**bright**)

1. The smoke had __________ the wall. (**black**)
2. David __________ his pace in order to catch up. (**quick**)
3. The army training __________ us up in no time. (**tough**)
4. He __________ with fright at the dreadful sound. (**stiff**)
5. We were __________ by the news of her death. (**sad**)
6. They have __________ the motorway by adding two lanes. (**wide**)
7. His face __________ with embarrassment. (**red**)
8. Things __________ up when the dancing started. (**live**)

-er, -or, -ar

These are all noun-forming endings.

The nouns created by them are 'doer' nouns, with the meaning 'someone or something that does a certain thing'.

-er

You can add **-er** to almost any verb to make a 'doer' noun:

call	*caller*	*desert*	*deserter*
labour	*labourer*	*paint*	*painter*
publish	*publisher*	*read*	*reader*
report	*reporter*	*ski*	*skier*
speak	*speaker*	*train*	*trainer*
walk	*walker*	*work*	*worker*

Handy Hint

Notice that a few **-er** 'doer' nouns are not formed from verbs, but from adjectives or nouns:

Britisher	*foreigner*
jeweller	*lawyer*
mariner	*prisoner*
sorcerer	*treasurer*

- When the verb ends in silent **e**, or in **-le** after one or more consonants, you just add **-r**:

advertise	*advertiser*	*argue*	*arguer*
bake	*baker*	*commute*	*commuter*
giggle	*giggler*	*invade*	*invader*
lecture	*lecturer*	*liquidize*	*liquidizer*
move	*mover*	*race*	*racer*
ramble	*rambler*	*seduce*	*seducer*
skate	*skater*	*tame*	*tamer*
weave	*weaver*		

- You double the final consonant of one-syllable verbs that have one vowel and end in one consonant; you also double the final consonant of verbs whose final syllable is stressed, even if this is not the main stress:

bid	*bidder*	*jog*	*jogger*
quit	*quitter*	*run*	*runner*
sit	*sitter*	*zip*	*zipper*
begin	*beginner*	*kidnap*	*kidnapper*
program	*programmer*		

Handy Hint

In American English the spellings **kidnaper** and **kidnapper** are both possible.

Handy Hint

In American English **l** does not usually double in an unstressed syllable before **-er**:

leveler *signaler*
traveler

Handy Hint

With **dry**, **fly** and **fry** there is a choice:

hair-drier or *hair-dryer*
high-flier or *high-flyer*
frier or *fryer*

- But **l** always doubles when it comes after a single vowel, even in an unstressed syllable, before **-er**:

control	*controller*	*level*	*leveller*
signal	*signaller*	*travel*	*traveller*

- A verb ending with **y** changes **y** to **i** before **-er**. But **y** stays if there is a vowel before it:

amplify	*amplifier*	*carry*	*carrier*
copy	*copier*	*fancy*	*fancier*
humidify	*humidifier*	*occupy*	*occupier*
photocopy	*photocopier*		

But there are some exceptions:

buy	*buyer*	*destroy*	*destroyer*
play	*player*	*stay*	*stayer*
lay	*mine-layer*	*pay*	*ratepayer*
slay	*giant-slayer*		

- A verb ending with **c** adds **k** before **-er**:

panic	*panicker*	*picnic*	*picnicker*

-or

Here is a list of 'doer' nouns ending with **-or**:

abductor	*accelerator*	*actor*
adjudicator	*administrator*	*aggressor*
ambassador	*ancestor*	*animator*
arbitrator	*auditor*	*author*
aviator	*bachelor*	*benefactor*
calculator	*captor*	*censor*
chancellor	*chiropractor*	*collaborator*
collector	*commentator*	*communicator*
compressor	*conductor*	*confessor*
conqueror	*conspirator*	*constructor*
contractor	*contributor*	*councillor*
counsellor	*creator*	*creditor*
curator	*cursor*	*decorator*
defector	*demonstrator*	*depositor*
debtor	*detonator*	*detractor*
dictator	*director*	*distributor*
doctor	*donor*	*duplicator*

editor
educator
elector
elevator
emperor
equator
escalator
excavator
executor
facilitator
factor
gladiator
governor
guarantor
illustrator
impersonator
impostor
incinerator
incubator
indicator
infiltrator
inheritor
initiator
inquisitor
inspector
instructor
interrogator
inventor
investigator
investor
invigilator
janitor
legislator
liberator
major
mayor
mediator
mentor
microprocessor
monitor
narrator
navigator
objector
operator
oppressor
orator
orchestrator
pastor
perambulator
perpetrator
persecutor
possessor
precursor
predator
predecessor
processor
professor
projector
proprietor
prosecutor
prospector
protector
purveyor
radiator
rector
reflector
refrigerator
regulator
sailor
selector
semiconductor
senator
solicitor
spectator
sponsor
suitor
supervisor
surveyor
survivor
tailor
testator
toreador
tractor
traitor
transgressor
transistor
translator
vector
vendor
ventilator
vibrator
victor
violator
visitor

Handy Hints

- Notice also the plural noun ***scissors***.
- Notice that silent **e** is dropped before **-or**:

communicate	*communicator*	*supervise*	*supervisor*
survive	*survivor*		

- Notice **councillor** and **counsellor** in British English, and usually **councilor**, **counselor** in American English.

- There are other nouns ending in **-or** that do not fit in the 'doer' class, for example:

alligator	*anchor*	*corridor*
horror	*languor*	*liquor*
motor	*pallor*	*phosphor*
stupor	*tenor*	*tremor*

- There are also some adjectives ending in **-or** which are originally Latin comparative adjectives:

major	*minor*	*inferior*
superior	*interior*	*exterior*
anterior	*posterior*	*ulterior*

There are a few 'doer' nouns ending with **-ar**.

beggar	*burglar*	*bursar*
friar	*liar*	*pedlar*
registrar	*scholar*	*vicar*

- Here are more nouns ending with **-ar** that do not fit in the 'doer' class:

altar	*calendar*	*caterpillar*
caviar	*cedar*	*cellar*
cigar	*collar*	*cougar*
dollar	*exemplar*	*grammar*
guitar	*hangar*	*hussar*
jaguar	*mortar*	*nectar*
pillar	*poplar*	*quasar*
radar	*seminar*	*sonar*
sugar	*vinegar*	

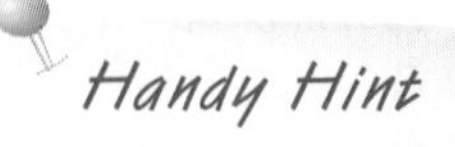

Notice also the plural noun **binoculars**.

- But **-ar** is also a common adjective-forming ending. Most adjectives that end with the sound /ə/ are spelt **-ar**.

  Here is a list of some frequent **-ar** adjectives:

angular	*avuncular*	*cellular*
circular	*consular*	*dissimilar*
familiar	*glandular*	*globular*
granular	*insular*	*irregular*
jocular	*jugular*	*linear*
lumbar	*lunar*	*molar*
molecular	*muscular*	*nuclear*
particular	*peculiar*	*perpendicular*
polar	*popular*	*rectangular*
regular	*secular*	*similar*
singular	*spectacular*	*stellar*
tabular	*triangular*	*tubular*
unfamiliar	*unpopular*	*vernacular*
vulgar		

DO IT YOURSELF

Fill in the correct singular or plural *-er* , *-or* or *-ar* noun in the following sentences.

1. The police are still looking for the __________ of the hoax. (**perpetrate**)
2. He got a job with a firm of __________. (**distil**)
3. Most **land**__________ don't welcome _______ . (**own, picnic**)
4. She was an amusing __________ of village life. (**chronicle**)
5. We must wait for the __________'s report. (**survey**)
6. The column of __________ was approaching the town centre.(**demonstrate**)
7. Some people are __________ and some are __________. (**do, facilitate**)
8. What proportion of households have a __________? (**tumble-dry**)
9. In America a baby's dummy is known as a __________. (**pacify**)
10. Are you a good __________? (**ski**)
11. The __________ of the story is a teenage girl. (**narrate**)
12. In the Isle of Man, the lieutenant __________ represents the Queen. (**govern**)
13. She works in a knitwear factory as a quality-__________. (**control**)
14. The __________ had broken in through the bathroom window. (**burgle**)

-ess

This is a noun-forming feminine ending.

Here is a table of masculine and feminine forms.

MASCULINE	FEMININE	MASCULINE	FEMININE
actor	*actress*	*millionaire*	*millionairess*
adulterer	*adulteress*	*murderer*	*murderess*
ambassador	*ambassadress*	*ogre*	*ogress*
author	*authoress*	*peer*	*peeress*
benefactor	*benefactress*	*poet*	*poetess*
clerk	*clerkess*	*priest*	*priestess*
conductor	*conductress*	*prince*	*princess*
count	*countess*	*prior*	*prioress*
duke	*duchess*	*procurer*	*procuress*
emperor	*empress*	*prophet*	*prophetess*
enchanter	*enchantress*	*proprietor*	*proprietress*
founder	*foundress*	*protector*	*protectress*
god	*goddess*	*sculptor*	*sculptress*
heir	*heiress*	*seducer*	*seductress*
host	*hostess*	*shepherd*	*shepherdess*
hunter	*huntress*	*sorcerer*	*sorceress*
instructor	*instructress*	*steward*	*stewardess*
leopard	*leopardess*	*tempter*	*temptress*
lion	*lioness*	*tiger*	*tigress*
manager	*manageress*	*traitor*	*traitress*
master	*mistress*	*waiter*	*waitress*
mayor	*mayoress*	*warder*	*wardress*

Did You Know?

Many feminines are dropping out of use. Female **sculptors**, **authors** and **poets** prefer those terms to the feminine forms; a **conductress** is found only on a tram or bus, not in front of an orchestra; a **mayoress** is usually the wife of a mayor, not a female mayor; an **ambassadress** tends to be a semi-official representative rather than a diplomat, as in 'cultural ambassadress'.

Handy Hints

- In keeping with the rule for doubling a final consonant when adding a suffix starting with a vowel to a *one-syllable, one-short-vowel* word ending in *one consonant*, you get:

  god *goddess*

- The endings *-der*, *-dor*, *-ter*, *-tor* become *-dress* or *-tress*:

  warder *wardress* | *ambassador* *ambassadress*
  waiter *waitress* | *proprietor* *proprietress*

  Notice also *tiger* *tigress*

- The ending **-erer** is changed to **-eress**:

  murderer *murderess* *sorcerer* *sorceress*

- After silent **e** you just add **-ss**:

  prince *princess* | *millionaire* *millionairess*

- The following do not conform to rules:

  duke *duchess* | *emperor* *empress*
  master *mistress* | *seducer* *seductress*

-ful

This is an adjective-forming and noun-forming ending.

As an adjective-forming ending **-ful** is added typically to nouns to make adjectives with the meaning 'having or showing a certain thing or quality'.

help	*helpful*	*glee*	*gleeful*
hurt	*hurtful*	*law*	*lawful*
rest	*restful*	*sin*	*sinful*
tact	*tactful*	*truth*	*truthful*

Nouns that end with silent **e** keep **e** before **-ful**.

care	*careful*	*hope*	*hopeful*
fate	*fateful*	*force*	*forceful*
hate	*hateful*	*shame*	*shameful*
spite	*spiteful*	*waste*	*wasteful*
woe	*woeful*		

Nouns ending in **y** change **y** to **i** before **-ful**.

beauty	*beautiful*	*bounty*	*bountiful*
duty	*dutiful*	*fancy*	*fanciful*
mercy	*merciful*	*pity*	*pitiful*

But they keep **y** if there is a vowel before **y**.

joy	*joyful*	*play*	*playful*

You can add the noun-forming ending **-ful** to any noun you want to, to give the meaning 'an amount contained in something'.

a spoonful of honey	*a jugful of water*
a mugful of coffee	*a handful of coins*
an armful of laundry	*a roomful of people*
a mouthful of food	*a shopful of customers*

Handy Hint

Notice also that **skill** and **will** drop an **l**:

skill *skilful*
will *wilful*

But in American English these words are spelt:

skillful *willful*

Handy Hint

An exception is:

awe *awful*

Handy Hint

Don't forget that you get **ll** when you add **-ly** for the adverb:

helpful *helpfully*
useful *usefully*

Handy Hints

- Don't forget that for the plural you add **s** after **-ful**:
  three teaspoonfuls of salt
  My hair came out in handfuls.
- You don't change **-y** to **i** before noun-forming **-ful**:
  bombs that wipe out whole cityfuls of people

DO IT YOURSELF

Fill in the correct -*ful* adjective, -*fully* adverb, or -*ful* noun in the following sentences.

1 Jimmy has such a __________ personality. (**force**)

2 I parked the car very __________ between a taxi and a truck. (**skill**)

3 Does **un**__________ mean the same as illegal? (**law**)

4 The precautions against flooding were __________ inadequate. (**woe**)

5 I received an __________ of complaints on my voicemail. (**ear**)

6 It was __________ quiet and __________ in the woods. (**delight**, **peace**)

7 There are __________ examples of this kind of error. (**plenty**)

8 Add two __________ of syrup to the mixture. (**tablespoon**)

9 Some suggestions were __________ silly. (**awe**)

10 Should you punish children who are __________ disobedient? (**will**)

11 __________, the animal did not suffer much. (**mercy**)

12 Anna sank __________ into an armchair. (**grace**)

13 I don't go along with all her __________ ideas. (**fancy**)

14 Kids are **dis**__________ **dis**__________ to their teachers nowadays. (**grace**, **respect**)

-hood

This is a noun-forming ending.

It can be added to nouns to mean the state or position of being a certain thing.

adulthood	*babyhood*	*boyhood*
brotherhood	*childhood*	*fatherhood*
girlhood	*knighthood*	*manhood*
motherhood	*parenthood*	*priesthood*
puppyhood	*sainthood*	*sisterhood*
widowhood	*womanhood*	

It is also added to a few adjectives.

false	*falsehood*	*hardy*	*hardihood*
likely	*likelihood*	*lively*	*livelihood*
unlikely	*unlikelihood*		

Handy Hint

Nouns ending with **-y** keep the **y** before **-hood**:

babyhood *puppyhood*

Handy Hint

Notice that adjectives ending with **-y** change **y** to **i** before **-hood**.

-ify, -efy

These are verb-forming endings, producing verbs with the meaning 'cause to become something'.

There are only four common verbs ending **-efy**.

liquefy *putrefy* *rarefy* *stupefy*

Here is a list of **-ify** verbs:

acidify	*amplify*	*beautify*	*calcify*
certify	*clarify*	*classify*	*deify*
dignify	*disqualify*	*diversify*	*edify*
electrify	*emulsify*	*exemplify*	*falsify*
gentrify	*glorify*	*gratify*	*horrify*
identify	*intensify*	*justify*	*magnify*
modify	*mortify*	*mummify*	*mystify*
notify	*pacify*	*personify*	*petrify*
prettify	*purify*	*qualify*	*quantify*
ratify	*sanctify*	*signify*	*simplify*
solidify	*specify*	*stratify*	*stultify*
syllabify	*terrify*	*testify*	*ransmogrify*
typify	*uglify*	*unify*	*verify*

Handy Hint

Nouns formed from **-efy** verbs end with **-faction**:

liquefaction
putrefaction
rarefaction
stupefaction

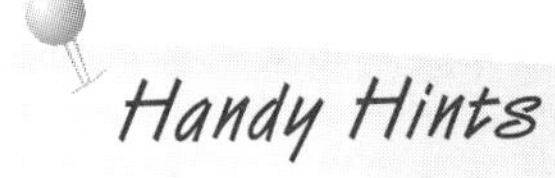

Handy Hints

- It is difficult to give rules about adding **-ify**, because this suffix in many cases has been attached to a Latin stem.

  Notice however that **y** is replaced by the **i** of **-ify**:

  beauty beautify | *gentry gentrify* | *pretty prettify* | *ugly uglify*
- Nouns formed from **-ify** verbs end with **-ification**:

  amplification classification identification simplification verification

  But notice that **petrification** and **petrifaction** are both possible.
- Notice also the slightly different formation of:

  satisfy satisfaction | *dissatisfy dissatisfaction*

-ious, -eous

These are adjective-forming endings, both pronounced /iəs/.

Most adjectives ending with this sound are spelt **-ious**:

abstemious	*acrimonious*	*amphibious*
censorious	*ceremonious*	*commodious*
compendious	*copious*	*curious*
delirious	*devious*	*dubious*
glorious	*harmonious*	*hilarious*
ignominious	*illustrious*	*impecunious*
imperious	*impervious*	*industrious*
ingenious	*injurious*	*laborious*
lascivious	*luxurious*	*melodious*
meritorious	*multifarious*	*nefarious*
notorious	*obsequious*	*obvious*
odious	*parsimonious*	*perfidious*
previous	*punctilious*	*rebellious*
salubrious	*sanctimonious*	*serious*
spurious	*studious*	*supercilious*
tedious	*uproarious*	*victorious*

Here is a smaller list of adjectives ending in **-eous**:

aqueous	*beauteous*	*bounteous*
consanguineous	*contemporaneous*	*courteous*
discourteous	*erroneous*	*extraneous*
gaseous	*heterogeneous*	*hideous*
homogeneous	*igneous*	*instantaneous*
miscellaneous	*nauseous*	*piteous*
simultaneous	*spontaneous*	*subcutaneous*

Handy Hint

gaseous can be pronounced /ˈgasɪəs/ or /ˈgeɪʃəs/.

The adjective-forming endings **-cious**, **-ceous**, **-tious**, all pronounced /ʃəs/, form a sound subgroup.

Handy Hint

Nouns that end in **-ce** replace **-e** with **-ious**:

avarice	*avaricious*
caprice	*capricious*
grace	*gracious*
space	*spacious*
vice	*vicious*

Handy Hint

There are many more adjectives in **-ceous** group, but they are scientific or technical, e.g.:

carbonaceous
cetaceous
iridaceous
liliaceous
sebaceous
siliceous

Here is a list of adjectives ending with **-cious**:

auspicious	*avaricious*	*capricious*
conscious	*delicious*	*efficacious*
gracious	*judicious*	*loquacious*
mendacious	*meretricious*	*pernicious*
perspicacious	*pertinacious*	*precocious*
spacious	*specious*	*suspicious*
unconscious	*vicious*	*vivacious*

Here are some adjectives ending with **-ceous**:

Cretaceous	*curvaceous*	*herbaceous*
predaceous		

Here is a list of adjectives ending with **-tious**:

ambitious	*bumptious*	*captious*
cautious	*conscientious*	*disputatious*
expeditious	*factious*	*fictitious*
flirtatious	*infectious*	*nutritious*
ostentatious	*pretentious*	*propitious*
repetitious	*scrumptious*	*seditious*
sententious	*superstitious*	*suppositious*
surreptitious	*unambitious*	*unpretentious*
vexatious		

The only adjective ending **-teous** with the sound /tʃəs/ is:

righteous

There are a very few adjectives ending **-xious** /kʃəs/:

anxious	*noxious*	*obnoxious*

The adjective-forming endings **-gious** and **-geous** (pronounced /dʒəs/) represent another sound subgroup.

Here are the adjectives ending in **-gious**:

contagious	*egregious*	*litigious*
prestigious	*prodigious*	*religious*
sacrilegious		

And here are the adjectives ending with -**geous**:

advantageous	*disadvantageous*	*courageous*
gorgeous	*outrageous*	

Handy Hint

Apart from **gorgeous**, these are words in which silent ***e*** has been kept to keep the ***g*** soft.

-ish

This is an adjective-forming ending, added mainly to adjectives or nouns to give the meaning 'rather something', 'like something', or 'inclined towards something'.

Here are some examples where **-ish** is just added to the base word:

amateurish	*bookish*	*boyish*
childish	*clownish*	*devilish*
fiendish	*freakish*	*impish*
kittenish	*oldish*	*outlandish*
roundish	*sheepish*	*stand-offish*
stiffish	*sweetish*	*tigerish*
toughish	*yellowish*	*youngish*

With one-syllable, one-short-vowel words ending in one consonant, the final consonant is doubled before **-ish**.

fat	*fattish*	*flat*	*flattish*
hot	*hottish*	*prig*	*priggish*
red	*reddish*	*slut*	*sluttish*
snob	*snobbish*	*thin*	*thinnish*
wet	*wettish*		

Words ending with silent **e**, or **le** after one or more consonants, drop **e** and add **-ish**.

ape	*apish*	*blue*	*bluish*
brute	*brutish*	*coquette*	*coquettish*
knave	*knavish*	*late*	*latish*
mode	*modish*	*purple*	*purplish*
rogue	*roguish*	*slave*	*slavish*
square	*squarish*	*tickle*	*ticklish*

Words ending with **y** keep the **y** before **-ish**.

babyish	*fiftyish*	*fortyish*
greyish	*puppyish*	

-ism

This is a noun-forming ending, producing nouns with the following meanings:

- attitude or behaviour of a certain kind: *racism, dogmatism, realism, racism*
- activity of a certain kind: *terrorism, criticism, hooliganism, tourism, vandalism*
- an occurrence of something: *heroism, symbolism, euphemism, colloquialism*
- belief in something: *Communism, Marxism, Taoism, Confucianism*
- a phenomenon: *magnetism*

Here are some well-known **-isms**:

agnosticism	*alcoholism*	*altruism*
amateurism	*anarchism*	*asceticism*
atheism	*bolshevism*	*capitalism*
careerism	*colloquialism*	*Communism*
Confucianism	*criticism*	*defeatism*
despotism	*dogmatism*	*dynamism*
egoism	*eroticism*	*euphemism*
fascism	*fanaticism*	*federalism*

feminism	*fetishism*	*hedonism*
heroism	*hooliganism*	*humanism*
hypnotism	*idealism*	*jingoism*
journalism	*Leninism*	*liberalism*
magnetism	*mannerism*	*Marxism*
masochism	*materialism*	*mechanism*
militarism	*modernism*	*monetarism*
mysticism	*narcissism*	*naturalism*
Nazism	*neutralism*	*opportunism*
optimism	*ostracism*	*pacifism*
patriotism	*pessimism*	*pragmatism*
puritanism	*racialism*	*rationalism*
realism	*satanism*	*scepticism*
sexism	*socialism*	*specialism*
Stalinism	*surrealism*	*symbolism*
Taoism	*terrorism*	*tokenism*
tourism	*tribalism*	*vandalism*

It is difficult to give rules for adding **-ism**, because in some cases it is added directly to whole English words (e.g. *defeatism, humanism, tokenism*), and in many other cases to the stem of Latin-derived or Greek-derived words (e.g. *feminism, dynamism*).

Notice however:

Silent **e** is dropped before **-ism**:

age	*agism*	*cube*	*cubism*
elite	*elitism*	*escape*	*escapism*
extreme	*extremism*	*Fauve*	*Fauvism*
future	*futurism*	*nature*	*naturism*
pure	*purism*	*race*	*racism*
Sade	*sadism*	*state*	*statism*
true	*truism*		

One-syllable, one-short-vowel words ending in one consonant double the consonant:

snob — *snobbism*

Final **y** stays before **-ism**:

Tory — *Toryism*

Handy Hint

agism and **ageism** are both possible.

Did You Know?

sadism is named after the Marquis de Sade, who in his novels described the kind of pleasure that comes from inflicting pain.

-ist

This is a noun-forming ending.

Many **-ist** nouns reflect **-isms**, and many of these can be used as adjectives.

atheist	*elitist*	*escapist*	*extremist*
feminist	*pacifist*	*racist*	*socialist*
sexist	*terrorist*		

Handy Hint

Notice these two spellings:

canoe *canoeist*
oboe *oboist*

But there are many other **-ist** nouns that have the meaning 'a person who does something' or 'an expert in something', or 'a performer on something'.

artist	*biologist*	*botanist*	*canoeist*
cellist	*chemist*	*colonist*	*copyist*
cyclist	*dentist*	*diarist*	*economist*
essayist	*finalist*	*flautist*	*geologist*
jurist	*machinist*	*novelist*	*oboist*
oculist	*pharmacist*	*physicist*	*pianist*
rapist	*soloist*	*typist*	*violinist*

-ity, -ety

Did You Know?

The word **safety** used to have three syllables, but the **e** is no longer pronounced separately.

These are noun-forming endings, pronounced /ɪti/ or /əti/.

Nearly all nouns ending with this sound are spelt **-ity**.

ability	*audacity*	*gravity*	*identity*
jollity	*morality*	*reality*	*sanctity*

Handy Hint

The **y** of **gay** changes to **i** before **-ety**: *gaiety*

A few nouns with this sound have the ending **-ety**.

entire	*entirety*	*gay*	*gaiety*
naive	*naivety*	*nice*	*nicety*
sure	*surety*		

l or **ll** before **-ity**?

You do not double **l** after a single short vowel before **-ity**:

brutal	*brutality*	*mortal*	*mortality*
equal	*equality*	*normal*	*normality*
final	*finality*	*plural*	*plurality*
legal	*legality*	*special*	*speciality*

Handy Hint

An exception is:

tranquil *tranquillity*

Notice that in American English the spelling can be *tranquility*.

-eity

A few nouns related to adjectives ending with **-eous** have the ending **-eity** /ˈiːɪti/.

homogeneous	*homogeneity*
instantaneous	*instantaneity*
spontaneous	*spontaneity*

-iety

Several nouns, some related to adjectives ending with **-ious**, have the ending **-iety** /ˈaɪəti/.

anxiety	*dubiety*	*impiety*	*impropriety*
notoriety	*piety*	*propriety*	*satiety*
sobriety	*society*	*variety*	

-ize, -ise

These are verb-forming endings, both pronounced /aɪz/.

Most verbs that end with this sound can be spelt either **-ize** or **-ise**.

criticize or *criticise*
idealize or *idealise*
maximize or *maximise*
minimize or *minimise*
modernize or *modernise*
recognize or *recognise*

The **-ize** spelling is possible wherever **-ize**/**-ise** is added to a base word as a true suffix.

If **-ise** is part of the main stem of the verb, and not a suffix, the **-ize** alternative is not possible.

-ise is part of the stem of the following verbs; none of these verbs can be spelt **-ize**.

advertise	*advise*	*apprise*
arise	*chastise*	*circumcise*
comprise	*compromise*	*despise*
devise	*disguise*	*excise*
exercise	*franchise*	*improvise*
incise	*revise*	*supervise*
surmise	*surprise*	*televise*

But **-ize** is part of the stem of the following verb, which must therefore always be spelt **-ize**.

capsize

Handy Hint

Two exceptions are:

crystal	*crystallize*
tranquil	*tranquillize*

Notice that *tranquilize* is the normal American English spelling.

You do not double **l** after a single short vowel before **-ize**/**-ise**.

brutal	*brutalize*	*equal*	*equalize*
final	*finalize*	*global*	*globalize*
idol	*idolize*	*legal*	*legalize*
penal	*penalize*	*plural*	*pluralize*
serial	*serialize*	*social*	*socialize*
special	*specialize*	*symbol*	*symbolize*
vandal	*vandalize*		

Handy Hint

These verbs are regularly spelt **-yze** in American English.

-yse, -yze

A few verbs are spelt **-yse** /aɪz/, not **-ize**/**-ise**:

analyse	*breathalyse*	*paralyse*
psychoanalyse		

-less

This is an adjective-forming ending.

It is added to nouns to give the meaning 'lacking something'.

cashless *colourless* *endless*
fearless *flawless* *humourless*
jobless *profitless* *tactless*
tailless

Silent **e** is kept before **-less**:

ageless *baseless* *careless*
guileless *hopeless* *loveless*
timeless *tuneless* *useless*

Final **y** is changed to **i** before **-less**.

mercy *merciless*
penny *penniless*
pity *pitiless*

But **y** is kept if there is a vowel before it:

joy *joyless*
money *moneyless*

-ment

This is chiefly a noun-forming ending.

It is added mainly to verbs to give the meaning 'the process of doing or experiencing something, or an instance of this'.

adjustment *adornment* *alignment*
allotment *amendment* *annulment*
assessment *enactment* *endowment*
enlightenment *equipment* *shipment*
treatment

Handy Hint

Notice that you get **ll** *when* **-less** *is added to a noun ending with* **l**:

tail *tailless*

Handy Hints

- But notice:

  argue *argument*

- And you have a choice with verbs ending **-dge**:

  acknowledgement or *acknowledgment*
  judgement or *judgment*

Handy Hints

- Notice:

  instal or *install* *instalment*

- In American English *fulfillment* is the usual spelling.

Silent **e** is kept before **-ment**:

amaze	*amazement*
amuse	*amusement*
elope	*elopement*
manage	*management*
move	*movement*
state	*statement*

Final consonants are not doubled before **-ment**:

inter	*interment*	*prefer*	*preferment*
fulfil	*fulfilment*		

Words ending in **y** change **y** to **i** before **-ment**

accompany	*accompaniment*
embody	*embodiment*
merry	*merriment*

But **y** is kept if there is a vowel before it.

employ	*employment*
enjoy	*enjoyment*
pay	*payment*

-ness

This is a noun-forming ending.

It is added to adjectives to give the meaning 'the state of being something'.

bitterness	*fairness*	*fitness*
madness	*raggedness*	*toughness*
usefulness	*willingness*	

Handy Hint

When you add **-ness** to an adjective ending with **n**, you get **-nn-**:

drunken	*drunkenness*
green	*greenness*
open	*openness*
plain	*plainness*
stern	*sternness*
sudden	*suddenness*

Silent **e** is kept before **-ness**:

awareness	*brittleness*	*denseness*
feebleness	*fineness*	*looseness*
niceness	*oneness*	*remoteness*
ripeness	*sameness*	*vagueness*

Final **y** changes to **i** before **-ness**:

airy	*airiness*	*cosy*	*cosiness*
edgy	*edginess*	*happy*	*happiness*
holy	*holiness*	*icy*	*iciness*
lazy	*laziness*	*oily*	*oiliness*
orderly	*orderliness*	*sexy*	*sexiness*
shapely	*shapeliness*	*silly*	*silliness*
sleepy	*sleepiness*	*tidy*	*tidiness*
ugly	*ugliness*	*wary*	*wariness*
worthy	*worthiness*		

Handy Hints

- Notice that the noun meaning 'the state of being busy' is usually spelt **busyness**, to distinguish it from **business**.
- Notice what happens with these adjectives that can be spelt **-ey**:

cagy or *cagey*	*caginess, cagyness* or *cageyness*
maty or *matey*	*mateyness* or *matiness*
phony or *phoney*	*phoniness*

- One-syllable adjectives ending with **y** keep **y** before **-ness**:

coyness	*dryness*	*greyness*	or	*grayness*
shyness	*slyness*	*spryness*		wryness

DO IT YOURSELF

A Fill in the correct *-less* adjective or *-lessly* adverb in the following sentences.

1 The accusation was completely ___________. (**base**)

2 Stacking supermarket shelves is a rather ___________ job. (**soul**)

3 The sun beat down ___________. (**mercy**)

4 A ___________ person is somebody who lacks cunning. (**guile**)

5 She slipped ___________ out of the room. (**noise**)

6 Some of my colleagues seem a bit ___________. (**clue**)

B Fill in the correct *-ment* noun in the following sentences.

1 Who was responsible for the ___________ of the book? (**abridge**)

2 I'll send the file as an ___________. (**attach**)

3 You'll find out in the next ___________. (**install**)

4 I'm reducing my ___________ with the company. (**involve**)

5 Her only concern was the ___________ of her own career. (**advance**)

6. The songs are set to a guitar ___________. (**accompany**)

C Fill in the correct *-ness* noun in the following sentences.

1 It's the ___________ and ___________ of kippers that puts people off them. (**bony, oily**)

2. Walking in the hills gives you a great feeling of ___________. (**alone**)

3 Nobody could accuse her of ___________. (**shy**)

4 We drove slowly because of the ___________ of the road surface. (**unneven**)

5 Scrooge was well known for his ___________. (**miserly**)

6. He had been well punished for his ___________. (**naughty**)

-our

This is a noun-forming ending.

Many nouns ending with **-our** are abstract qualities (for example *candour, honour, splendour*) but others have more concrete meanings (*armour, harbour, neighbour*).

armour	*behaviour*	*candour*	*clamour*
clangour	*colour*	*demeanour*	*disfavour*
dishonour	*endeavour*	*favour*	*fervour*
flavour	*glamour*	*harbour*	*honour*
humour	*labour*	*neighbour*	*odour*
rancour	*rigour*	*rumour*	*saviour*
savour	*splendour*	*succour*	*tumour*
valour	*vapour*	*vigour*	

Handy Hints

- Several of these nouns are used as verbs:

  clamour, colour, dishonour, endeavour, favour, flavour, harbour, honour, humour, labour, savour, succour.

- In American English all except one of these words are spelt with **-or** instead of **-our**:

  armor, behavior, candor, etc.

  The exception is **glamour**, which is spelt **-our** in American English.

Several of these nouns form adjectives by adding **-ous**, but notice that they drop the **u** from **-our** when they do so.

clamour	*clamorous*	*clangour*	*clangorous*
glamour	*glamorous*	*humour*	*humorous*
odour	*odorous*	*rancour*	*rancorous*
rigour	*rigorous*	*tumour*	*tumorous*
valour	*valorous*	*vapour*	*vaporous*
vigour	*vigorous*		

Handy Hints

- Notice also:

  labour *laborious*

- Also notice:

  amour /əˈmʊə/ *amorous*

- But **u** is not dropped when **-able** is added:

colour	*colourable*	*favour*	*favourable*
honour	*honourable*	*dishonour*	*dishonourable*

  In American English the spelling is:

  favorable, honorable, etc.

- In addition, notice these spellings:

colour	*coloration* or *colouration*	*colourist*
honour	*honorarium* or *honorary*	*honorific*
labour	*labourer*	
savour	*savoury*	

Handy Hints

- The ending **-ous** is in some cases added to an English noun, for example:

  gluttonous, hazardous, poisonous, thunderous, villainous

  but in many more cases to a Latin or Greek stem.

- Notice however that silent **e** is dropped in:

adventure	*adventurous*
desire	*desirous*
gangrene	*gangrenous*
rapture	*rapturous*

- The **e** in **-er** is dropped in:

disaster	*disastrous*
wonder	*wondrous*

- **ll** is doubled in:

libel	*libellous*
marvel	*marvellous*

  But **l** is not doubled in:

credulous	*frivolous*
garrulous	*meticulous*
miraculous	*querulous*
ridiculous	*scandalous*
scrupulous	*scurrilous*

Did You Know?

There are some nouns ending with **-us**, that have a related **-ous** adjective, for example:

callus	*callous*
citrus	*citrous*
fungus	*fungous*
mucus	*mucous*

-ous

This is an adjective-forming ending.

For adjectives with the endings **-ious** and **-eous**, see the section **-ious**, **-eous** above (page 79); for adjectives ending **-orous** see the section **-our** below (page 91).

Here are some of the well-known adjectives ending with **-ous**:

adulterous	*adventurous*	*ambiguous*
amorphous	*androgynous*	*anonymous*
arduous	*assiduous*	*autonomous*
barbarous	*boisterous*	*cacophonous*
cadaverous	*calamitous*	*callous*
cancerous	*cantankerous*	*carnivorous*
cavernous	*chivalrous*	*circuitous*
conspicuous	*contemptuous*	*contiguous*
continuous	*covetous*	*credulous*
dangerous	*deciduous*	*decorous*
desirous	*dexterous*	*disastrous*
disingenuous	*enormous*	*erogenous*
exiguous	*famous*	*fatuous*
felicitous	*fibrous*	*fortuitous*
frivolous	*gangrenous*	*generous*
garrulous	*glutinous*	*gluttonous*
gratuitous	*grievous*	*hazardous*
heinous	*herbivorous*	*horrendous*
impetuous	*incestuous*	*incongruous*
incredulous	*indigenous*	*infamous*
ingenuous	*iniquitous*	*innocuous*
jealous	*joyous*	*lecherous*
libellous	*libidinous*	*ludicrous*
luminous	*magnanimous*	*marvellous*
mellifluous	*meticulous*	*miraculous*
mischievous	*momentous*	*monogamous*
monotonous	*mountainous*	*monstrous*
murderous	*mutinous*	*necessitous*
nervous	*nitrous*	*numerous*
obstreperous	*ominous*	*omnivorous*
onerous	*perilous*	*poisonous*
pompous	*ponderous*	*porous*
portentous	*posthumous*	*precipitous*

presumptuous	*promiscuous*	*prosperous*
querulous	*rapturous*	*ravenous*
ridiculous	*riotous*	*ruinous*
scandalous	*scrupulous*	*scurrilous*
sensuous	*slanderous*	*solicitous*
sonorous	*strenuous*	*stupendous*
sumptuous	*superfluous*	*synchronous*
synonymous	*tautologous*	*tempestuous*
tenuous	*thunderous*	*timorous*
tortuous	*treacherous*	*tremendous*
tremulous	*tumultuous*	*tyrannous*
ubiquitous	*unanimous*	*unctuous*
unscrupulous	*vacuous*	*venomous*
verminous	*villainous*	*virtuous*
vociferous	*voluminous*	*voluptuous*
wondrous	*zealous*	

A few **-ous** adjectives form nouns by adding **-ity**. But notice that they lose the **u** of **-ous** when they do so.

curious	*curiosity*	*generous*	*generosity*
impetuous	*impetuosity*	*luminous*	*luminosity*
monstrous	*monstrosity*	*pompous*	*pomposity*
porous	*porosity*		

Handy Hints

- Many other **-ous** adjectives form nouns by adding **-ness**, for example:

  adventurousness *covetousness*
  nervousness *strenuousness*

- **Virtuosity**, meaning skill in playing a musical instrument, is the noun corresponding to the adjective **virtuoso** rather than the adjective **virtuous**; you use **virtue** or **virtuousness** to mean 'goodness'.

- **Callosity**, meaning a hard patch or **callus** on the skin, corresponds to a specialized meaning of the adjective **callous**, describing hard skin; you use **callousness** to mean 'coldhearted cruelty'.

- **Monstrosity** means 'a monstrous thing'; use **monstrousness** to mean the quality of being monstrous.

- **Scrupulosity** is sometimes used as the noun from **scrupulous**, but **scrupulousness** is much commoner.

DO IT YOURSELF

Fill in the correct adjective or noun in the following sentences.

1 You're wearing a very ________ outfit. (**glamour**)

2 Thank you for your ________. (**generous**)

3 You should take ________ exercise every day. (**vigour**)

4 P G Wodehouse was a writer of ________ stories. (**humour**)

5 The inspectors sent in a ________ report on the school. (**favour**)

6 ________ killed the cat. (**curious**)

7 They are all ________ men. (**honour**)

8 Your ________ will lead you into big trouble one day. (**impetuous**)

9 ________ is the quality of being unsympathetic or cold-hearted. (**callous**)

10 These samples have been subjected to ________ testing. (**rigour**)

11 The compartment was full of ________ schoolchildren. (**clamour**)

12 How is the ________ of stars measured? (**luminous**)

13 ________ is self-important language or behaviour. (**pompous**)

14 The new supermarket is just a hideous ________. (**monstrous**)

-some

This is an adjective-forming ending, but it is not much used as a 'living suffix' to form new words. Most of the adjectives ending in **-some** are rather old words.

The suffix **-some** is added to verbs and nouns to produce adjectives with the meaning 'inclined towards something'.

awesome	*bothersome*	*burdensome*
cumbersome	*fearsome*	*gruesome*
handsome	*irksome*	*loathsome*
lonesome	*meddlesome*	*quarrelsome*
tiresome	*toilsome*	*troublesome*
venturesome	*wearisome*	*wholesome*

Handy Hint

- Notice that silent **e** is kept before **-some**:

awe	*awesome*
lone	*lonesome*
meddle	*meddlesome*

Loathsome looks like an exception, but it comes not from the verb *loathe*, but from an old noun *loath*, meaning 'disgust'.

- Notice that final **y** becomes **i** before **-some**:

  weary *wearisome*

- The word **handsome** once literally meant 'easy to handle', which explains its formation.

-tion, -sion, -cion

These are noun-forming endings, attached mainly to Latin stems, and producing mainly abstract nouns.

-cion and **-tion** are both pronounced /ʃən/.

There are only two words you need to know that end with **-cion**:

coercion *suspicion*

-sion is pronounced /ʒən/ after a vowel.

So you can be sure that if the pronunciation is /ʒən/, the spelling must be **-sion**:

abrasion	*adhesion*	*circumcision*
cohesion	*collision*	*collusion*
concision	*conclusion*	*confusion*
contusion	*corrosion*	*decision*
delusion	*derision*	*diffusion*
disillusion	*dissuasion*	*division*
effusion	*elision*	*erosion*

Did You Know?

Gruesome comes from a dialect verb *grue* meaning to shudder.

Did You Know?

- The following **-sion** words are also verbs:
  disillusion occasion provision
- American English has the verb **envision,** meaning 'visualize'.

evasion	*excision*	*exclusion*
explosion	*fusion*	*illusion*
imprecision	*incision*	*inclusion*
infusion	*intrusion*	*lesion*
occasion	*persuasion*	*precision*
protrusion	*provision*	*revision*
seclusion	*subdivision*	*suffusion*
supervision	*television*	*transfusion*
vision		

But **-ssion** is pronounced /ʃən/.

- You get **-ssion** nouns formed from verbs ending with **-cede** or **-ceed**:

accede	*accession*
cede	*cession*
concede	*concession*
intercede	*intercession*
precede	*precession*
proceed	*procession*
recede	*recession*
secede	*secession*
succeed	*succession*

- You get **-ssion** nouns formed from verbs ending with **-mit**:

admit	*admission*
commit	*commission*
emit	*emission*
omit	*omission*
permit	*permission*
remit	*remission*
submit	*submission*
transmit	*transmission*

- You get **-ssion** nouns related to verbs ending in **-ss**:

aggress	*aggression*	*compress*	*compression*
concuss	*concussion*	*confess*	*confession*
depress	*depression*	*digress*	*digression*
discuss	*discussion*	*express*	*expression*

impress	*impression*	*obsess*	*obsession*
oppress	*oppression*	*percuss*	*percussion*
possess	*possession*	*profess*	*profession*
progress	*progression*	*regress*	*regression*
repress	*repression*	*suppress*	*suppression*
transgress	*transgression*		

Handy Hint

In addition, notice the following **-ssion** nouns:

compassion *fission*
mission *passion*
session

Otherwise, if the pronunciation is /ʃən/ after a vowel, you can be sure that the spelling is **-tion**, for example:

addition	*aeration*	*ambition*	*audition*
aviation	*caution*	*citation*	*creation*
deletion	*devotion*	*dilation*	*dilution*
donation	*duration*	*edition*	*elation*
emotion	*equation*	*fixation*	*fruition*
gyration	*ignition*	*legation*	*libation*
ligation	*location*	*lotion*	*munition*
mutation	*nation*	*negation*	*notation*
notion	*oration*	*ovation*	*petition*
position	*relation*	*rotation*	*sedation*
sedition	*solution*	*station*	*taxation*
tuition	*vacation*	*vexation*	*vocation*
volition			

After a consonant **-sion** and **-tion** are both pronounced /ʃən/.

- After **l** the spelling is always **-sion**:

compulsion *convulsion* *expulsion*
propulsion *repulsion* *revulsion*

- After **n** the spelling is often **-sion**:

apprehension	*ascension*	*comprehension*
condescension	*declension*	*dimension*
dissension	*distension*	*emulsion*
expansion	*extension*	*hypertension*
incomprehension	*mansion*	*misapprehension*
pension	*pretension*	*scansion*
suspension	*tension*	

Handy Hints

- But notice:

abstain	*abstention*
detain	*detention*
retain	*retention*
attend	*attention*
contend	*contention*
intend	*intention*
convene	*convention*
intervene	*intervention*
invent	*invention*
prevent	*prevention*

- Also notice:

mention

Handy Hints

- But notice:

abort	*abortion*
assert	*assertion*
contort	*contortion*
desert	*desertion*
distort	*distortion*
exert	*exertion*
extort	*extortion*
insert	*insertion*

- Also notice:

portion
proportion

Handy Hints

- After **s**, **-tion** is pronounced /tʃən/, as in:

combustion, *congestion*, *digestion*, *exhaustion*, *indigestion*, *question*, *suggestion*

- Some **-ction** nouns are sometimes spelt **-xion**:

connection or *connexion*
flection or *flexion*
inflection or *inflexion*

- A few nouns are always spelt **-xion**:

complexion, *crucifixion*, *fluxion*, *transfixion*

- Notice that the final sound /ʃən/ is also heard with **-cian**, the ending of a group of 'profession' nouns mainly formed from nouns ending **-ic** or **-ics**, for example:

beautician	*diagnostician*
dietician	*logician*
magician	*mathematician*
mortician	*obstetrician*
optician	*physician*
politician	*statistician*
tactician	*technician*

- After **r** the spelling is often **-sion**:

aspersion	*aversion*	*conversion*	*dispersion*
diversion	*excursion*	*extroversion*	*immersion*
perversion	*incursion*	*introversion*	*submersion*
subversion	*version*		

- Otherwise, after a consonant, the spelling is **-tion**, for example:

absorption	*action*	*affection*
attraction	*auction*	*benefaction*
caption	*collection*	*combustion*
concoction	*congestion*	*conjunction*
connection	*consumption*	*contraption*
conviction	*deception*	*defection*
dejection	*description*	*destruction*
diction	*digestion*	*disruption*
distinction	*eruption*	*exception*
exemption	*exhaustion*	*fiction*
fraction	*function*	*gumption*
indigestion	*infection*	*injunction*
inscription	*interruption*	*obstruction*
option	*perception*	*presumption*
question	*reaction*	*reception*
redemption	*restriction*	*satisfaction*
section	*subscription*	*suggestion*

-Y

This is an adjective-forming ending.

It is a 'living suffix', added mainly to nouns, but also to some verbs and adjectives, to produce adjectives with the meaning 'characterized by something', or 'like something in quality'.

airy	*brainy*	*bulky*	*chalky*
cloudy	*dusky*	*fishy*	*fluffy*
foxy	*frilly*	*fuzzy*	*grassy*
healthy	*inky*	*jerky*	*leaky*
marshy	*meaty*	*milky*	*moody*
oily	*patchy*	*risky*	*sandy*

sexy	*silky*	*silvery*	*slangy*
smelly	*spooky*	*steamy*	*stormy*
trashy	*watery*	*wealthy*	*windy*
woody	*wordy*		

- Silent **e** is dropped before **-y**:

ache	*achy*	*bounce*	*bouncy*
breeze	*breezy*	*bubble*	*bubbly*
chance	*chancy*	*ease*	*easy*
flake	*flaky*	*fleece*	*fleecy*
grease	*greasy*	*groove*	*groovy*
pebble	*pebbly*	*rose*	*rosy*
scale	*scaly*	*shake*	*shaky*
smoke	*smoky*	*sponge*	*spongy*
smudge	*smudgy*	*snake*	*snaky*
spice	*spicy*	*wave*	*wavy*
wire	*wiry*	*wobble*	*wobbly*

- One-syllable words with one short vowel, ending in one consonant double the final consonant before **-y**, for example:

bag	*baggy*	*bog*	*boggy*
chat	*chatty*	*chum*	*chummy*
crag	*craggy*	*fad*	*faddy*
flop	*floppy*	*fun*	*funny*
knot	*knotty*	*mud*	*muddy*
pal	*pally*	*snap*	*snappy*

- Words ending in **-ic** add **k** before **-y**:

panic *panicky*

- The **e** in *anger*, *hunger* and *winter* drops out before **-y**:

angry *hungry* *wintry*

- Words that already end with **y** have to add **-ey** instead of **-y**:

clay *clayey*
spray *sprayey*

Handy Hints

- Final **e** is kept in these words before **-y**:

blue	*bluey*
clique	*cliquey*
dice	*dicey*
glue	*gluey*
hole	*holey*
same	*samey*
smile	*smiley*

It is also often kept in the following words:

cage	*cagey* or *cagy*
dope	*dopey* or *dopy*
home	*homey* or *homy*
joke	*jokey* or *jokey*
mange	*mangey* or *mangy*
mate	*matey* or *maty*
pace	*pacey* or *pacy*
plague	*plaguey* or *plaguy*
price	*pricey* or *pricy*
stage	*stagey* or *stagy*

- Notice also:

phoney or *phony*

Handy Hints

- Notice also

wool *woolly*

- Consonants are not doubled after an unstressed syllable, except for **l**:

fidget	*fidgety*
tinsel	*tinselly*
weasel	*weaselly*

and you have a choice with:

Christmas
Christmasy or *Christmassy*

DO IT YOURSELF

Form -*y* adjectives from the words supplied, to fill the gaps in the following sentences.

1 The food all tastes rather ____________. (**garlic**)

2 It's hard to hem ____________ fabric like this. (**fray**)

3 I'd better go and wash my ____________ hands. (**paint**)

4 She was wearing a ____________ white shawl. (**lace**)

5 He can't resist making ____________ remarks. (**cat**)

6 They say that drinking gin gives you a ____________ voice. (**gravel**)

7 The sky turned a ____________ shade of grey. (**purple**)

8 His hair was a ____________ red colour. (**carrot**)

9 She's got a new ____________ hairstyle. (**spike**)

10 The material had a ____________ texture. (**cotton**)

11 Thank you for your nice ____________ letter. (**gossip**)

12 He slipped and fell on the ____________ path. (**ice**)

13 It happened one ____________ day in February. (**snow**)

14 The ground was soft, wet and ____________. (**bog**)

-y or -ie?

-ie (pronounced /i/), rather than **-y**, is a common noun-forming ending.

It is added to a whole word or to a shortened stem, to produce informal or diminutive nouns.

aunt	*auntie*
Australian	*Aussie*
bookmaker	*bookie*
budgerigar	*budgie*
cab-driver	*cabbie* or *cabby*
conscientious objector	*conchie* or *conchy*
daft	*daftie*
dear	*dearie*
girl	*girlie* or *girly*
goalkeeper	*goalie*
good	*goodie*
handkerchief	*hankie* or *hanky*
lass	*lassie*
left	*leftie*
mean	*meanie*
mounted policeman	*mountie*
moving picture	*movie*
old	*oldie*
quick	*quickie*
soft	*softie* or *softy*
sweet	*sweetie*
weep	*weepie*

Silent **e** is dropped before **-ie**:

horse	*horsie*

Final consonants are doubled after a short vowel:

big	*biggie*	*cab-driver*	*cabbie* or *cabby*
chap	*chappie*	*cigarette*	*ciggie*
dog	*doggie*	*hip*	*hippie* or *hippy*
lad	*laddie*	*picture*	*piccie* (/ˈpɪki/)
present	*pressie* or *prezzie*	*transistor radio*	*trannie*

Handy Hints

- Notice also:

  free *freebie*

- And notice these other diminutives:

  brownie
  cookie
  groupie
  junkie or *junky*
  pixie or *pixy*
  walkie-talkie

- And these, connected with golf:

  birdie
  brassie
  caddie or *caddy*
  mashie
  stymie

Handy Hints

Diminutives ending **-ie** are typical of Australian English:

swimming costume : *cossie* or *cozzie*

mosquito : *mossie* or *mozzie*

5 WORD BEGINNINGS: Some Spelling Points

This section deals with some *prefixes* (word beginnings) that cause spelling problems.

anti- or ante-?

These prefixes are both pronounced /anti/.

ante- means 'before' as in:

antecedent (something that precedes)
antechamber, anteroom (a small room that leads to a large and more important one)
antedate (to date a cheque or other document earlier than the actual date)
antediluvian (belonging to a time before the biblical Flood)
antenatal (belonging to pregnancy or the period before birth)

Handy Hint

Sometimes a hyphen is used to separate ***anti-*** *from a following vowel (****anti-aircraft****,* ***anti-inflammatory****), and sometimes just for extra clarity (****anti-hero****).*

anti- means:

- against or opposed to something :

antivivisectionist *antislavery*

- attacking something :

anti-aircraft *antiballistic* *antipersonnel*
antitank

- preventing something:

antifreeze *anti-inflammatory* *antiperspirant*
antiseptic

- the opposite of something:

anticlimax *anticyclone* *anti-hero*

dis-

dis- is used as a negative prefix, is added to **verbs** to mean:

- to reverse a process or do the opposite of something:

disagree *disallow* *disappear*
disapprove *disbelieve* *disconnect*
disentangle *disfranchise* *dishearten*
dishonour *disintegrate* *dislike*
dislodge *dismount* *disobey*
disoblige *disorient* *disown*
displace *displease* *dispossess*
disprove *disqualify* *disregard*
dissociate *dissuade* *disunite*

- to remove something:

disarm *disillusion* *disrobe*

dis- is added to **nouns** to mean 'the opposite of something':

disadvantage *discontent* *disfavour*
dishonesty *dishonour* *disincentive*
disinclination *disinformation* *disorder*
displeasure *disquiet* *disrepair*
disrepute *disrespect* *dissatisfaction*
disservice *distaste* *distrust*
disunion *disuse*

Handy Hint

Remember that when **dis-** is added to a word beginning with **s**, you get **-ss-**:

dis- + *satisfied* = *dissatisfied*
dis- + *service* = *disservice*
dis- + *similar* = *dissimilar*

dis- is added to adjectives or past participles to mean 'not something':

dishonest	*disloyal*	*disorderly*
disingenuous	*disjointed*	*disobedient*
disorganized	*dispassionate*	*disreputable*
dissatisfied	*distasteful*	*disused*

for- or fore-?

These are both pronounced /fɔː/, or when unstressed, /fə/.

fore- means:

- before or previously:

forecast	*foresee*	*foreshadow*
foresight	*foretell*	*forewarn*

- in front:

forecourt	*forefinger*	*forefoot*
forehead	*foreleg*	*forepaw.*

for- is an old prefix, not used nowadays to create new words. It expresses:

- prohibition or prevention:

forbid

- omission; not doing something:

forget	*forgive*
forgo	*forsake*

- extremeness:

forlorn

Handy Hints

- **forbear** is a verb meaning to refrain from doing something, often from politeness or kindness:

  *I **forbore** to mention her mistake.*

  The noun **forbearance**, meaning tolerance, comes from it.

  Your **forebears** are the previous members of your family, your ancestors.

  But notice that the spelling **forbears** is sometimes used.

- Notice the difference in spelling between the adverb **forward** (shortened from an old word *forthward*) and the noun **foreword**, meaning an introduction to a book.

Handy Hints

To **forgo** something you want is not to have it:

*I shall have to **forgo** my usual holiday.*

But notice the **fore-** spelling and the 'before' meaning of **foregoing** and **foregone**:

*in my **foregoing** remarks*
*a **foregone** conclusion*

in-, il-, im-, ir-

in- is a Latin prefix, attached mainly to Latin-derived words.

It has two meanings:

- 'not', or 'the opposite of, or lack of, something':

inaccurate *incompatible* *incompetent*
incomplete *incomprehensible* *inconceivable*
inconclusive *incongruous* *inconsiderate*
inconsistent *inconsolable* *inconspicuous*
inconvenient *incorrect* *incredible*
incredulous *incurable* *indecent*
indecipherable *indecision* *indefinite*
indelicate *independent* *indescribable*
indestructible *indigestion* *indignity*
indirect *indiscipline* *indiscreet*
indispensable *indisputable* *indistinct*
indistinguishable *ineducable* *ineffective*
ineffectual *inefficient* *inelastic*
inelegant *ineligible* *inequality*
inescapable *inessential* *inevitable*
inexact *inexcusable* *inexpensive*
inexperience *inexpert* *inexplicable*
inexpressible *inextinguishable* *infamous*
infertile *infidelity* *inflexible*
infrequent *ingratitude* *inharmonious*
inhospitable *inhuman* *inhumane*
inhumanity *injudicious* *injustice*
innumerable *innumeracy* *inoffensive*
inoperable *inoperative* *inopportune*
inorganic *insane* *insanitary*
insatiable *insecure* *insensible*
insensitive *inseparable* *insoluble*
instability *insufficient* *intangible*
intolerable *invariable* *invertebrate*
invisible *involuntary* *invulnerable*

Handy Hint

Notice that when **in-** is added to a word beginning with **n**, you get **-nn-**:

in- +numeracy = innumeracy

Notice also the spelling of:

innocent *innocuous*
innuendo *innumerable*

- 'in' or 'into':

incorporate	*incriminate*	*incubate*
indebted	*indoctrinate*	*infiltrate*
inflate	*inflict*	*influx*
infuse	*ingredient*	*inhabit*
inhale	*inherent*	*inject*
innate	*inoculate*	*inscribe*
inscription	*inseminate*	*insertion*
inspire	*install* or *instal*	*intrude*
invade	*invite*	*involve*

il-

Before **l**, **in-** becomes **il-**, so you get **ill-**, for example:

in- + legal = *illegal*
in- + literate = *illiterate*
in- + logical = *illogical*

so you also get:

illegible	*illicit*	*illuminate*
illusion	*illustrate*	

im-

Before **m**, **in-** becomes **im-**, so you get **imm-**, for example:

in- + mature = *immature*
in- + migrate = *immigrate*
in- + mobile = *immobile*

so you also get:

immaterial	*immeasurable*	*immediate*
immense	*immerse*	*imminent*
immoderate	*immodest*	*immoral*
immortal	*immovable*	*immune*

Before **b** and **p**, **in-** becomes **im-**, for example:

in- + balance	=	*imbalance*
in- + partial	=	*impartial*
in- + plant	=	*implant*
in- + practical	=	*Impractical*

so you also get:

imbecile	*imbibe*	*imbue*
impact	*impalpable*	*impassable*
impassive	*impatient*	*impenetrable*
impenitent	*imperceptible*	*imperfect*
imperil	*impermanent*	*impersonal*
implicit	*impolite*	*import*
impregnate	*impress*	*imprint*
imprison	*improbable*	*improper*
impure		

ir-

Before **r**, **in-** becomes **ir-**, so you get **irr-**, for example:

in- + radiate	=	*irradiate*
in- + rational	=	*irrational*
in- + regular	=	*irregular*

so you also get:

irreconcilable	*irrecoverable*	*irreducible*
irrefutable	*irrelevant*	*irreparable*
irreplaceable	*irrepressible*	*irreproachable*
irresistible	*irresolute*	*irrespective*
irresponsible	*irretrievable*	*irreverence*
irreversible	*irrevocable*	*irrigate*
irritable	*irritate*	

Handy Hints

- But notice that **in-** is also a native English prefix, added to English words, with the meaning 'in' or 'into'.

  The native English prefix **in-** remains unchanged before **l**, **m**, **b**, **f** or **r**:

  in + lay = nlay   *in + mate = inmate*   *in + born = inborn*
  in + patient = inpatient   *in + road = inroad*

- Notice the difference between **impatient** meaning 'not patient', and **inpatient**, meaning a patient admitted to a hospital ward.

Handy Hint

When **mis-** is added to a word beginning with **s**, you get **ss**:

misshapen *misspell*
misspend

mis-

mis- is added to verbs to mean 'do something badly or 'wrongly':

misbehave	*miscast*	*misjudge*
miscalculate	*misfire*	*midirect*
mishit	*misguided*	*misinform*
misinterpret	*mismanage*	*misquote*
misrepresent	*misshapen*	*misspell*
misspend	*mistake*	*mistime*
misunderstand	*misuse*	

mis- is added to nouns to mean 'bad or wrong something', or 'the lack of something':

misadventure	*misapprehension*	*mischance*
misconception	*misconduct*	*misdemeanour*
mishap	*misnomer*	*misrule*
mistake	*mistrust*	*misuse*

Handy Hints

- In British English, **non-** is often separated from the base word by a hyphen. In American English the prefix **non-** and the base word are often written as a single word. For example:

  nonstandard *nonstarter*
  nonstop
- If you choose to write non- words as single words, remember you get **-nn-** when the base word starts with **n**:

  nonnative *nonnegotiable*
  nonnuclear
- Some **non-** words are already fully established as single words, for example:

  nonconformist *nonentity*
  nonsense

non-

non- is added to adjectives and nouns to mean 'not something', or 'the lack of something', or 'the reverse or opposite of something':

non-alcoholic	*non-allergenic*	*nonconformist*
non-controversial	*non-event*	*non-existent*
non-fiction	*non-flammable*	*non-member*
non-native	*non-negotiable*	*non-nuclear*
non-smoking	*non-standard*	*non-starter*
non-violence		

non- is added to some verbs to produce adjectives that mean 'not doing something' or 'designed not to do something':

non-drip *non-slip* *non-stick* *non-stop*

re-

re- is added mainly to verbs to mean 'do something again', or 'do something in a new way':

rearrange	*reborn*	*rebuild*
reboot	*recapture*	*redirect*
redo	*redevelop*	*refit*
refresh	*regroup*	*rehouse*
reimburse	*rejoin*	*relocate*
renegotiate	*renew*	*reorder*
reorganize	*rephrase*	*replay*
reprint	*reproduce*	*reschedule*
resurface	*retell*	*reuse*
rewind	*reword*	*rewrite*

Handy Hints

- When **re-** is added to a base word that begins with **e**, a hyphen is sometimes used for clarity:

  re-echo *re-enter*
  re-export

- Notice the use of a hyphen to distinguish the following:

  recreation (=relaxing activity)

  but *re-creation* (= creating again)

  reform (= to change and improve)

  but *re-form* (= to form again).

un-

un- has two meanings.

- It is a negative prefix, added mainly to adjectives, past and present participles, and nouns, to mean 'not something', or 'the opposite of something' or 'the lack of something':

unable	*unacceptable*	*unaccustomed*
unaided	*unappealing*	*unattractive*
unarmed	*unashamed*	*unavoidable*
unbalanced	*unbeatable*	*unaware*
unbelievable	*unbreakable*	*unceasing*
uncertain	*uncertainty*	*unchangeable*
uncivilized	*uncomfortable*	*uncommon*
uncomplaining	*unconcerned*	*unconditional*
unconscious	*unconstitutional*	*uncontrollable*
unconventional	*unconvincing*	*uncritical*
uncultivated	*undecided*	*undemocratic*
undesirable	*undignified*	*undrinkable*
unemployment	*unending*	*unenterprising*
unequal	*unethical*	*uneven*
uneventful	*unexpected*	*unfailing*
unfaithful	*unfamiliar*	*unfavourable*
unfeeling	*unfinished*	*unfit*
unfortunate	*unfriendly*	*unfurnished*

ungenerous	*ungovernable*	*ungracious*
ungrateful	*unhappy*	*unharmed*
unhealthy	*unheard-of*	*unhelpful*
unhurt	*unhygienic*	*unidentified*
unimaginative	*unimportant*	*unimpressed*
uninhabited	*uninspiring*	*uninterested*
uninteresting	*uninterrupted*	*uninvited*
unjust	*unkind*	*unknowable*
unknown	*unlawful*	*unlicensed*
unlike	*unlikely*	*unlimited*
unlit	*unloved*	*unlucky*
unmanageable	*unmanned*	*unmatched*
unmentionable	*unmissable*	*unmistakable*
unmoved	*unnatural*	*unnecessary*
unnumbered	*unobserved*	*unobtainable*
unobtrusive	*unoccupied*	*unofficial*
unorthodox	*unpaid*	*unparalleled*
unpardonable	*unperturbed*	*unpleasant*
unpopular	*unprecedented*	*unprepared*
unprofessional	*unprofitable*	*unpronounceable*
unqualified	*unrealistic*	*unreasonable*
unreliable	*unrepeatable*	*unrepresentative*
unresponsive	*unrewarding*	*unripe*
unrivalled	*unsatisfactory*	*unsaturated*
unsavoury	*unscientific*	*unscripted*
unscrupulous	*unseeded*	*unseemly*
unseen	*unselfish*	*unsentimental*
unshakable	*unshaven*	*unsociable*
unsolicited	*unsophisticated*	*unsound*
unspeakable	*unspoilt*	*unspoken*
unstable	*unsteady*	*unstoppable*
unstressed	*unsuccessful*	*unsuitable*
unsure	*unsuspecting*	*untaught*
unthinkable	*unthinking*	*untidy*
untimely	*untold*	*untouchable*
untrue	*untrustworthy*	*untruth*
untruthful	*unusable*	*unused*
unusual	*unutterable*	*unvoiced*
unwaged	*unwanted*	*unwary*
unwashed	*unwavering*	*unwelcome*
unwell	*unwilling*	*unwise*
unwonted	*unworkable*	*unworldly*
unworn	*unworthy*	

- **un-** is added to verbs, with the meaning 'reverse a process', 'do the opposite of something', or 'remove something':

unblock	*unbuckle*	*unbutton*
unclasp	*uncover*	*undo*
undress	*unearth*	*unfasten*
unfix	*unfold*	*unfreeze*
unfurl	*unhook*	*unlace*
unlearn	*unleash*	*unload*
unlock	*unmask*	*unnerve*
unpack	*unpeg*	*unpick*
unpin	*unplug*	*unquote*
unravel	*unroll*	*unsaddle*
unscramble	*unscrew*	*unseat*
unsettle	*unshackle*	*unsheathe*
unstick	*unstop*	*untangle*
untie	*unveil*	*unwind*
unwrap	*unyoke*	*unzip*

Handy Hint

When **un-** is added to a word starting with **n**, you get **-nn-**:

unnatural *unnecessary*
unnerve *unnumbered*

DO IT YOURSELF

Notice that when a prefix is added to an irregular verb, the verb remains irregular, for example:

mis- + take = mistake: *Who was the man who **mistook** his wife for a hat?*
un- + do = undo: *Jack **undid** his jacket.*

Fill in the correct verb forms in the following sentences.

1 I __________ the voicemail message you left last night. (**misunderstand**)

2 You should have __________ the lamp before taking the bulb out. (**unplug**)

3 The whole area was __________ and __________ after the war. (**rebuild, redevelop**)

4 It's dangerous to walk about with your shoelaces __________. (**undo**)

5 When she __________ her story to the police, she altered some details. (**retell**)

6 Later that night he __________ the tape and __________ it. (**rewind, replay**)

7 They had __________ my name as usual. (**misspell**)

8 He was __________ from driving for a whole year. (**disqualify**)

9 I prefer __________ the knots to cutting the string. (**untie**)

10 My thesis will have to be partly __________ and then __________. (**rewrite, resubmit**)

11 The kids love __________ their birthday presents and showing them to everyone. (**unwrap**)

12 Speed restrictions will be in force during the __________ of the road. (**resurface**)

13 'Phew, I'm boiling,' said Mike, __________ his jacket. (**unbutton**)

14 She was __________ as Ophelia; she should have been playing Gertrude. (**miscast**)

6 SOME WORD COMPONENTS: Latin, Greek and Other Elements

There are some elements that you often find forming the beginnings, middles or ends of words. Many of these come from Greek and Latin.

Here is a list of some common word components or 'combining forms':

acr or **acro**
top, height, extremity: *acronym, acropolis*

aer or **aero**
air, aircraft: *aerated, aerobics, aeroplane, aeronautic, aerobatics*

agr, agri or **agro**
farming: *agrarian, agriculture, agrochemical*

algia
pain: *neuralgia, nostalgia*

alter or **altern**
other, change: *alteration, alternative*

alti or **alto**
high: *altitude, alto* (higher than tenor)

ambi or **amphi**
on both sides or all round: *ambidextrous, amphibian, amphitheatre*

andr, andro, anthrop or **anthropo**
man or human: *android, anthropoid*

anim
spirit, breath, soul: *animal, animate*

ante
before: *antedate, antenatal*

anth or **antho**
flower: *polyanthus, anthology*

anti
against, the opposite of: *anti-British, antibiotic, anticlimax, anticlockwise, antifreeze*

aqua, **aque** or **aqui**
water: *aqualung, aquarium, aquatic, aqueduct aquiculture*

arch or **archy**
rule, control, chief: *archbishop, anarchy, monarch*

archae or **archai**
old, ancient: *archaeology, archaic*

astr or **astro**
star: *astral, astronaut, astrology, astronomy, astrophysics*

audi or **audio**
hearing: *audible, audience, audiovisual, audiotape*

aut or **auto**
(1) self, working by itself: *autism, autobiography autograph, automatic, automobile, autoteller*
(2) relating to cars or motor bikes: *autoroute, autosport*

bene
good, well: *benefactor, benefit, benevolent*

bi or **bin**
two, twice: *biannual, biennial, bicycle, bilingual bilateral, binary, binoculars, bisect*

bibl or **biblio**
book: *bible, bibliography, bibliophile*

bio, biosis or **biot**
life, living, organism: *antibiotic, biography, biology, bioengineering, symbiosis*

capit
head, chief: *capital, decapitate*

cardi or **cardio**
heart: *cardiac, cardiograph, cardiology*

carn or **carni**
flesh: *carnal, carnivorous*

cent or **centi**
a hundred or a hundredth: *centenary, centigrade, centimetre, centipede*

chrom, chromat, chrome, chromo
colour: *chromatic, monochrome*

chir or **chiro**
hand: *chiromancy, chiropody, chiropractic*

chron or **chrono**
time: *chronic, chronicle, chronology*

cid or **cide**
killing: *genocide, homicide, insecticide, suicidal*

circum or **circu**
round: *circulate, circumference, circumnavigate*

civi or **civili**
city, citizen, citizenship, society: *civic, civilian, civilization*

co
together: *co-operation, coexistence, coincidence*

cosm or **cosmo**
the world, the universe: *cosmic, cosmology, cosmonaut*

counter
against, opposite: *counteract, counterattack*

cracy, crat
rule, ruler, power: *bureaucrat, democracy, aristocracy*

credi, credu or **credit**
trust, belief: *credible, creditworthy, credulous*

crypt or **crypto**
hidden, secret: *cryptic, cryptogram*

cyber
machine communication, Internet navigation: *cyberspace*

cycl or **cyclo**
circle, wheel, rotation: *cycle, cyclic, cyclometer, cyclone*

cyte or **cyto**
cell: *cytoplasm, erythrocyte*

de
reverse or undo a process: *decontaminate, defrost*

dec, deca, decem or **deci**
ten, tenth: *decade, decagon, December, decilitre*

demo
people: *democratic, demography*

dendr or **dendro**
tree: *dendrochronology*

dent or **denti**
tooth: *dental, dentist*

derm, dermat or **dermato**
skin: *dermatitis, dermatologist, pachyderm*

di
two, twice: *dilemma, diode, diphthong*

dia
across, through: *diagonal, diameter, diarrhoea*

dox, doxo or **doxy**
opinion, belief: *doxology, orthodox*

du or **duo**
two: *dual, duologue*

duc or **duct**
lead: *aqueduct, conduct, deduction, education*

dys
trouble, difficulty: *dyslexia, dysfunction*

ectomy
the surgical removal of a part of the body: *appendicectomy, tonsillectomy*

enter or **entero**
intestines: *enteritis, gastroenterology*

ep or **epi**
outer, extra, additional, on, over: *epicentre, epidermis, epilogue, epiphyte*

equi
equal: *equilateral, equinox*

ethn or **ethno**
race, people: *ethnic, ethnology*

ex
(1) out: *expatriate, export*
(2) no longer something: *ex-president, ex- husband*

extra
outside: *extracurricular, extraterrestrial*

ferous
bearing: *coniferous, resiniferous*

fold
multiplied a certain number of times: *twofold, tenfold*

fore
(1) front: *foreleg, forename*
(2) before, earlier, previously: *forecast, foretell*

fratern or **fratri**
brother: *fraternity, fraternize, fratricide*

gam or **gamy**
marriage or mating: *monogamous, polygamy*

gastr or **gastro**
stomach: *gastritis, gastronomic*

gen
birth, producing: *genetic, cytogenesis, erogenous, pathogenic*

genea or **geno**
race: *genealogy, genocide*

gener
kind, class, birth: *generic, general, generation*

geo
the earth: *geology, geography*

gon
angle: *hexagon, polygon*

gram
something written, drawn, or recorded: *anagram, diagram, telegram, electrocardiogram*

graph
an instrument for writing or recording something, or a record, image or piece of writing: *electrocardiograph, tachograph telegraph, autograph, photograph*

gyn, gyno, gynaec or **gynaeco** (or **gynec**, **gyneco** in American English):
woman: *gynaecologist, misogyny*

haem, haemo, haemat or **haemato** (or **hem**, **hemo**, etc in American English)
blood: *haematology, haemoglobin*

hemi
half: *hemisphere*

hepat or **hepato**
liver: *hepatitis*

hept or **hepta**
seven: *heptagon*

hetero
other: *heterosexual*

hex or **hexa**
six: *hexagon*

holo
whole, complete: *holocaust*

homoeo (or **homeo** in American English) or **homo**:
the same: *homoeopathy* (or *homeopathy*), *homophone, homosexual*

hydr or **hydro**
water: *hydrant, hydroelectricity*

hyper
over or above, or more than normal: *hyperlink, hypersensitive, hypercritical*

hypo
under, or less than normal: *hypodermic, hypothermia*

iatr or **iatro**
doctor: *geriatrics, iatrogenic, psychiatry*

ideo
idea: *ideology*

idio
own, individual: *idiosyncrasy*

igne or **igni**
fire: *igneous, ignition*

infra
below, under: *infrastructure, infrared*

inter
between: *international, interactive, intercom*

intra
within, inside: *intravenous*

iso
equal: *isobar, isosceles*

itis
inflammation in a part of the body: *appendicitis, arthritis, tonsillitis*

kilo
a thousand: *kilometre, kilobyte, kilowatt*

let
something small or young: *booklet, leaflet, piglet, starlet*

ling
something small or young or unimportant: *duckling, seedling, weakling*

lith or **litho**
stone: *Neolithic, lithograph*

logi or **logo**
word, reason, ratio: *logic, logistics, logorrhoea*

logue (or **log** in American English):
(1) discourse, conversation: *dialogue, monologue*
(2) a collection: *catalogue*

logy
(1) the study of something: *archaeology, bacteriology, psychology*

(2) something expressed in words: *apology, tautology, terminology*
(3) a collection: *anthology*

macro
long, great: *macroeconomics, macrobiotic*

mancy
divination: *chiromancy, necromancy, ornithomancy*

manu
hand: *manual, manufacture, manuscript*

matern or **matri**
mother: *maternity, matricide*

mega or **megalo**
big, large, great, (or sometimes) a thousand: *megalith, megalomania, megabyte, megaton*

meso
middle, average: *Mesolithic, mesomorph, mesosphere*

meter
(1) a measuring device: *speedometer, thermometer, barometer*
(2) a certain distance or length that can be measured: *diameter, perimeter*

micro
small: *microchip, microcircuit, microcomputer, microprocessor, microscope*

mid
the middle of something, or halfway through something: *midday, midnight, midsummer, midway, midweek, midwinter*

mill or **milli**
a thousand or a thousandth: *millennium, millipede, millimetre*

mini
very small or short: *minicab, minidisk, minidress*

mono
one, single: *monogamy, monolingual, monologue, monorail*

morph
shape: *mesomorph*

mort
death: *mortal, mortician, mortuary*

multi
many: *multicoloured, multicultural, multimedia, multitasking*

my or **myo**
muscle: *myalgia*

myco
fungus: *mycology, mycoprotein*

myel or **myelo**
marrow, spinal cord: *myelitis*

nat
birth: *natal, nativity*

naut
sailor, navigator, sailing: *astronaut, cosmonaut*

nav or **navi**
ship: *nave, navigate, navy*

necr or **necro**
corpse, dead: *necromancy*

neo
new, most recent: *Neolithic, neologism*

nephr or **nephro**
kidney: *nephritis, nephrology*

neur
nerve: *neuralgia, neuritis, neurotic*

nona or **novem**
nine: *nonagenarian, November*

oct, octa or **octo**
eight: *octave, octagon, October, octopus*

oid
having the shape or appearance of something: *anthropoid, android, asteroid, tabloid*

omni
all, everything: *omnipotent, omniscient, omnivorous*

onym
a name or word: *synonym, antonym, pseudonym, eponym*

ophthalm or **ophthalmo**
eye: *ophthalmic, ophthalmologist*

opia, **opt**
vision, sight: *myopia, optic, optician, optometry*

ornith or **ornitho**
bird: *ornithology*

orth or **ortho**
straight, right, correct: *orthodontics, orthodox orthoptics, orthopaedic*

osis
(1) an illness or bodily condition: *fibrosis, neurosis, psychosis, thrombosis*
(2) a process: *hypnosis, metamorphosis, osmosis*

oste or **osteo**
bone: *osteopath, osteoporosis*

ot or **oto**
ear: *otalgia, otitis*

over
(1) over, above or across: *overhead, overseas*
(2) too much, more than normal: *overdo, overwork, overload*

paed or **paedo** (or in American English **ped, pedo**)
child: *orthopaedics, paediatrics, paedophile*

palae or **palaeo** (or in American English **pale**, **paleo**):
ancient, primitive: *Palaeolithic, Palaeozoic*

pan
all: *panacea, panorama*

patern or **patr**
father: *paternal, patricide*

path, patho or **pathy**
illness, suffering, feeling: *neuropathy, pathology, psychopathic, sympathy, telepathy*

ped, **pede** or **pedo**
foot: *quadruped, centipede, pedal, pedestrian pedometer*

pent or **penta**
five: *pentathlon, pentagon*

per
through: *pervade*

peri
round: *perimeter, peripheral*

phag, phago, phage or **phagy**
eating, feeding on something: *anthropophagy, phagocyte*

phil, phile or **philo**
liking or loving something: *bibliophile, philharmonic, philosophy*

phobe or **phobia**
fearing or hating something: *claustrophobia, technophobe, xenophobia*

phon, phone or **phono**
sound, voice, speaking: *phonetic, phonic, phonology, microphone, megaphone, telephone saxophone, xylophone, anglophone*

phor, phore or **phorous**
bearing, carrying: *phosphor, semaphore*

photo
(1) light: *photoelectric, photosynthesis*
(2) photograph: *photocopy*

physi or **physio**
nature: *physical, physiology, physiotherapy*

phyt, **phyte** or **phyto**
plant, growth: *epiphyte, phytoplankton, phytotoxin*

pneumo, pneumat, pneumato, pneumon or **pneumono**
air, gas, breathing, lungs: *pneumatic, pneumonia*

pod
foot, walking: *arthropod, gastropod, podiatry podium*

poly
many: *polygamy, polygon, polysyllabic*

post
after: *postgraduate, postscript, postmortem*

pre
before: *prefix, premature, preview*

pro
in favour of something: *pro-American, pro-democracy*

proof
protected against something, or not letting something get in or out: *fireproof, foolproof, mothproof, rustproof, soundproof, waterproof*

prot or **proto**
first: *prototype, protozoa*

pseud or **pseudo**
false: *pseudonym*

psych or **psycho**
mind: *psychiatry, psychoanalysis, psychology*

pter or **ptero**
wing: *helicopter, lepidopterist, pterodactyl*

pyr or **pyro**
fire, fever: *pyretic, pyrotechnics*

py or **pyo**
pus: *pyaemia, pyorrhoea*

quadr, quadri or **quadru**
four: *quadrangle, quadrilateral, quadruplet*

quasi
giving the impression of being something: *quasi-official*

quinqu, quint or **quintu**
five: *quinquennium, quintet, quintuplet*

rect, recti or **recto**
straight, right, upright: *rectangle, rectilinear, rectum*

retro
back, backwards: *retrograde, retrospective*

rhin or **rhino**
nose: *rhinitis, rhinoceros, rhinoplasty*

rrh
flow; discharge: *diarrhoea, haemorrhage, catarrh*

rupt
burst, break: *disrupt, interrupt, rupture*

sci
know, knowledge: *conscious, science, omniscient*

scrib or **script**
write, writing: *scribble, scribe, script, scripture*

scope
an instrument for looking at something: *microscope, periscope, stethoscope, telescope*

sect
cut: *bisect, dissect, insect, section, sector*

semi
half, partially: *semi-automatic, semicircle, semiconductor, semifinal, semicolon, semi-precious*

sept or **septem**
seven: *septet, September*

sex, sext or **sextu**
six: *sexagenarian, sextet, sextuplet*

ship
(1) a role, position or rank: *citizenship, directorship, governorship, membership*
(2) ability in a certain activity: *horsemanship, marksmanship, musicianship, salesmanship seamanship, sportsmanship, statesmanship workmanship*
(3) a connection between people: *friendship, relationship, companionship, comradeship, partnership*

soci or **socio**
people, society, or the community: *social, sociology*

spect
look, view: *aspect, inspect, prospect, spectacle spectator*

stat
instrument for regulating something: *thermostat*

stereo
three-dimensional, solid: *stereophonic, stereovision*

sub
under or below: *subaquatic, submarine, subtitle*

super
(1) over or above: *superintendent, supervisor, supersonic*
(2) greater than others: *Superman, superpower, superhighway*

sym or **syn**
together with: *sympathy, syndrome, syndicate, synonyms*

techn or **techno**
(1) practical skill, practical science: *technician, technique, technology*
(2) electronic: *technomusic*

tele
distant: *telecommunications, telephone, television*

tetr or **tetra**
four: *tetragonal*

theo
god: *theology*

therm or **thermo**
heat: *thermal, thermostat*

tomy
the surgical cutting of a part of the body: *phlebotomy, tracheotomy*

tox, toxi, toxic, toxico, or **toxo**
poison: *intoxicate, toxaemia, toxicology, toxin*

trans
across, through, over: *transpacific, transparent transport, transmit*

tri
three: *triangle, tricycle*

ultra
beyond: *ultrasonic, ultraviolet*

under
(1) below or underneath: *underclothes, undergrowth, underwater*
(2) too little, or less than normal: *underestimate, undervalue, undernourished, underprivileged*

uni
one, single: *unicorn, unilateral*

vice-
deputy: *vice-president*

video
seeing, or images: *videocassette, videotape, videophone*

visi or **visu**
seeing: *television, visible, vision, visual*

vor, vore or **vorous**
eating, feeding on a certain thing: *carnivore, herbivorous, omnivorous, voracious*

ways
in a certain direction, or a certain way round: *lengthways, sideways*

wise
in a certain direction, or a certain way round: *anticlockwise, clockwise, crosswise*

worthy
(1) describing the proper condition of vehicles: *airworthy, roadworthy, seaworthy*
(2) deserving a certain thing: *blameworthy, praiseworthy, trustworthy*

xeno
strange, foreign: *xenophobia*

xer or **xero**
dry: *xerography, Xerox*

xyl or **xylo**
wood: *xylophone*

zo or **zoo**
animal: *Palaeozoic, protozoa, zodiac, zoology*

7 ABBREVIATIONS and ACRONYMS

When do they need full points?

The tendency is to use points only where they are needed for clarity.

- Abbreviations that include the final letter of the abbreviated word are usually written without a point:

  Mr *Thomson;* ***Mrs*** *Freeman;* ***Dr*** *Saunders*
  7, Rankeillor ***St****; 6 Hetherington* ***Rd****; 8 Hardy* ***Ave****;*
  St *Andrew's Church;* ***Mt*** *Kenya*
  Ben aged 3 ***yrs*** *and 5* ***mths****; a measurement of 4* ***ft*** *and 3* ***ins***

  Abbreviations of ordinal numbers are written without points:

  Sessions have been scheduled for ***1st*** *September,*
  2nd *October,* ***3rd*** *November and* ***4th*** *December.*

- Abbreviations of metric measurements are usually written without points:

  21 cm; 6 km; 10 g; 5 kg; 20 dl; 30 ml

- Chemical symbols are written without points:

  Al *(aluminium);* ***Ca*** *(calcium);* ***Mg*** *(magnesium);* ***O*** *(oxygen);*
  Ra *(radium)*

- Abbreviations written wholly in capitals, for example those that represent countries, states or organizations, are usually written without points, especially if they are pronounced as words:

  EC; EEC; ERM; GB;
  IMF; IMO (International Maritime Organization);
  NSW (New South Wales);
  UK; UN; USA; USSR; WHO (World Health Organization)
  EFTA; FIFA; NATO; UNESCO; UNICEF

- Here are some other types that are usually written without points:

  AGM;CD; CD-ROM;
  ECG (electrocardiograph);
  EFL; ELT; EIA (estimated time of arrival); GHQ; GM foods;
  PC (personal computer; politically correct);
  VCR (videocassette recorder); VDU (visual display unit);
  Did you include your DOB in your CV?
  Is she an MP?

- Degrees, qualifications, titles and awards are increasingly written without points:

  KG (Knight of the Order of the Garter);
  OBE (Order of the British Empire);
  BA; BSc; DPhil; MA

- A reliable principle is to add points to small-letter abbreviations, and to those that start with a capital, if the last letter is not included in the abbreviation:

  adj.(adjective); adv. (adverb); prep.(preposition);
  12th-cent. music; approx.; doz. (dozen); max.; min.;
  chap. (chapter); vol. (volume); Jan.; Feb.; Mon.; Tues.

Handy Hint

In many cases these abbreviations would be clear in context without points, and you can leave them out:

*Could you send me the agenda for **Thurs** 7 **Aug**?*
*I can't remember if that reference occurs in **Vol** 1 or **Vol** 2.*

Handy Hints

Notice that when you put abbreviations composed of capitals into the plural, you do not need an apostrophe before adding **-s**:

my collection of CDs;
free CD-ROMs;
five different CVs;
several MPs.

- Some abbreviations are in the form of words, called **acronyms**, composed of the initial one or two letters of the words that make up the full form; these are always written without points:

*AIDS (**a**cquired **i**mmune-**d**eficiency **s**yndrome)*
*Basic (**b**eginners' **a**ll-purpose **s**ymbolic **i**nstruction **c**ode)*
*laser (**l**ight **a**mplification by **s**timulated **e**mission of **r**adiation)*
*radar (**ra**dio **d**etection **a**nd **r**anging)*
*scuba (**s**elf-**c**ontained **u**nderwater **b**reathing **a**pparatus)*
*sitcom (**sit**uation **com**edy)*

8 APOSTROPHES

Apostrophes have two uses:

- in *contracted words*, to show where letters have been omitted;
- to create *possessive forms* for proper names and nouns.

Contractions

There are two sets of contractions:

- pronoun + auxiliary verb
- auxiliary verb + not

PRONOUN + AUXILIARY VERB

CONTRACTION	FULL FORM	CONTRACTION	FULL FORM
I'm	*I am*	*it's*	*it is* or *it has*
I've	*I have*	*it'll*	*it will*
I'll	*I will* or *I shall*	*it'd*	*it had* or *it would*
I'd	*I had* or *I would*	*we're*	*we are*
you're	*you are*	*we've*	*we have*
you've	*you have*	*we'll*	*we will* or *we shall*
you'll	*you will*	*we'd*	*we had* or *we would*
you'd	*you had* or *you would*	*they're*	*they are*
he's	*he is* or *he has*	*they've*	*they have*
he'll	*he will*	*they'll*	*they will*
he'd	*he had* or *he would*	*they'd*	*they had* or *they would*
she's	*she is* or *she has*	*there's*	*there is* or *there has*
she'll	*she will*	*there'll*	*there will*
she'd	*she had* or *she would*	*there'd*	*there had* or *there would*

AUXILIARY VERB + NOT

CONTRACTION	FULL FORM	CONTRACTION	FULL FORM
aren't	*are not* or *am not*	*won't*	*will not*
isn't	*is not*	*wouldn't*	*would not*
wasn't	*was not*	*shan't*	*shall not*
weren't	*were not*	*shouldn't*	*should not*
haven't	*have not*	*can't*	*cannot*
haven't	*have not*	*couldn't*	*could not*
hasn't	*has not*	*daren't*	*dare not*
hadn't	*had not*	*mightn't*	*might not*
don't	*do not*	*mustn't*	*must not*
doesn't	*does not*	*needn't*	*need not*
didn't	*did not*	*oughtn't*	*ought not*

Grammar Help

- Contractions using **be** and **have** are also acceptable when they act as ordinary verbs:
  *I **haven't** an idea. It **isn't** here.*
- The contraction **'s** for **is** or **has** can be used also after nouns, proper names, other pronouns, **wh**- question words and **here**:
  *The **road's** closed. **Dad's** arrived. **That's** done it! **What's** happened? **Here's** George.*
- **Aren't** is used in British English for **am not**, but only in the inverted form **aren't I**?: ***Aren't I** an idiot?*
- Instead of **she isn't**, **they won't**, **I haven't**, etc, you can use **she's not**, **they'll not**, **I've not**, etc:
  He'd** not* (or *he **wouldn't) *want to lose his job.*
  There'd** not* (or *there **hadn't) *been any rain for a week.*
  We'll** not* (or *we **won't) *need any more milk.*
- Remember that **I'm not** is the only possible contraction for **I am not**.
- Although there are letters missing in two places in the contractions **shan't** (for *shall not*) and **won't** (for *will not*), you only use one apostrophe.
- Notice also the contraction **let's** for **let us**:
  ***Let's** meet at 1.30 at the Festival Theatre.*

DO IT YOURSELF

The full form of question forms such as **don't you**?, **won't he**?, **hadn't they**? *and so on is* **do you not**?, **will he not**?, **had they not**? *and so on* (NOT *do not you?, will not he?, had not they?*)

A In the following sentences, replace the full forms with a suitable contraction.

1 **It is** going to rain.

2 I **was not** concentrating.

3 **They had not** noticed.

4 You **ought not** to be working so late.

5 **Could you not** sell the car?

6 **We have** eaten all the cheese.

7 **Jean has** checked the figures.

8 I **shall not** be able to come.

9 **How is** your sister?

10 You **must not** get so angry.

B In the following sentences, replace the contraction with the full form.

1 I **haven't** finished my shopping yet.

2 **We'd** not been home very long.

3 **Where's** the rice?

4 I **don't** want any fuss.

5 **It'll** be fine tomorrow.

6 **You'd** have laughed if **you'd** seen her.

7 **We'll** wait till next week.

8 **There's** not been any rain for weeks.

9 You **needn't** look so pleased with yourself.

10 **Won't you** stay for supper?

11 **Doesn't he** realise the trouble **he's** caused?

12 **Let's** call a taxi.

Possessive Apostrophe

You add **'s** (apostrophe +s) or **'** (apostrophe alone) after nouns and proper names to make possessive forms.

General Rules

- Add **'s** after singular nouns and names:

  the headteacher's *room*
  Andrew's *desk*

- Add **'** (apostrophe alone) after plural nouns and names:

  the students' *assignments*
  the Robinsons' *apartment*
  the waitresses' *aprons*

- Add **'s** after irregular plural nouns that do not end with **s**:

  the men's *cloakroom*
  my children's *birthdays*
  people's *prejudices*
  women's *magazines*

Singular Nouns and Names ending with *s*

- Add **'s** in the regular way to singular nouns that end with **s**:

  the princess's *clothes*
  my boss's *timetable*
  the class's *attention*

- Add **'s** in the regular way to names ending with **s**:

  James's *coat*
  Thomas's *books*
  Mr Jones's *bicycle*
  Mary Jenkins's *car*
  Robert Burns's *poems*

- With Greek names ending with **s**, such as *Aristophanes*, *Euripides, Aeschylus, Sophocles, Archimedes, Socrates*, and biblical names such as *Jesus* and *Moses*, people sometimes just add an apostrophe to form the possessive:

  Euripides' *plays*
  Moses' *leadership*

  But if you prefer you can add **'s** in the regular way:

  Moses's *journey*
  Jesus's *teachings*
  Sophocles's *tragedies*

- You can use **'s** with time expressions:

  Saturday's *match*
  last year's *reunion*
  next week's *appointments*

  You can use **'s** with expressions for an amount of time:

  The computer crashed and I lost ***three hours'*** *work.*
  I think I'll take ***a week's*** *holiday.*
  He was sentenced to ***four years'*** *imprisonment.*

- You can use the possessive form of a sum of money with *worth* to give the cost of something:

  Rioters did ***10,000 dollars'*** *worth of damage.*

- You can add **'s** to 'occupation' words such as **baker**, **grocer**, **doctor**, **dentist**, to mean their shop or workplace:

  Get me a loaf from ***the baker's****.*
  I've an appointment at ***the dentist's*** *at 10.00.*

DO IT YOURSELF

Fill in the correct singular or plural possessive form, ending with *'s* or *s'*, in the following sentences:

For example: Seven _*hours'*_ work should complete the job. (**hour**)

1 This is every ________ dream kitchen. (**hostess**)

2 Somebody broke into Mrs ________ house last night. (**Williams**)

3 Troublemakers like you make the ________ task even harder. (**police**)

4 I'm owed several ________ leave. (**week**)

5 Men's and ____ fashions are in the basement; ________, ________ and junior ________ fashions are on the ground floor. (**boy, lady, child, miss**)

6 Has anyone found ________ purse? (**Frances**)

7 ________ ideas vary a great deal on this subject. (**people**)

8 Do you know what the venue is for next ________ gig? (**month**)

9 He delivered flowers to the three leading ________ dressing rooms. (**actress**)

10 Do you stock ________ cots at this shop? (**baby**)

9 HYPHENS

Hyphens have two functions:

- to punctuate what you have written so that it is clear to the reader.
- to divide words at the end of a line of text.

Hyphens for Clarity

You sometimes need to join words with a hyphen so that the reader knows that they represent a compound unit, and doesn't have to hesitate and re-read bits of text.

Notice the difference in clarity between these two sentences:

She teaches thirty five year old children.
She teaches thirty five-year-old children.

In the second example, the compound adjective *five-year-old* is made clearly visible to the reader by the hyphens.

It will be useful here to divide compound words into word classes, and show when they need hyphens and when they don't.

Compound Nouns

Many compound nouns can be written as one word:

classroom; teacup; fireman; payphone; sweatshirt; wallpaper; waveband.

Look up the compounds in a dictionary to discover if the one-word spelling is possible.

Compound nouns that are not written as one word do not need a hyphen if the first word qualifies the second like an adjective:

book club; fire alarm; signal box; railway bridge; singles bar.

Combinations such as *dining room* don't *need* a hyphen:

dancing shoes; swimming costume; shopping centre; spinning wheel; washing machine.

> **Handy Hints**
>
> Some people prefer to write *dining-room, dancing-shoes, swimming-costume*, etc.

With a large number of other compound nouns the first word is grammatically the object of the second word. These can in many cases be written as one word:

screwdriver; firefighter; dishwasher; lawnmower.

If they are written as two words they are clearer if written with a hyphen than without:

taxi-driver; word-processor; book-keeper; book-collector; cash-dispenser; smoke-inhalation.

Compound nouns that are formed from phrasal verbs can in some cases be written as one word:

breakdown; breakthrough; flyover; flypast; layout; singalong; takeover.

But compounds using the shorter particles are usually written with a hyphen:

sit-in; passers-by; runner-up; break-in; break-out; break-up; take-off; take-up.

Certain compound nouns represent a combination or mixture of two things and are usually hyphenated:

a shampoo-conditioner.

Treat compound military ranks like this too:

lieutenant-colonel; sergeant-major; major-general.

Compound nouns consisting of a string of words need to be kept together with hyphens:

my mother-in-law; the Queen's ladies-in-waiting;
a bunch of forget-me-nots; caught in no-man's-land.

Compound Adjectives

Compound adjectives that come before the noun should usually be hyphenated. Use the types below as models:

eye-catching designs; a much-overused word;
a long-awaited announcement; clear-cut ideas;
well-thumbed pages; ill-educated people;
never-ending complaints; the short-term view;
short-legged dogs; a bad-tempered teacher;
panic-stricken passengers; snow-capped peaks;
index-linked pensions; mind-bending drugs;
lemon-yellow walls; waist-deep water;
shoulder-length hair; rock-hard sandwiches;
a door-to-door salesman; a yellow-and-black-striped insect;
a fruit-and-vegetable stall; the balance-of-payments deficit;
a four-page leaflet; ten-year-old children;
a three-bedroomed apartment; a three- or four-week delay;
four- to six-week-old babies; off-piste skiing;
an up-to-date report; a never-to-be-repeated performance;
their longed-for release; the knock-on effects;
a bricked-up archway.

Adjectival phrases using a **-ly** adverb do not need a hyphen when used before a noun:

a beautifully illustrated book

Handy Hint

Some of these combinations also need hyphens when they come after the noun, and some don't. Use the following models:

designs that are eye-catching
a word that is much overused
ideas that are clear-cut
pages that are well thumbed
people that are ill educated
The list is never-ending.
He's rather bad-tempered.
They were panic-stricken.
All pensions are index-linked.
The walls are lemon-yellow.
Her hair is shoulder-length.
The sandwiches are rock-hard.
a report that is up to date
The archway is bricked up.

When not in the pre-noun position combinations like the following do not require hyphens:

an expression that is much overused
books that are well written
a report that is up to date
He is better known as an actor.
The tomb has been bricked up for the last 40 years.
Which books are most frequently asked for?
There is good skiing off piste.

But keep hyphens in cases like the following where there is an underlying, sometimes compressed, syntactical structure:

All pensions are index-linked. (= linked to an index)
The passengers were panic-stricken. (= stricken with panic)
The possibilities are mind-blowing. (= mind is the object of blow)
The situation is not as clear-cut as that. (clear is not a -ly adverb)
She wears her hair shoulder-length. (= the length that reaches to her shoulders)
The whole thing is crystal-clear. (= as clear as crystal)
I was standing waist-deep in the snow. (= as deep as my waist)
The walls are lemon-yellow. (= yellow like lemons)
That remark was uncalled-for. (un- governs the whole expression called for)

-like and other combining elements:

Some **-like** words are well-established as single words, for example: *childlike, ladylike*. It is safer to hyphenate less-recognized combinations, whether before the noun or not:

an owl-like expression
Her fingers were long and claw-like.

Notice **-aware**, **-conscious**, **-friendly**, **-looking**, **-sensitive**, **-sounding**, **-specific** also used after a hyphen, whether before the noun or not:

fashion -aware kids

environment-friendly washing powders

a strange-sounding name

an attractive-looking neighbourhood

Is this dialogue box case-sensitive?

Are the British as class-conscious as ever?

gender-specific nouns such as 'waitress'

Compound Verbs

These should be written either as one word or hyphenated:

Who masterminded the scheme?

Haven't you stage-managed a play before?

'Awaken' is cross-referred to 'waken'.

The plane nose-dived into the sea.

Handy Hint

But notice that you don't hyphenate phrasal verbs:

*Couldn't you **share out** (not share-out) the sweets?*

Other Issues

Compounds formed with prefixes are normally written as one word:

redo decontaminate uncover precondition postdate

Considerations of appearance and clarity in some cases require a hyphen to be inserted between the prefix and base word:

anti-aircraft co-opt ex-wives non-native a semi-invalid

Dictionaries have their individual preferences but give some guidance.

The combining element **self**- always requires a hyphen:

self-control self-effacing self-important

Handy Hint

A hyphen is needed to distinguish between certain pairs of words to avoid ambiguity:

recover (= get better)
re-cover (= to put a new cover on something)

recreation (= relaxation)
re-creation (= the process of creating something anew)

reform (= improve)
re-form (= to form afresh).

A hyphen is needed after the prefix if the following word begins with a capital:

un-American   *un-British*

You have a choice with:

e-mail or *email* (short for *electronic mail*)

People occasionally use hyphens to avoid slightly awkward letter juxtapositions, for example:

heart-throb (rather than *heartthrob*);
book-keeping (rather than *bookkeeping*);
re-emerge (rather than *reemerge*).

Figures and fractions:

Compound numbers and fractions are hyphenated:

twenty-seven   *thirty-first*   *three-quarters*

Hyphens in Word Division

Where a word has to be broken by a hyphen at the end of a line, make sure that the part before the break gives readers the best possible guidance about the rest of the word, to enable them to read on fluently. Avoid breaks that mislead the reader into a pronunciation that will have to be adjusted.

Here are some right and wrong line-end word-divisions:

RIGHT		WRONG	
knowl-	*edge*	*know-*	*ledge*
magi-	*cian*	*magic-*	*ian*
to-	*tal*	*tot-*	*al*
na-	*tion*	*nat-*	*ion*
met-	*al*	*me-*	*tal*
rec-	*ognize*	*re-*	*cognize*

Handy Hint

Where a break is needed at a double consonant, the hyphen comes between the two:

flam- mable   *chat- ter*
cof- fee

but:

chuck- le

DO IT YOURSELF

A Insert hyphens if needed into the following sentences.

1 The next morning I called my sister in law.

2 It was one of those never to be forgotten evenings.

3 The staff at the embassy were friendly and not at all status conscious.

4 In came the Fairy Queen with her splendidly dressed attendants.

5 A twelve month old child can be quite adventurous.

6 Patients may have a six or seven week wait before seeing a doctor.

7 That timetable is out of date.

8 I want to get this job finished before the preChristmas rush.

9 He went brick red with embarrassment.

10 Our office is that odd looking building on the corner.

11 When we returned from our cruise the grass in the garden was waist high.

12 Most teenagers are a bit self conscious.

B Show with a vertical line where you would divide the following words if they came at the end of a line of text.

reckon; comedy; traffic; tradition; malice; acknowledgement; college; gracious; passage.

10 A NOTE ON THE BEHAVIOUR OF LETTER L

The letter **l** differs from other consonants in its behaviour in English, so it will be useful here to sum up its various habits.

-ll at the end of *one-syllable, one-vowel words*

Handy Hint

There are only a few exceptions to this rule:
gal (an informal spelling of *girl*)
gel *nil* *pal*

Letter **l** is normally double at the end of single-syllable words where the vowel is a single letter:

all	*ball*	*bell*	*bill*	*bull*	*call*
cell	*chill*	*drill*	*droll*	*dull*	*dwell*
fall	*fell*	*fill*	*frill*	*full*	*grill*
gull	*ill*	*mill*	*null*	*pill*	*pull*
roll	*shall*	*skill*	*smell*	*spell*	*stall*
still	*tall*	*tell*	*till*	*wall*	*well*

Letter **l** is usually single after a double vowel, and after a one-vowel final syllable:

boil	*civil*	*coil*	*equal*	*fool*	*foul*
fuel	*haul*	*model*	*patrol*	*pistol*	*parallel*
prevail	*repeal*	*sandal*	*soul*	*symbol*	*trail*
travel	*trial*	*vowel*	*wool*		

But when the words in the one-syllable **-ll** list above form part of a compound word, or have a prefix added, they usually keep **-ll**:

skill	*deskill*	*mill*	*flourmill*	*fall*	*pitfall*
stall	*install*	*call*	*recall*	*fill*	*refill*
tell	*retell*	*pull*	*ringpull*		

Handy Hint

But note that the following verbs end in a single **l**:

annul *appal*
distil *enrol*
enthral *fulfil* *instil*

Install can also be spelt **instal**.

In American English these verbs are all spelt with a final **-ll**, with the exception of *annul*.

Doubling l before adding word endings

Words with a final syllable that ends with **l** and has a single vowel double the **l** before the following endings: **-ant, -ation, -ed, -ent, -ing, -er, -ery, -ion, -ious, -ous, -y**.

This happens whether the final syllable is stressed or unstressed:

appal	*appalled*	*appalling*			
cancel	*cancellation*	*cancelled*	*cancelling*		
cavil	*cavilled*	*caviller*	*cavilling*		
channel	*channelled*	*channelling*			
control	*controlled*	*controller*	*controlling*		
council	*councillor*				
counsel	*counselled*	*counselling*	*counsellor*		
cruel	*crueller*				
dial	*dialled*	*dialling*			
distil	*distillation*	*distilled*	*distiller*	*distillery*	*distilling*
duel	*duelled*	*dueller*	*duelling*		
enamel	*enamelled*	*enameller*	*enamelling*		
enrol	*enrolled*	*enrolling*			
equal	*equalled*	*equalling*			
excel	*excelled*	*excellent*	*excelling*		
fuel	*fuelled*	*fuelling*			
gospel	*hot-gospeller*				
gravel	*gravelly*				
grovel	*grovelled*	*groveller*	*grovelling*		
hostel	*youth-hosteller*	*youth-hostelling*			
instal(l)	*installation*	*installed*	*installing*		
jewel	*jewelled*	*jeweller*	*jewellery*		
level	*leveller*				
libel	*libelled*	*libeller*	*libelling*	*libellous*	
marshal	*marshalled*	*marshalling*			
marvel	*marvelled*	*marvelling*	*marvellous*		
medal	*medallion*				

model	*modelled*	*modeller*	*modelling*		
patrol	*patrolled*	*patrolling*			
pedal	*pedalled*	*pedalling*			
pencil	*pencilled*	*pencilling*			
propel	*propellant*	*propelled*	*propellent*	*propeller*	*propelling*
rebel	*rebelled*	*rebelling*	*rebellion*	*rebellious*	
repel	*repellant*	*repelled*	*repellent*	*repelling*	
revel	*revelled*	*reveller*	*revelling*		
signal	*signalled*	*signaller*	*signalling*		
stencil	*stencilled*	*stencilling*	*stencilled*		
travel	*travelled*	*traveller*	*travelling*		
tunnel	*tunnelled*	*tunnelling*			
yodel	*yodelled*	*yodeller*	*yodelling*		

Handy Hint

Parallel *is an exception:*

parallel
paralleled
paralleling

American English doubles the final **l** only in a syllable that is stressed:

patrol *patrolled* *patrolling*

but:

signal *signaled* *signaler* *signaling*

Notice that the following do not double the **l** before **-ous**:

scandal *scandalous*
peril *perilous*

And note that these other adjectives have single **l** before **-ous**:

credulous	*fabulous*	*frivolous*	*garrulous*
meticulous	*miraculous*	*pendulous*	*populous*
querulous	*ridiculous*	*scrupulous*	*scurrilous*
tremulous			

Handy Hint

American English allows **wooly**, *and prefers* **woolen**.

Final **l** does not usually double after a double vowel, but the following is an exception:

wool *woolly* (notice also *woollen*)

Final **l** is not doubled before word endings **-ism**, **-ist**, **-ity**, **-ize** (or **-ise**):

brutal	*brutalism*	*brutalist*	*brutality*	*brutalize*
civil	*civility*	*civilize*		
equal	*equality*	*equalize*		
final	*finalist*	*finality*	*finalize*	
formal	*formalism*	*formalist*	*formality*	*formalize*
fossil	*fossilize*			
general	*generality*	*generalize*		
legal	*legalism*	*legality*	*legalize*	
moral	*moralist*	*morality*	*moralize*	
plural	*plurality*	*pluralize*		
scandal	*scandalize*			
special	*specialism*	*specialist*	*speciality*	*specialize*
symbol	*symbolism*	*symbolize*		

Handy Hint

But there are the following exceptions:

crystal	*crystallize*
medal	*medallist*
panel	*panellist*
tranquil	*tranquillity*
	tranquillize

In American English these derivatives are all spelt with a single **l**, with the exception of ***crystallize***.

Dropping one l from -ll

Adjectives ending in **-ll** have to drop one **l** when adding **-ly**:

droll *drolly* | *dull* *dully* | *full* *fully*

Words ending **-ll** sometimes drop an **l** before a second element beginning with a consonant:

all	*almighty, almost, already, also, although, altogether, always*	*bell*	*belfry*
chill	*chilblain*	*full*	*fulfil, fulsome*
install	*instalment*	*skill*	*skilful*
smell	*smelt*	*spell*	*spelt*
spill	*spilt*	*thrall*	*thraldom*
well	*welcome, welfare*	*will*	*wilful*

Words ending **-ll** sometimes drop an **l** when they form the final element of a combination:

all	*withal*
fill	*fulfil*
full	*beautiful, cupful, handful, useful, wonderful, etc.*
till	*until*

Handy Hints

- American English prefers:

  fulfill *installment*
  skillful *willful*

- **-ll** is kept before **-ness**:

  dull *dullness*
  full *fullness*
  still *stillness*

DO IT YOURSELF

Combine the supplied base word and suffix into the correctly spelt derivative (using British-English spelling) to fill the gap in each of the following sentences.

1 They found the __________ remains of dinosaurs in the canyon. (**fossil, -ized**)

2 Give me time to __________ my ideas. (**crystal, -ize**)

3 They were happy to get home after their __________ journey. (**peril, -ous**)

4 She has decided on a career in __________ . (**model, -ing**)

5 We visited a large whisky __________ in the Scottish Highlands. (**distil, -ery**)

6 She has to take __________ to keep her calm. (**tranquil, -izers**)

7 He __________ that he was ready to start recording. (**signal, -ed**)

8 The __________ took their places on the winners' podium. (**medal, -ists**)

9 I never feel very __________ in this job. (**fulfil, -ed**)

10 In the __________ of the night you could have heard a pin drop. (**still, -ness**).

11 I didn't expect to be amongst the __________. (**final, -ists**)

12 It was a __________ tale of bribery and intrigue. (**scandal, -ous**)

13 I've already __________ in the date of the meeting. (**pencil, -ed**)

14 The dove usually __________ peace. (**symbol, -izes**)

11 A NOTE ON AMERICAN-ENGLISH SPELLING

ll and l

American English attempts to iron out the idiosyncrasies that letter **l** has in British English, and make it conform to the general rules for doubling consonants.

American English usually spells the following words with **ll** where British English has (or, as in the case of *instal*(*l*), can have) **l**.

appall	*distill*	*enroll*	*enthrall*
fulfill	*install*	*instill*	*installment*
skillful	*willful*		

When adding the endings that cause final **l** to double in British English, American English tends to double final **l** only in stressed syllables.

patrol	*patrolled*	*patrolling*	
propel	*propelled*	*propeller*	*propelling*
rebel	*rebelled*	*rebelling*	

But:

cancel	*canceled*	*canceling*	
council	*councilor*		
counsel	*counseled*	*counseling*	*counselor*
dial	*dialed*	*dialing*	
jewel	*jeweled*	*jeweler*	
libel	*libeled*	*libeling*	*libelous*
marvel	*marveled*	*marveling*	*marvelous*
pedal	*pedaled*	*pedaling*	
travel	*traveled*	*traveler*	*traveling*

Handy Hint

But **crystallize** and **crystalline** have **ll**, as in British English.

Where British English has an irregular **ll**, American English has **l**:

medalist *panelist* *tranquility* *tranquilize* *woolen*

pp and p

The spellings *kidnaped, kidnaping, kidnaper* and *worshiped, worshiping, worshiper* are possible in American English.

But notice *handicapped, handicapping*, as in British English.

Handy Hint

Notice the following, spelt **-lyse** in British English, but **-lyze** in American English:

analyze
breathalyze
electrolyze
paralyze

-ize and -ise

American English prefers **-ize** wherever **-ize** is a valid alternative to **-ise**:

idealize *maximize* *modernize* *recognize*

Handy Hint

glamour, spelt **-our** in American English, is an exception.

-or and -our

American English has **-or** where British English has **-our**:

armor	*behavior*	*candor*	*color*	*endeavor*
favor	*flavor*	*harbor*	*honor*	*humor*
labor	*neighbor*	*savior*	*savor*	

-er and -re

Many words that end in **-re** in British English are spelt **-er** in American English:

caliber	*center*	*fiber*	*goiter*
liter	*luster*	*meager*	*meter*
maneuver	*miter*	*reconnoiter*	*saber*
scepter	*specter*	*theater*	

Handy Hints

- But where **c** precedes **-re**, the spelling **-re** is kept in American English:
  acre *lucre*
  massacre *mediocre*
  wiseacre
- Notice also that ***macabre*** *and* ***ogre*** *are spelt as in* British English.

-log and -logue

Words that end with **-logue** in British English can be spelt **-log** in American English:

analog	*catalog*	*dialog*	*epilog*
homolog	*monolog*	*prolog*	

Handy Hints

- ***Encyclopedia*** *and* ***medieval*** *are now commoner spellings in* British English than ***encyclopaedia*** *and* ***mediaeval***.

  You will even hear ***medieval*** pronounced as three syllables (/mə'di:vəl/) instead of four (/medɪ'i:vəl/). The latter is correct.
- **Fetus** is used in technical contexts in preference to **foetus**.

oe, ae and e

In American English **e** normally replaces both **ae** and **oe** in words derived from Greek and Latin:

BRITISH	AMERICAN
aeon	*eon*
anaesthesia	*anesthesia*
aesthetic	*esthetic*
diarrhoea	*diarrhea*
encyclopaedia	*encyclopedia*
foetus	*fetus*
gonorrhoea	*gonorrhea*
haemoglobin	*hemoglobin*
homoeopathy	*homeopathy*
leukaemia	*leukemia*
mediaeval	*medieval*
oedema	*edema*
oesophagus	*esophagus*
oestrogen	*estrogen*

-se and -ce

practice: this is the usual spelling for both the noun and the verb in American English.

license: this is the usual spelling for both the verb and the noun in American English.

The nouns **defence**, **offence** and **pretence** are usually spelt **defense**, **offense** and **pretense** in American English.

ss and s

The plurals *busses* and *gasses* are possible in American English.

Random variations

Note the spelling differences in the following words:

BRITISH	AMERICAN
aluminium	*aluminum* (/əˈluːmɪnəm/)
axe	*ax*
cheque	*check*
cosy	*cozy*
jewellery	*jewelry*
manoeuvre	*maneuver*
mold, moldy	*mould, mouldy*
plough	*plow*
prise (to lever)	*prize*
programme	*program*
sceptic	*skeptic*
sulphur	*sulfur*
tyre	*tire*
vice (gripping tool)	*vise*

ENGLISH
LANGUAGE
TOOLBOX
Understanding Spelling

12 WORDS THAT CAUSE SPELLING PROBLEMS

In the following list, spelling reminders have been added in bracketed italics.

An entry such as '***wagon*** or ***waggon***' means that both spellings are acceptable.

abandoned, abandoning *(-n-)*
abattoir *(-b- -tt-)*
abbreviation *(-bb-)*
abhorrent *(-bh-, -rr-, -e)*
abominable *(-min-)*
abscess *(-sc-)*
absence, absent, absentee *(-s-)*
absorption *(-p-)*
abyss *(-b-, -ss)*
abysmal, abysmally *(-s- ,-ally)*
academically *(-ally-)*
academy *(-dem-)*
accede *(-cede)*
accelerate, accelerator *(-or)*
accessible *(-ible)*
accessory *(-ory)*, ***accessories***
accidentally *(-ally)*
accommodate *(-cc-, -mm-)*
accommodation *(-cc-, -mm-)*
accompaniment *(-cc- -ni-)*
accumulate *(-cc-, -mu-)*
accumulation, accumulator *(-or)*
accuracy, accurate *(-cc-, -r-)*
accustomed *(-cc-)*
ache *(-ch-)*
achieve, achievement *(-ie-)*
acknowledge *(-ckn-)*
acknowledgement or ***acknowledgment***
acquaint, acquaintance *(-cqu-)*
acquiesce, acquiescent *(-cqu-, -sc-)*
acquire, acquisition, acquisitive *(-cqu-)*
acquit, acquitted, acquittal *(-cqu-, -tt-)*
acreage *(-re- -age-)*
across *(-c-)*
additional *(-dd-)*
address *(-dd-)*
adequate, adequacy *(-de-)*
admissible *(-ible)*
admittance *(-tt-, -ance)*
admitted, admitting *(-tt-)*
adolescence, adolescent *(-sc-, -en-)*
advertise, advertisement *(-ise-)*
advantageous *(-eous)*
advise *(-ise)*

aerate *(aer-)*
aerial *(ae-)*
aeroplane *(ae-)*
aerosol *(ae-)*
aesthetic *(ae-)*
affiliate, affiliation *(-ff-, -l-)*
afforestation *(-ff-)*
aggravate, aggravation *(-gg-)*
aggregate *(-gg-, -re-)*
aggression, aggressive *(-gg-)*
aghast *(-gh-)*
agoraphobia *(-g-, -ora-)*
agree, agreeable, agreed *(-g-)*
aisle *(-sl-)*
alcohol *(-co-)*
alibi, alibis *(-li-, -bis)*
align, alignment *(-gn-)*
allege, allegation *(-lleg-)*
allegiance *(-llegi-)*
allergic *(-ll-)*
alligator *(-ll-)*
alliteration *(-ll-)*
allotment *(-ll-)*
almond *(alm-)*
already *(-l-)*
although *(-l-)*
altogether *(-l-)*
aluminium *(-l-)*
amateur *(-m-, -eur)*
amethyst *(-me-, -yst)*
ambulance *(-ance)*
amiable *(ami-)*
ammunition *(-mm-)*
amount *(-m-)*
anachronism *(-n-, -ch-)*
anaesthetic *(-aesth-)* or (in American English) ***anesthetic***
analyse or (in American English) ***analyze, analysis, analyst*** *(-ly-)*
ancestor *(-ces-, -or)*, ***ancestry***
angrily *(-ily)*
anguish *(-gu-)*
annihilate *(-nn-, -ihil-)*, ***annihilation***
announcement *(-nn-)*
annulled *(-nn-, -ll-)*
annulment *(-nn-, -l-)*
anonymous *(-nym-)*
answer *(-sw-)*, ***answered***
antedate *(ante-)*
antibiotic *(anti-)*
anticlimax *(anti-)*
antithesis *(-thes-)*
Antarctic *(-ct-)*
apartheid *(-p-, -theid)*
apologize or ***apologise, apology*** *(-p-, -log-)*
appalling *(-pp- -ll-)*
apparatus *(-pp-)*
apparent *(-pp-,-r-, ent)*
appearance *(-pp-, -ance)*
appendicitis *(-pp-, -citis)*
appearance *(-pp-, -ance)*
appreciate *(-pp-)*
appropriate *(-pp-)*
approval *(-pp-)*
aquarium *(aqu-)*
arbitrary *(-trary)*
archaeology *(-ch-, -ae-)* or (in American English) ***archeology***
architect *(-chi-)*
Arctic *(-ct-)*
arguably, argument *(-gu-)*
arrangement *(-rr-)*
arrival *(-rr-)*
arson *(-son)*
ascendant or ***ascendent*** *(-sc-)*
ascendancy or ***ascendency*** *(-sc-)*
ascertain *(-sc-)*
asphyxiate *(-sphyx-)*
aspirin *(-pir-)*
arthritis *(ar-)*
asphalt *(-sphalt)*
asphyxiate, asphyxiation *(-sphy-)*
assassin, assassinate *(-ss-, -ss-)*
assessment *(-ss-, -ss-)*
assignment *(-ss-, -gn-)*
assimilate *(-ss-, -mi-)*
assistance, assistant *(-ance, -ant)*

associate *(-ss-, -c-)*
asthma *(-sthm-)*
atheist *(-ei-)*
atoll *(-t-, -ll)*
atlas, *(-s)* ***, atlases***
atrocious *(-cious)*
attach, attachment *(-tt-, -ach-)*
attendant *(-tt-, -ant)*
attitude *(-tt-)*
attorney *(-tt-, -or-, ey),* ***attorneys***
audience *(-ence)*
augur *(-ur)*
autumn *(-mn)*
awful, awfully *(aw-)*
awkward *(aw-)*
awesome *(awe-)*

bachelor *(-ach-)*
baggage *(-gg-)*
bailiff *(-l-, -ff)*
balloon *(-ll-)*
baptize or ***baptise***
barbecue *(-cue)*
barrister *(-rr-)*
basically *(-ally)*
bassoon *(-ss-)*
battalion *(-tt-, -l-)*
beautiful, beautifully *(-eau-, -fully)*
beggar *(-ar)*
beginner, beginning *(-nn-)*
beguile *(-gu-)*
beleaguer, beleaguered *(-gu-)*
belief, believe *(-ie-)*
belligerent *(-ll-, -g-, -ent)*
beneficial *(-ici-)*
benefited, benefiting *(-t-)*
bequeath *(-eath)*
berserk *(ber-)*
besiege *(-ie-)*
biases, biased, biasing *(-s-)*
bicycle *(bi-, cy-)*
bigoted *(-g-, -t-)*
biscuit *(-cui-)*
bisect *(-s-)*
bivouac, bivouacked, bivouacking *(-ou-, -ck-)*
bizarre *(-z-, -rr-)*
blancmange *(-ncm-)*
blaspheme, blasphemous, blasphemy *(-ph-)*
boatswain *(-swain)*
bodily *(-ily)*
boulder *(-ou-)*
boundary *(-ary)*
bouquet *(-ou, -quet)*
bourgeois *(-ou-, -geois)*
boutique *(-ou-, -ique)*
boycott *(-tt)*
bracketed *(-t-)*
braise *(-s-)*
brassiere *(-ss-, -ere)* or ***brassière***
breadth *(-ea-)*
breathalyse or ***breathalyze***
brief *(-ie-)*
brigadier *(-ier)*
Britain *(-t-, ain)*
British *(-t-)*
Briton *(-t-)*
Brittany *(-tt-)*
broccoli *(-cc- -l-)*
brochure *(-ch-)*
bronchitis *(-nch-)*
bruise *(-ui-)*
brusque *(-que)*
buccaneer *(-cc-, -n-)*
Buddhist *(-ddh-)*
budgeted, budgeting *(-t-)*
bulletin *(-ll-, -t-)*
bulwark *(-l-, -wark)*
bumptions *(-mpti-)*
buoyancy, buoyant *(buo-, -an-)*
bureaus or ***bureaux***
bureaucracy, bureaucratic *(-eau-)*
burglar *(-ar)*
bused, busing or ***bussed, bussing***
buses *(plural)*
business *(-i-)*
buttoned *(-tt-, -n-)*

caffeine *(-ff-, ei-)*
calendar *(-en-, -ar)*
camouflage *(-ou-)*
campaign *(-gn)*
cancelled, cancelling *(-ll-)* or (in American English) ***canceled, canceling***
cancellation *(-ll)* or (in American English) ***cancelation***
cannabis *(-nn-)*
cannibal *(-nn-, -bal)*
canoeing, canoeist *(-oe-)*
capillary *(-p-, -ll-)*
capsize *(-ize)*
carburettor or ***carburetter*** *(-tt-)* or (in American English) ***carburetor***
career *(-r-)*
caress *(-r-)*
Caribbean *(-r-, -bb-, -ean)*
carriage *(-rri-)*
cartilage *(-til-, -age)*
cashier *(-ier)*
casual, casually, casualty *(-ua-)*
catarrh *(-rrh)*
catechism *(-tech-)*
category *(-teg-)*
caterpillar *(-ter-, -ll-, -ar)*
cauliflower *(caul-)*
ceiling *(-ei-)*
Celsius *(-s-)*
cemetery *(-ery)*
certainty *(-tain-)*
chandelier *(-ier)*
chameleon *(ch-, le-)*
chancellor *(-ll-)*
changeable *(-eable)*
chaos, chaotic, chaotically *(ch-, -ao-, -ally)*
character *(ch-)*
characteristically *(-ally)*
chasm *(ch-, asm)*
chauffeur *(-au-, -ff-)*
chauvinism *(-au-, -vi)*
cheque or (in American English) ***check***
chief, chiefly *(-ie-)*
chilblain *(-l-)*
chimneys *(-eys)*
chisel, chiselled *(-s-, -ll-)*
chocolate *(-co-)*
chronically *(-ally)*
chrysanthemum *(chrys-, -the-)*
cinnamon *(-nn-, -mon)*
circuit *(-uit)*
cistern *(-ern)*
civilian *(-l-)*
claustrophobia *(claustro-)*
clientele *(-tele)*
coalesce, coalescing *(-oa-, -esc-)*
cocoa *(-oa)*
coconut *(coco-)*
coconut *(-o-)*
coincidence *(-ence)*
collaborate, collaborator *(-ll-, -b- ,-or)*
collapsible *(-ll-, -ible)*
colleague *(-eague)*
college *(-ege)*
colonel *(-olo-)*
colossal *(-l-, -ss-)*
column *(-l-, -mn)*
commemorate *(-mm-, -m-)*
commission *(-mm-)*
commitment *(-mm- -t-)*
committed, committing *(-mm-, -tt-)*
committee *(-mm-, -tt-, -ee)*
commuter *(-er-)*
comparative *(-para-)*
comparison *(-pari-)*
compatible *(-ible)*
competent *(-pe-, -tent)*
competitive, competitor *(-petit-, -or)*
complexion *(-x-)*
concede *(-cede)*
conceit, conceited *(-ei-)*
conceive *(-ei-)*
condemn *(-mn)*
condescend *(-desc-)*
confectionery *(-ery)*
conference *(-fer- -ence)*
confusable *(-able)*

congregate, congregation *(-greg-)*
conjure *(-jure)*
connoisseur *(-nn-, -oi-, -ss-, -eur)*
connotation *(-nn)*
conscience *(-sci-)*
conscientious *(-sci-, -tious)*
conscious *(-sci-)*
consign, consignment *(-ign-)*
consistent, consistency *(-en-)*
conspiracy *(-acy)*
consumption *(-mp-)*
contemporary *(-rary)*
continent *(-ti-, -ent)*
controversial *(-tro-)*
convalescence, convalescent *(-val-, -sc-, -en-)*
convertible *(-ible)*
coolly *(-ll-)*
corduroy *(-dur-)*
coronary *(-ary)*
corps *(-ps)*
correspondence, correspondent *(-rr-, -en-)*
corroborate *(-rr-, -b-, -r-)*
corrugated *(-rrug-)*
counterfeit *(-ei-)*
coup *(-p)*
courageous *(-geous)*
courteous *(-teous)*
courtesy *(-tesy)*
coxswain *(-swain)*
crescent *(-sc-)*
critically *(-ally)*
crochet, crocheted, crocheting *(-et-)*
crucifixion *(-x-)*
cruelly, crueller, cruellest *(-ll-)*
cruise *(-ui-)*
cryptic *(-y-)*
crystalline *(-ll-)*
crystallize or ***crystallise*** *(-ll-)*
cuisine *(cui-)*
cupboard *(-pb-)*
cupola *(-ol-)*
currency, currencies *(-rr-, en-)*
curriculum *(-rr-, -c-)*
curtsy, curtsying, curtsies, curtsied *(-tsy)*
cygnet *(cy-)*
cylinder *(cy-, -li-)*
cynic, cynical, cynicism *(-cyn-)*
cyst *(cy-)*
Czech *(cz-, -ch)*

daffodil *(-ff-, -d-, -l)*
dahlia *(-h-)*
dais *(-ai-)*
debris *(-s)*
debt, debtor *(-bt, -or)*
debut *(-t)*
deceit, deceive *(-ei-)*
decide, decision, decisive *(dec-)*
defence *(-ce)* or (in American English) ***defense***
defendant *(-ant)*
defensive *(-s-)*
deferred, deferring *(-rr-)*
definite, definitely *(-ite-)*
deign *(-gn)*
deliberate *(de-)*
delicatessen *(-t-, -ss-)*
demeanour *(-our)*
democracy *(-acy)*
deodorant *(-or-)*
dependant *(-ant* for noun, or, in American English, *-ent)*
dependence *(-ence)*
dependent *(-ent* for adjective*)*
depth *(-pth)*
derelict *(-rel-)*
descend *(-sc-)*
descendant *(-sc-, -ant)*
describe, description *(des-)*
desiccated *(-s-, -cc+)*
despair *(des-)*
despatch or ***dispatch*** *(-tch)*
desperate *(-per-)*
despise *(-ise)*
detach, detached, detachable *(-ach)*

deterred, deterring *(-rlr-)*
deterrent *(-rr-)*
deuce *(-eu-)*
develop *(-lop)*
developed, developing *(-p-)*
development *(-lopm-)*
dexterous or ***dextrous***
diagrammatic *(-mm-)*
diamond *(-ia-, -mo-)*
diaphragm *(-gm)*
diarrhoea *(-rrh-, -oe-)* or (in American English) ***diarrhea***
differed, differing *(-r-)*
difference, different *(-fer-)*
digestible *(-ible)*
dilemma *(-l-, -mm-)*
dilettante *(-l-, -tt-)*
diocese *(dio-, -cese)*
diligence, diligent *(-lig-)*
diphtheria *(-phth-)*
diphthong *(-phth-)*
disadvantageous *(-geous)*
disagree *(-g-)*
disappear, disappearance *(-s-, -pp-, -ance)*
disappoint, disappointed *(-s-, -pp-)*
disapprove, disapproval *(-s-, -pp-)*
disastrous *(-tr-)*
disbelief *(-ie)*
disc or (especially computing) ***disk***
discernible *(-ible)*
discipline, disciplinary *(-sc-, -ary)*
discourteous *(-cour-, -teous)*
discrepancy *(-cy)*
disguise *(-ui-)*
dishevelled *(-ll-)* or (in American English) ***disheveled***
disillusioned *(-s-, -ll-)*
dishonourable or (in American English) ***dishonorable***
disk or ***disc***
dispatch or ***despatch*** *(-tch)*
dispensable *(-able)*
dispossess *(-s-, -ss-, -ss)*
dissatisfaction, dissatisfied *(-ss-)*
dissect *(-ss-)*
dissent *(-ss-)*
dissimilar *(-ss-)*
dissolve *(-ss-)*
dissuade *(-ss-)*
distil *(-il)* or (in American English) ***distill***
distillation, distilled. distilling *(-ll-)*
distraught *(-aught)*
divisible *(-ible)*
do's *('s)*
donkeys *(-eys)*
don'ts *(-n'ts)*
doubt, doubtful *(-bt)*
drastically *(-ally)*
draught *(-ght)*
drunkenness *(-nn-)*
dryer or ***drier*** *(-y-* or *-i-* for noun; *-i-* for comparative adjective*)*
dryly or ***drily***
duly *(-uly)*
dumbfounded *(-mb-)*
dungeon *(-geon)*
dutiful *(-i-)*
dysentery *(dys-)*

earnest *(ear-)*
earring *(-rr-)*
eccentric *(-cc-)*
ecclesiastical *(-cc-)*
ecstasy, ecstatic *(-cs-. -asy)*
eczema *(-cze-)*
eerie, eerily, eeriness *(-ie, -ily, -iness)*
effective *(-ff)*
effervesce, effervescence *(-ff-, -sc-, -en-)*
efficacious *(-ff-, -cious)*
efficient *(-ff-)*
effrontery *(eff-, -ery)*
eighth *(-ghth)*
either *(ei-)*
elaborate *(el-, -bor-)*
elegance, elegant *(-leg-, -an-)*
eligible *(-lig-, -ible)*, ***eligibility***
elliptical *(-ll-)*

emanate, emanation *(-man-)*
embarrass, embarrassment *(-rr-, -ss-)*
Emmanuel *(-mm-, -n-)*
encumbrance *(-br-)*
encyclopaedia or ***encyclopedia***
endeavour *(-ea- -our)*
enquire or ***inquire***
enrol, enrolment *(-l-)* or (in American English) ***enroll, enrollment***
enrolled, enrolling *(-ll-)*
enthusiastically *(-ally)*
envelop *(-lop* for verb*)*, ***enveloped, enveloping*** *(-p-)*
envelope *(-lope* for noun*)*
environment *(-nm-)*
equalize or ***equalise*** *(-l-)*
equalled, equalling *(-ll-)*
equatorial *(-quat-)*
equipment *(-p-)*
equipped, equipping *(-pp-)*
equivalent *(-val-, -ent)*
erratic *(-rr-, -t-)*
erroneous *(-rr-, -eous)*
estuary *(-uary-)*
etiquette *(-t-, -qu- -tt-)*
exaggerate, exaggeration *(-gg-)*
exalt, exaltation *(-xal-)*
exasperate, exasperation *(-per)*
exceed, exceedingly *(-ceed-)*
excel *(-xc-, -el)*
excellence, excellent *(-xc-, -ll-)*
except *(-xc-)*
excerpt *(-xc-, -pt)*
exchequer *(-xch-, -qu-)*
excise *(-xc-)*
exciting, excitement *(-xc-)*
exercise *(-cise)*
exhale, exhalation *(-xhal-)*
exhaust, exhaustion *(-xh-)*
exhibit, exhibition *(-xh-)*
exhibited, exhibiting *(-xh-, -t-)*
exhilarate, exhilaration *(-xh-)*
exhort, exhortation *(-xh-)*
exhume *(-xh-)*
expense *(-se)*
extension *(-sion)*
extraneous *(-eous)*
extraordinary *(-aor-)*
extravagance, extravagant *(-vag-)*
extravert or ***extrovert***

façade or ***facade***
facetious *(-ious)*
faeces *(-ae-)* or (in American English) ***feces***
fallacious *(-ll-, -cious)*
fallible *(-ible)*
family *(-ily)*
fascicule *(-sc-)*
fascinate, fascination *(-sc-)*
favourable *(-our-)* or (in American English) ***favorable***
favourite *(-our-)* or (in American English) ***favorite***
fearsome *(fear-)*
feasible *(-ea-, -ible)*
February *(-ru-)*
feign *(-gn)*
feisty *(-ei-)*
ferocious *(-r-, -cious)*
feudal *(-eu-, -al)*
fidgeted, fidgeting *(-dg-, -t-)*
field *(-ie-)*
fiend *(-ie-)*
fierce *(-ier-)*
fiery *(-ier-)*
finesse *(-n-, -esse)*
finish *(-n-)*
fiord or ***fjord***
flabbergasted *(-bb-, -g-)*
flaccid *(-cc-)*
flavour *(-our)* or (in American English) ***flavor***
fledgling *(-dgl-)*
flotilla *(-t-, -ll-)*
fluorescent *(fluor-, -sc-)*
fluoride *(fluor-)*
focused, focuses, focusing
foetus *(-oe-)* or (in American English) ***fetus***
foliage *(-l-)*

foreboding *(fore-)*
foreign *(-ei-, -gn)*
forestall *(fore-, -ll)*
forfeit *(for-, ei-)*
forgiveness *(-n-)*
forgo *(for-)*
fortuitous *(-ui-)*
forty *(for-)*
fossilize or ***fossilise*** *(-ss-, -l-)*
fourteen *(four-)*
frailty *(-ai-)*
franchise *(-ise)*
frantically *(-ally)*
fraught *(-gh-)*
freight *(-eigh-)*
friend *(-ie-)*
frolicked, frolicking *(-ck-)*
fulfil *(ful-, -fil)* or (in American English) ***fulfill***
fulfilled, fulfilling *(-ful-,-ll-)*
fulfilment *(-l-, -l-)*
fullness *(-ll-)*
fulsome *(ful-)*
fundamental *(-da-)*
fuselage *(-se-)*

gaiety *(-aiet-)*
gaily *(-ai-)*
galloped, galloping *(-ll-, -p-)*
gaol *(-ao-)*
garrison, garrisoned *(-rr-)*
gases *(-s- for plural)*
gassed, gassing *(-ss-)*
gateaus or ***gateaux***
gauge *(-au-)*
gazetteer *(-z-, -tt-)*
geisha *(-ei-)*
genealogy, genealogist *(-neal-)*
ghastly *(gh-)*
gherkin *(gh-)*
ghetto *(gh-)*
ghettos or ***ghettoes***
ghost, ghostly *(gh-)*
ghoul, ghoulish *(gh-)*
gimmick *(-mm-, -ick)*
gipsy or ***gypsy***
giraffe *(-r-, -ff-)*
glamorous *(-or-)*
glamour *(-our* in British and American English*)*
glimpse, glimpsing *(-mps-)*
globally *(-ally)*
gluttonous, gluttony *(-tt-, -n-)*
glycerine *(-y-, -ine)*
gnat *(gn-)*
gnarled *(gn-)*
gnash *(gn-)*
gnaw *(gn-)*
gnome *(gn-)*
goal *(-oa)*
goddess *(-dd-)*
gonorrhoea *(-n-, -rrh-, -oe-)*
gorgeous *(-eous)*
gorilla *(-r-, -ll-)*
gossiped, gossiping *(-ss-, -p-)*
government *(-nm-)*
governor *(-or)*
graffiti *(-ff-, -t-)*
grammar *(-ar)*
gramophone *(-mo-)*
grandeur *(-eur)*
gratuitous *(-tui-)*
gray or ***grey***
grief, grieve, grievance *(-ie-)*
grievous *(-ie-, -vous)*
grotesque *(-esque)*
grovel, grovelled, grovelling *(-el, -ll-)*
gruesome *(-ue-)*
guarantee *(gu-, -r-)*
guard, guardian *(gu-)*
guerrilla *(gu-, -rr-, -ll-)*
guess *(gu-)*
guest *(gu-)*
guide, guidance *(gu-, -ance)*
guillotine *(gu-, -ll-)*
guilt, guilty *(gu-)*
guinea *(gu-, -ea)*

gullible *(-ible)*
gymkhana *(-y-, -kh-)*
gynaecology *(-ae-)* or (in American English) ***gynecology***
gypsy or ***gipsy***

haemoglobin *(-aemo-)* or (in American English) ***hemoglobin***
haemorrhage *(-ae-, -mo-, -rrh-)* or (in American English) ***hemorrhage***
halcyon *(-cy-)*
hallucination *(-ll-, -c-)*
handicapped, handicapping *(-pp-)*
handkerchief *(hand-)*
happened, happening *(-pp-, -n-)*
harangue, haranguing *(-r-, -gu-)*
harass, harassed, harassment *(-r-, -ss-)*
harpsichord *(-ch-)*
harridan *(-rr-)*
haughty *(-gh-)*
havoc *(-oc)*
hazard, hazardous *(-z-)*
hearse *(-ear-)*
height *(-ei-)*
heinous *(-ei-)*
heifer *(-ei-)*
height *(-ei)*
heinous *(-ei)*
heir, heiress *(-ei-)*
heist *(-ei-)*
herbaceous *(-ceous)*
herbalist *(-l-)*
hereditary *(-ary)*
heroes *(-oes)*
heyday *(-ey-, -ay)*
hiccup or ***hiccough***
hiccuped, hiccuping *(-p-)* or (in American English) ***hiccupped, hiccupping***
hideous *(-eous)*
hierarchy *(-ie-, -ch-)*
hieroglyphic *(-ie-, -yph-)*
hindrance *(-dr-)*
hippopotamus *(-pp-, -p-, -t-)*
honorary *(-or-, -ary)*
honourable *(-our-)* or (in American English) ***honorable***
horizon *(-r-, -z-)*
horrible *(-rr-, -ible)*
humorous *(-or-)*
humour *(-our)* or (in American English) ***humor***
Hungary *(-ary)*
hurricane *(-cane)*
hyacinth *(hya-, -c-)*
hydraulic *(hy-, -draul-)*
hygiene, hygienic *(-ie-)*
hypochondria, hypochondriac *(-y-, -ch-)*
hypocrisy *(hyp-, -isy)*
hypocrite *(hyp-, -ite)*
hypotenuse *(hy-, -ten-, -use)*
hysterically *(hys-, -ally)*

iconoclasm, iconoclast *(icono-)*
identical *(-cal)*
ideological *(ideo-)*
idiosyncrasy *(-syn-, -asy)*
idyllic *(-yll-)*
illegal *(-ll-)*
illicit *(-ll-, -c-)*
illegible *(-ll-, -ible-)*
illegitimate *(-ll-, -g-, -t-)*
illiterate *(-ll-)*
imaginary *(-ary)*
imitate *(-m-)*
immaculate *(-mm-, -cu-)*
immediate, immediately *(-mm-)*
immense *(-mm-)*
immigrant, immigration *(-mm-)*
imminent *(-mm-)*
immoral, immorality *(-mm-)*
immortal *(-mm-)*
immovable *(-mm-, -vable)*
immune *(-mm-)*
impasse *(-asse)*
impeccable *(-cc-)*
impervious *(-vious)*
implement *(-le-)*
impostor *(-or)*

impresario *(-s-)*
impropriety *(-priety)*
improvise, improvisation *(-s-)*
inaccessible *(-cc-, -ss-, -ible)*
inaccurate *(-n-, -cc-)*
inadmissible *(-ible)*
inappropriate *(-pp-)*
incandescent *(-sc-, -ent)*
incessant *(-c-, -ss-, -ant)*
incidentally *(-ally)*
incipient *(-c-, -ent)*
incredible *(-ible)*
incompatible *(-ible)*
incompetent *(-ent)*
incontrovertible *(-tro-, -ible)*
incorrigible *(-rr-, -ible)*
incur, incurred, incurring *(-rr-)*
indefinitely *(-ite-)*
independent, independence *(-en-)*
indestructible *(-ible)*
indict, indictment *(-ct-)*
indifference, indifferent *(-fer-)*
indigenous *(-gen-)*
indigestible *(-ible)*
indignant *(-ant)*
inefficient, inefficiency *(-ff-, -en-)*
ineligible *(-ible)*
indiscreet *(-ee-)*
indispensable *(-able)*
inexhaustible *(-h-, -ible)*
infallible *(-ible)*
inflammable *(-mm-, -able)*
inflammation, inflammatory *(-mm-)*
ingredient *(-ent)*
inhabitant *(-ant)*
inhibited *(-b-, -t-)*
initial, initialled, initialling or (in American English) ***initialed, initialing***
innocence, innocent *(-nn-)*
innocuous *(-nn-)*
innumerable *(-nn-)*
inoculate *(-n-)*
inquire, inquiry or ***enquire, enquiry***
inseparable *(-par-)*
insincere *(-cere)*
insistent, insistence *(-en-)*
install or ***instal***
intallation *(ll-)*
instalment *(-l-)* or (in American English) ***installment***
instantaneous *(-eous)*
instil *(-l)* or (in American English) ***instill***
instilled, instilling *(-ll-)*
instrument, instrumental *(-stru-)*
insular *(-ar)*
intellect, intellectual *(-ll-)*
interested, interesting *(-ter-)*
interference *(-ence)*
internecine *(-nec-)*
interpolate, interpolation *(-pol-)*
interregnum *(-rr-)*
interrogate, interrogation *(-rr-)*
interrupt, interruption *(-rr-)*
intricacy *(-acy)*
intrigue *(-gue)*
intrinsically *(-s-, -ally)*
introduce, introduction *(-tro-)*
inveigh *(-eigh)*
inveigle *(-ei-)*
irascible *(-r-, -sc-, -ible)*
iridescence *(-r-, -sc-, -ence)*
irregular *(-rr-)*
irrelevant *(-rr-, -lev-, -ant)*
irreplaceable *(-eable)*
irresistible *(-rr-, -ible)*
irresponsible *(-rr-, -ible)*, ***irresponsibility***
irritable *(-rr-, -able)*
isosceles *(-sc-)*
issue, issuing *(-ss-)*
isthmus *(-sthm-)*
itinerary *(-rary)*

jealous *(-ea-)*
jeopardize or ***jeopardise, jeopardy*** *(-eo-)*
jerseys *(-eys)*
jettison, jettisoned *(-tt-, -s-)*
jeweller *(-ll-)* or (in American English) ***jeweler***

jewellery or (in American English) ***jewelry***
jockeys *(-eys)*
jodhpurs *(-dh-)*
journalism, journalist *(-our)*
journeys *(-our-, -eys)*
jubilant *(-l-, -ant-)*
jubilee *(-l-)*
judgement or ***judgment***

kaleidoscope *(-ei-)*
kaolin *(-ao-)*
karaoke *(-ao-)*
keenness *(-nn-)*
khaki *(kh-)*
kidnapped, kidnapper, kidnapping *(-pp-)* or (in American English) ***kidnaped, kidnaper, kidnaping***
kidneys *(-eys)*
knowledgeable *(-dge-)*

label, labelled, labelling or (in American English) ***labeled, labeling***
laboratory *(-tory)*
laborious *(-or-)*
labyrinth *(-by-, -ri-)*
laconic, laconically *(-c-, -ally)*
lacquer *(-cqu-)*
laid *(-aid)*
language *(-gua-)*
languor, languorous *(-guor-)*
larceny *(-c-)*
larynx, laryngitis *(-yn-)*
lascivious *(-sc-)*
lassitude *(-ss-)*
lasso *(-o)*, ***lassos, lassoing*** or ***lassoes, lassoeing***
latitude *(-t-)*
laughter *(-augh-)*
launderette *(-der-)*
lavatory *(-tory)*
league *(-gue)*
leanness *(-nn)*
ledger *(-dg-)*
legendary *(-g-, -ary)*
legible *(-g-, -ible)*
leisure *(-ei-)*
length, lengthen *(-ngth-)*
leopard *(-eo-)*
leukaemia *(-eu-, -k-, -ae-)*or (in American English) ***leukemia***
level, levelled, levelling *(-ll-)* or (in American English) ***leveled, levelling***
liaise, liaison *(-ai-)*
libellous *(-ll-)* or (in American English) ***libelous***
library *(-rary)*
licence *(-ce* for noun*)* or (in American English) ***license***
license *(-se* for verb*)*
licentious *(-t-)*
lieu *(-ieu)*
lieutenant *(-ieu-)*
lightning *(-tn-* for noun*)*
likelihood *(-li-)*
limousine *(-ou-)*
lineage *(-eage)*
liquefy *(-efy)*
liqueur *(-qu-, -eur)*
liquor *(-qu-, -or)*
liquorice *(-qu-, -or-, -ice)*
listened, listening *(-st-)*
literate, literature *(liter-)*
livelihood, liveliness *(-li-)*
lonely *(-ely)*
loneliness *(-eli-)*
longitude *(-ngi-)*
lose, verb *(-o-)*
luggage *(-gg-)*
lumbar *(-ar)*
luncheon *(-eon)*
luscious *(-sc-)*
luxury *(-xur-)*

Madeira *(-ei-)*
maelstrom *(-ae-)*
magnanimous *(-nim-)*
mahogany *(-gan-)*
maintain *(-ai-, -ai-)*

maintenance *(-ai-, -ten-)*
malign *(-gn)*
manageable *(-eable)*
manilla or ***manila***
manoeuvre *(-oeu-)* or (in American English) ***maneuver***
mantelpiece *(-tel-)*
margarine *(-gar-)*
marketed, marketing *(-t-)*
marmalade *(-mal-)*
maroon *(-r-)*
marquess *(-quess)*
marriage, marriageable *(-iag-, -eable)*
martyr *(-tyr)*
marvellous *(-ll-)* or (in American English) ***marvelous***
massacre *(-ss-)*
mayonnaise *(-nn-)*
meagre *(-ea-, -gre)* or (in American English) ***meager***
medallist *(-ll-)* or (in American English) ***medalist***
medicine *(-di-)*
mediaeval or ***medieval***
Mediterranean *(-d-, -t-, -rr-, -ean)*
melancholy *(-ch-)*
melee *(-l-, ee)*
memento *(mem-)*, ***mementos*** or ***mementoes***
meringue *(-ingue)*
messenger *(-en-)*
meteorologist, meteorology *(-eor-)*
mezzanine *(-zz-, -n-)*
miaow or ***meow***
midday *(-dd-)*
migraine *(-aine)*
milage or ***mileage***
milieu *(-ieu)*
millennium *(-ll-, -nn-)*
millionaire, millionairess *(-ll-, -n-)*
mimicked, mimicking *(-ck-)*
mimicry *(-cry)*
miniature *(-ia-)*
ministry *(-stry)*
minuscule *(-nu-)*
minute *(-ute)*
miscellaneous *(-sc-, -ll-, eous)*
mischief *(-ie-)*
mischievous *(-ie-, -vous)*
mishap *(-sh-)*
misogynist *(-gyn-)*
misshapen *(-ssh-)*
misspelt *(-ss-, -l-)*
misspent *(-ss-)*
mistletoe *(-stl-)*
mnemonic *(mne-)*
moccasin *(-cc-, -s-)*
model, modelled, modelling *(-ll-)* or (in American English) ***modeled, modeling***
monarch *(-ch)*
monastery *(-ery)*
monkeys *(-eys)*
morgue *(-gue)*
mortgage *(-tg-)*
mortgagor *(-tg-, -gor)*
mosaic *(-aic)*
mould, mouldy or (in American English) ***mold, moldy***
moustache *(mou-)*
mountainous *(-tain-)*
municipal *(-pal)*
murderous *(-der-)*
murmur, murmured, murmuring *(-ur-, -ur-)*
muscle *(-scl-)*
mustn't *(-stn-)*
myopic *(my-)*
myrrh *(-yrrh)*
mystify *(my-, -ti-)*

naif or ***naïf, naive*** or ***naïve***
naivety or ***naïvety*** *(-ety)*
naphtha *(-phth-)*
naughty, naughtiness *(-aught-)*
nausea *(-ea)*
necessary *(-c-, -ss-)*
negligence, negligent *(-li-, -en-)*
negligible *(-li-, -ible)*

negotiate *(-ti-)*
neighbour *(-eigh-, -our)*
neither *(-ei-)*
niece *(-ie-)*
ninth *(-nth)*
no one or ***no-one***
noticeable *(-ceable)*
notoriety *(-iety)*
nought or (in American English) ***naught***
nuisance *(-ui-, -ance)*
numb *(-mb)*
nutritious *(-tious)*

oblique *(-que)*
obscene, obscenity *(-sc-)*
obstetrician *(-stet-, -ician)*
obstreperous *(-per-)*
occasion, occasional, occasionally *(-cc-, -s-)*
occupancy, occupation, occupy *(-cc-, -p-)*
occur *(-cc-)*
occurred, occurrence, occurring *(-cc-. -rr-)*
offence *(-ce)* or (in American English) ***offense***
offensive *(-s-)*
offered, offering *(-r-)*
omelette *(-mel-, -ette)* or in American English) ***omelet***
omit, omission *(-m-)*
omitted, omitting *(-m-, -tt-)*
oneself
onomatopoeia *(ono-, mato-, -oeia)*
opaque *(-p-, -que)*
ophthalmic, opthalmology *(-phth-)*
opinion *(-p-, -n-)*
opossum *(-p-, -ss-)*
opponent *(-pp-, -n-, -ent)*
opportunity *(-pp-)*
opposite, opposition *(-pp-, -s-)*
opprobrium *(opp-)*
ordinary *(-ary)*
oscillate, oscillation *(-sc-, -ll-)*
outfitter *(-tt-)*
outrageous *(-eous)*
overrated *(-rr-)*
overrule *(-rr-)*
overrun *(-rr)*
overwrought *(-wrought)*

pageant *(-geant)*
paid *(-ai-)*
pallor *(-or)*
pamphlet *(-mphl-)*
panacea *(-cea)*
panicked, panicking, panicky *(-ck-)*
paraffin *(-r-, -ff-)*
parallel *(-r-, -ll-, -l)*
paralleled, paralleling *(-r-, -ll-, -l-)*
parallelogram *(-r-, -ll-, -l-)*
paralyse *(-r-, -l-, -yse)* or (in American English) ***paralyze***
paralysis, paralytic *(-r-, -ly-)*
paraphernalia *(-phern-)*
parcelled, parcelling *(-ll-)* or (in American English) ***parceled, parcelling***
parliament, parliamentary *(-lia-)*
paroxysm *(-oxysm)*
particularly *(-larly)*
partridge *(-idge)*
passenger *(-eng-)*
pastime *(-s-)*
patrol, patrolled, patrolling *(pat-, -ll-)*
pattern *(-ern)*
pavilion *(-l-)*
peaceable *(-eable)*
pedal *(ped-, al)*
pedalled, pedalling *(-ll-)* or (in American English) ***pedaled, pedaling***
pedlar *(-ar)* or (in American English) ***peddler***
pencilled, pencilling *(-ll)* or (in American English) ***penciled, penciling***
pendant *(-ant* for noun*)*
penicillin *(-n-, -ll-)*
peninsula *(-n-)*, ***peninsular*** *(-ar* for adjective*)*
perceptible *(-ible)*

perennial *(-r-, -nn-)*
perilous *(-r-, -l-)*
permanent *(-ent)*
permissible *(-ible)*
permitted, permitting *(-tt-)*
persistence, persistent *(-en-)*
personnel *(-nn-)*
Pharoah *(-oah)*
phlegm *(-gm)*
physically *(phys-, -ally)*
physician *(phys-, -ic-)*
physique *(phys-, -que)*
pianos *(-os)*
picnicked, picnicking *(-ck-)*
picturesque *(-esque)*
piece *(-ie-)*
pigeon *(-geo-)*
pinafore *(-n-, -fore)*
piteous *(-eous)*
pitiful *(-ti-)*
pivoted, pivoting *(-t-)*
plague *(-gue)*
plaintiff *(-ff)*
plait *(-ai-)*
plaque *(-que)*
plateaus or ***plateaux***
plausible *(-ible)*
playwright *(-wright)*
pleurisy *(-eu-, -isy)*
pneumonia *(pn-, -eu-)*
poignancy, poignant *(-gn-)*
poisonous *(-n-)*
pollution *(-ll-)*
porpoise *(-oise)*
porridge *(-rr-, -idge)*
Portuguese *(-gu-)*
possess, possession, possessive *(-ss-, -ss-)*
possible *(-ss-, -ible)*, ***possibility***
posthumous *(-sth-)*
potatoes *(-oes)*
poultry *(-ou-)*
practice *(-ce* for noun*)*
practise *(-se* for verb*)* or (in American English) ***practice***
precede *(-cede)*
precinct *(-c-)*
predecessor *(-c-, -ss-, -or)*
predominance *(-ance)*
preferable *(-r-, -able)*
preference *(-r-, -ence)*
preferred, preferring *(-rr-)*
prejudice *(-ju-)*
preparation *(-par-)*
preponderance *(-ance)*
presence *(-s-, -ence)*
prestige, prestigious *(-ig-)*
presumably *(-mably)*
prevalent *(-ent)*
priest *(-ie-)*
primitive *(-m-)*
privilege *(-l-, -ege)*
probably *(-bab-)*
procedure *(-ced-)*
proceed, proceedings *(-ceed-)*
profession *(-f-, -ss-)*
professor *(-f-, -ss-)*
proffer, proffered, proffering *(-ff-, -r-)*
profited, profiting *(-t-)*
programme (in British English), ***program*** (in American English and computing)
programmed, programming *(-mm-)* (or in American English sometimes ***programed, programing****)*
pronunciation *(-nun-)*
propaganda *(-pag-, -da)*
propellant (noun), ***propelled, propelling*** *(-ll-)*
propeller *(-ll-)*
prophecy *(-cy* for noun*)*
prophesy *(-sy* for verb*)*
prosaic *(-ai-)*
protein *(-ei-)*
protrude *(-tru-)*
protuberance *(-tu-)*
prove, verb *(-o-)*

prowess *(-ss)*
psalm *(ps-, -al-)*
pseudonym *(pseud-)*
psychiatric, psychiatrist, psychiatry *(ps-, -ch-)*
psychological. psychologist, psychology *(ps-, -ch-)*
publicly *(-cly)*
pumice *(-m-, -ice)*
pursue *(-pur-)*, ***pursuit*** *(-uit)*
pyjamas (in British English), ***pajamas*** (in American English)
pyramid *(pyr-)*

quarrelled, quarrelling *(-ll-)* or (in American English) ***quarreled, quarreling***
quarter *(-art-)*
quay *(-ay)*
questionnaire *(-nn-)*
queue *(-eue)*, ***queuing*** *(-eu-)*
quiescent *(-sc-, -ent)*
quietly *(-ie-)*
quizzes *(-zz-)*

racketeering *(-t-)*
raspberry *(-pb-)*
ravenous *(-ven-)*
really *(-ll)*
realm *(-eal-)*
rebelled, rebelling *(-ll-)*
recede *(-cede)*
receipt *(-ei-, -pt)*
receive *(-ei-)*
recipe *(-c-, -pe)*
recognize or ***recognise*** *(-cogn-)*
recommend, recommendation *(-c-, -mm-)*
reconnaissance *(-c-, -nn-, -ss-, -ance)*
reconnoitre *(-c-, -nn-, -tre)* or (in American English) ***reconnoiter***
recruit *(-ui-)*
recurred, recurrence, recurring *(-rr-)*
redundancy, redundant *(-ant)*
referral, referred, referring *(-rr-)*
referee *(-r-)*
reference *(-r-. -ence)*
refrigerator *(-frig-)*
refuelled, refuelling or (in American English) ***refueled, refueling***
regrettable, regretted, regretting *(-tt-)*
rehearsal *(-hears-)*
reign *(-gn)*
reiterate *(-ei)*
relevance, relevant *(-l-, -an-)*
relief, relieve *(-ie-)*
religious *(-ious)*
reminiscence, reminiscent *(-min-, -sc-, -en)*
remittance, remitted, remitting *(-tt-)*
renaissance *(-n-, -ss-)*
rendezvous *(-ez-, -ous)*
repaid *(-ai-)*
repentance, repentant *(-an-)*
repertoire *(-per-, -oire)*
repetition *(-pet-)*
repetitive *(-tit-)*
reprieve *(-ie)*
require *(requ-)*
rescind *(-sc-)*
resemble. resemblance *(-s-, -ance)*
reservoir *(-er-, oir)*
resign *(-gn)*
resistance, resistant *(-an-)*
responsible *(-ible)*, ***responsibility***
restaurant *(-taur-)*
resurrect, resurrection *(-s-,-u-, -rr-)*
resuscitate *(-sci-)*
retrieve *(-ie)*
reveille *(-eille)*
reversible *(-ible)*
rhapsodize or ***rhapsodise, rhapsody*** *(rh-)*
rhetoric, rhetorical *(rh-)*
rheumatism *(rh-, eu-)*
rhinoceros *(rh-, -c-, os)*
rhododendron *(rh-, -do-)*
rhubarb *(rh-)*

rhyme *(rh-, -y-)*
rhythm, rhythmic *(rh-, -y-, -thm)*
ridiculous *(ri-)*
rigorous *(-or-)*
rivalled, rivalling *(-ll-)* or (in American English) ***rivaled, rivaling***
riveted, riveting *(-t-)*
rogue *(-gue)*
role or ***rôle***

sabotage *(-bot-)*
saccharine *(-cch-)*
sachet *(-et)*
sacrilege, sacrilegious *(-cri-, -leg-)*
said *(-ai-)*
salmon *(-alm-)*
saloon *(-l-)*
sandal *(-al)*
sapphire *(-pph-)*
satellite *(-t-, -ll-)*
satisfactory *(-ory)*
sausage *(-au-, -s-)*
scaffolding *(-ff-)*
scandalize *or* ***scandalise, scandalous*** *(-l-)*
scary *(-ry)*
scene, scenery *(-sc-, -ery)*
sceptic, sceptical *(sc-)* or (in American English) ***skeptic, skeptical***
sceptre or (in American English) ***scepter*** *(sc-)*
schedule *(sch-)*
scheme *(sch-)*
schizophrenia *(sch-, -z-)*
sciatica *(sc-)*
science, scientific, scientifically *(sc-, -ally)*
scissors *(sc-)*
scourge *(-our-)*
scrupulous *(-pu-)*
scurrilous *(-rr-, -l-)*
scythe *(sc-, -y-)*
seance *or* ***séance***
secondary *(-ary)*
secretary *(-tary)*
sedentary *(-ent-)*
segregate *(-greg-)*
seize, seizure *(-ei-)*
semblance *(-ance)*
sensible *(-ible)*
sentence *(-ence)*
sentinel *(-el)*
separable, separate, separation *(-par-)*
septic *(se-)*
serenade *(-re-)*
sergeant *(ser-, -eant)*
series *(-ies)*
serrated *(-rr-)*
serviceable *(-eable)*
settee *(-tt-)*
several *(-ver-)*
sheikh *(-ei-, -kh)*
shepherd *(-ph-)*
sheriff *(-r-, -ff)*
shield *(-ie-)*
shovelled, shovelling *(-ll-)* or (in American English) ***shoveled, shoveling***
shyer, shyest, shyly, shyness *(-y-)*
siege *(-ie-)*
sieve *(-ie-)*
sigh *(-igh)*
signalled, signalling or (in American English) ***signaled, signaling***
silhouette *(-h-)*
similar, similarity, similarly *(-m-)*
simultaneous *(-ult-, -eous)*
sincerely *(-cere-)*
sinecure *(-nec-)*
singeing *(-ge-)*
sinusitis *(-us-)*
skein *(-ei-)*
skied, skiing
skilful *(-l-)* or (in American English) ***skillful***
slanderous *(-der-)*
slaughter *(-gh-)*
sleigh *(-eigh)*
sluice *(-ui)*

slyer, slyest, slyly or ***slily, slyness***
smelt *(-l-)*
sobriety *(-ie-)*
soiree or ***soirée*** *(-oir-)*
sojourn *(-journ)*
soldier *(-ier)*
solecism *(-lec-)*
solemn *(-mn)*
solicitor *(-l-, -or)*
solstice *(-l-, -ice)*
sombre or (in American English) ***somber***
somersault *(somer-)*
sorbet *(-et)*
souvenir *(-ir)*
sovereign, sovereignty *(-ei-, -gn)*
spaghetti *(-gh-)*
spaniel *(-iel)*
spasm *(-asm)*
species *(-ies)*
specifically *(-ally)*
spectacles *(-tac-)*
speech *(-ee-)*
spelt *(-l-)*
sphinx *(sph-, -inx)*
spilt *(-l-)*
spinach *(-ach)*
spontaneity *(-ei-)*
spontaneous *(-eous)*
sporadic, sporadically *(spor-, -ally)*
sprightly *(-ight-)*
squalor *(-or)*
squirrel, squirrelled, squirrelling *(-rr-, -ll-)* or (in American English) ***squirreled, squirreling***
staccato *(-cc-)*
stalk *(-lk)*
stallion *(-ll-)*
stalwart *(-l-, -wart)*
steadfast *(-ea-)*
stealth *(-ea-)*
stencilled, stencilling *(-ll-)* or (in American English) ***stenciled, stenciling***
stereos *(-os)*
stirrup *(-rr-)*
stoic, stoicism *(-oi-)*
stomach *(-ch)*
strategically *(-ally)*
strength, strengthen *(-ngth)*
stupefy *(-efy)*
stupor *(-or)*
suave *(-ua-)*
subjugate *(-ju-)*
subpoena, subpoenaed *(-oe-)*
subterranean *(-rr-, -ean)*
subtle, subtlety, subtly *(-bt-)*
succeed *(-cc-, -ceed)*
success, successfully *(-cc-)*
succession, successive, successor *(-cc-)*
succinct *(-cc-)*
succulent *(-cc-, -lent)*
succumb *(-cc-, -mb)*
suddenness *(-nn-)*
suede *(-ue-)*
sufferance, suffering *(-er-)*
suffocate *(-ff-, -oc-)*
suggest, suggestion *(-gg-)*
sulphur *(-ph-, -ur)* or (in American English) ***sulfur***
summarize or ***summarise, summary*** *(-mm-, -ar-)*
summoned, summoning *(-mm-, -n-)*
supercilious *(-cil-)*
superintendent *(-dent)*
supersede *(-sede)*
superstitious *(-tious)*
supervise, supervisor *(-is-, -or)*
supplant *(-pp-)*
supplementary *(-pp-)*
suppose, supposing *(-pp-)*
surgeon *(-geon)*
surrogacy, surrogate *(-rr-, -og-, -acy)*
surprise, surprised, surprising *(-is-)*
surroundings *(-rr-)*
surveillance *(-ei-, -ll-, -ance)*
surveyor *(-veyor)*
survivor *(-or)*
susceptible *(-sc-, -ible)*
suspicious *(-cious)*

sustenance *(-te-, -ance)*
sword *(sw-)*
sycamore *(sy-, -ca-, -more)*
sycophant *(sy-, -co-, -ph-)*
syllable, syllabic *(sy-, -ll-)*
syllabus *(sy-, -ll-, -us),* ***syllabuses*** or ***syllabi***
symbol, symbolic, symbolize or ***symbolise*** *(sym-, -l-)*
symmetrical, symmetrically, symmetry *(sy-, -mm-)*
sympathetic, sympathy *(sym-)*
symposium *(sym-)*
synagogue *(syn-, -ag-, -gue)*
synchronize or ***synchronise*** *(-syn-, -chr-)*
synonym *(syn-, -o-, -nym)*
synthesis, synthesize *or* ***synthesise, synthetic*** *(-syn-)*
syphilis *(sy- -phi-)*
syringe *(-sy-, -rin-)*
syrup, syrupy *(syr-)*
system *(sys-)*
systematically *(sys-. -ally)*

tableau *(-eau),* ***tableaus*** or ***tableaux***
taciturn *(-c-, -urn)*
tambourine *(-ou-)*
targeted, targeting *(-t-)*
tariff *(-r-, ff)*
tarpaulin *(-ar-, -au-, -in)*
tattoo *(-tt-)*
teat *(-ea)*
taxied, taxiing
technically *(-chn-, -ally)*
technique *(-chn-, -que)*
televise *(-ise)*
temperamental *(-per-)*
temperature *(-per-)*
temporary *(-rary)*
tenant, tenancy *(-an-)*
tendency *(-ency)*
termagant *(-gant)*
terrestrial *(-rr-)*
terrible, terrify, terror *(-rr-)*
territory *(-rr-, -ory)*
tertiary *(-ti-, -ary)*
theatre or (in American English) ***theater***
therapeutic *(-eu)*
thesaurus *(-au-),* ***thesauruses*** or ***thesauri***
thief, thieves *(-ie-)*
thigh *(-gh)*
thinness *(-nn-)*
thorough, thoroughfare, thoroughly *(-or-, -ough)*
threatened, threatening *(-ea-)*
threshold *(-sh-)*
throughout *(-ough-)*
tingeing *(-ge-)*
thwart *(-art)*
thyroid *(thy-)*
tissue *(-ss-)*
titillate, titillating *(-t-, -ll-)*
tobacco, tobacconist *(-b-, -cc-)*
toboggan, tobogganed, tobogganing *(-b-, -gg-, -n-)*
tomatoes *(-oes)*
tomorrow *(-rr-)*
tonsil, tonsillitis *(-ll-)*
tortoise, tortoiseshell *(-oise)*
total, totalled, totalling *(-ll-)* or (in American English) ***totaled, totaling***
towelling *(-ll-)* or (in American English) ***toweling***
trafficked, trafficking *(-ck-)*
tragedy, tragic, tragically *(-g-, -ally)*
tranquil, tranquillity or (sometimes in American English) ***tranquility***
tranquillize *or* ***tranquillise*** *(-ll-)* or (in American English) ***tranquilize***
transcend *(-sc-)*
transferable, transference *(-r-)*
transferred, transferring *(-rr-)*
transmitted, transmitter, transmitting *(-tt-)*
transparency, transparent *(-en-)*
trapeze *(-z-)*

travelled, traveller, travelling *(-ll-)* or (in American English) ***traveled, traveler, traveling***
travesty *(-ve-)*
treacherous, treachery *(-ea-)*
treasure, treasury *(-ea-, -sur-)*
treble *(-b-)*
trespass, trespasser *(-s-, -ss-)*
triple *(-p-)*
trousseau *(-ss-, -eau),* ***trousseaus*** or ***trousseaux***
truly *(-uly)*
tsar *(ts-)*
tsetse *(ts-)*
tuberculosis *(-cu-)*
tumour *(-our)* or (in American English) ***tumor***
tunnel, tunnelled, tunnelling *(-ll)* or (in American English) ***tunneled, tunneling***
turnstile *(-ile)*
turquoise *(tur-, -qu-, -oise)*
twelfth *(-lfth)*
tyranny *(-r-, -nn-)*
tyre *(-y-)* or (in American English) ***tire***

unanimous *(-n-, -n-, -m-)*
unconscious *(-sc-, -ious)*
underprivileged *(-leg-)*
underrate, underrated *(-rr-)*
undoubted *(-bt-)*
unduly *(-uly)*
unequalled *(-ll-)* or (in American English) ***unequaled***
unfasten *(-st-)*
unforgettable *(-tt-)*
uninterrupted *(-rr-)*
unique *(-que)*
unmistakable *(-kable)*
unnatural *(-nn-)*
unnecessary *(-nn-, -c-, -ss-)*
unparalleled *(-ll-, -l-)*
until *(-l)*
upbraid *(-pb-)*
upheaval *(-ph-, -ea-)*
upholstery *(-ph-)*
uproarious *(-oa-)*
usually *(-ua-, -lly)*
usury *(-sur-)*
utensil *(-l)*

vaccinate, vaccination *(-cc-)*
vacuum *(-c-, -uu-)*
vague *(-gue-)*
valleys *(-eys)*
valuable *(-ua-)*
vanguard *(-gu-)*
vanilla *(-n-, -ll-)*
variegated *(-ie-)*
vegetable *(-get-)*
vehement *(-ehe-)*
vehicle *(-hi-)*
veneer *(-eer)*
venereal *(-eal)*
vengeance *(-eance)*
ventriloquist *(-lo-)*
verruca *(-rr-, -c-)*
vertebra *(-te-),* ***vertebrae*** *(-ae)*
vestige *(-ige)*
vetoes *(-oes)*
viable *(-ia-)*
vicissitude *(-c-, -ss-)*
videos *(plural) or (3rd person singular)* ***videoes***
vigorous *(-or-)*
villain *(-ll-, -ain)*
vinegar *(-eg-, -ar)*
viscount *(vis-)*
visitor *(-or)*
vociferous *(-c-)*
volleys *(-eys)*
voluntary *(-lun-, -tary)*
volunteer *(-lun-, -teer)*
voyeur *(-oy-, -eur)*

wagon or ***waggon***
walloped, walloping *(-p-)*
walrus, walruses *(-l-)*
waltz *(-ltz)*

weapon *(-ea-)*
Wednesday *(-nes)*
weigh, weight *(-ei-, -gh-)*
whale *(wh-)*
weir *(-ei-)*
weird *(-ei-)*
whereabouts *(-ea)*
whilst *(-lst)*
whisky or (in Ireland and in American English) ***whiskey***
wholesale *(-le-)*
wholesome *(-le-)*
wholly *(-lly)*
whooping cough *(wh-)*
wield *(-ie-)*
wiry *(-ry)*
withhold *(-thh-)*
woollen, woolly *(-ll-)* or (in American English) ***woolen, wooly***
worshipped, worshipping *(-pp-)* or (in American English) ***worshiped, worshiping***
wretched *(wr-, -tch-)*

xenophobia *(xen-)*
xylophone *(xy-, -lo-)*

yacht *(-cht)*
yield *(-ie-)*
yeoman *(-eo-)*
yoghurt or ***yoghourt***
yolk *(-lk* for the egg centre*)*

zealous *(-ea)*
zephyr *(-phyr)*
zeroes or ***zeros***
zigzagged *(-gg-)*
zoology *(-oo-)*

13 WORDS SOMETIMES CONFUSED

aboard, abroad

- **Aboard** means on board a ship, aircraft, etc:

  We weren't allowed aboard till the baggage had been loaded.

- **Abroad** means 'to or in a foreign country':

  We usually take a holiday abroad during the summer.

accede, exceed

- You **accede** to something when you agree to it:

  He acceded readily to our suggestion.

- One amount **exceeds** another if it is greater:

  Don't let your expenditure exceed your income.

  You're exceeding the speed limit.

accept, except

- You **accept** something when you receive it gladly, or agree to it:

  Please accept this gift.

  They accepted our proposal.

- **Except** is a preposition meaning 'not including':

  I finished all the questions except the last one.

  Except can also be a verb:

  Some folk are terribly lazy, present company excepted, of course.

access, excess

- You have **access** to materials or data when you are able to see them or use them:

  Who could have gained access to the files?

  An **access** of something is a sudden fit of it:

  In an access of generosity he offered to pay for lunch.

- An **excess** of something is too much of it:

  In general people have an excess of fat in their diet.

  Excesses are outrageous acts:

  the excesses of the Pol Pot regime

adapter, adaptor

- An **adapter** is a person who adapts something, e.g. a play for television.
- An **adaptor** is a fitting into which an electric plug can be inserted.

addition, edition

- An **addition** is something new or extra:

  We're expecting an addition to the family in April.

- An **edition** of a book is the set of copies that are printed at one time:

  The first edition had a few errors which we corrected in the second edition.

adverse, averse

- **Adverse** circumstances, conditions, or criticism are unfavourable:

  He coped amazingly well in adverse circumstances.

- You say you are not **averse** to something if you don't object to it:

  I'm not averse to a small whisky at bedtime.

advice, advise

- **Advice** is a noun:

  Your bank will give you sound advice.

- **Advise** is a verb:

  Your bank will advise you.

aesthetic, ascetic

- **Aesthetic** matters relate to appearance, beauty, or artistic appreciation:

  These wheeled dustbins in the street may be practical but they are a disaster from the aesthetic point of view.

- People who lead **ascetic** lives severely restrict their pleasures and physical comforts, for example the amount that they eat and drink.

affect, effect

- **Affect** is a verb: you **are affected** by something if it changes or alters things for you:

  Nobody over 40 will be affected by the new legislation.

- **Effect** is a noun:

  What effect will the new legislation have on those under 40?

  Effect can also be a verb: to **effect** something is to make it happen:

  The alterations to the traffic flow will be effected as soon as possible.

aid, aide

- **Aid** is a noun or verb meaning 'help':

  Various charities are involved in organizing aid for the refugees.
  Aided by an extraordinary memory, she was a frequent winner of general-knowledge quizzes.

- A president's or prime minister's **aides** are his or her close personal advisors.

aisle, isle

- An **aisle** is a passageway, for example between shelves of goods in a supermarket, or between blocks of seating in a theatre:

  Please don't leave trolleys blocking the aisles.

- **Isle** is a poetic word for an island, often found in the names of islands:

  the Isle of Man; the Isles of Scilly.

allay, alley, ally

- To **allay** somebody's fear, hunger, etc, is to make it less:

  This new piece of information served to increase rather than allay her suspicions.

- An **alley** is a narrow street or gangway:

  a bowling alley

- An **ally** is a friend, especially a political one:

  Britain and France were allies during the war.

  Ally can also be a verb:

  Italy had allied herself to Germany.

allude, elude

- To **allude** to something is to refer to it:

  I'm alluding to your recent Broadway success.

- Something **eludes** you when it escapes you:

  His name eludes me.

  The perpetrators of the hoax have so far eluded detection.

allusion, delusion, illusion

- You make an **allusion** to something when you refer to it:

  You find plenty of allusions to contemporary politics in his plays.

- A **delusion** is a false belief that may be a result of mental unbalance:

  You begin to suffer from the delusion that everyone is against you.

- An **illusion** is a wrong impression, often a visual one:

  I have no illusions about the school — it is in need of far-reaching reforms.

  You can use mirrors to create an illusion of space.

altar, alter

- An **altar** is the sacred table in a church, temple, etc.
- **Alter** is a verb; to **alter** something is to change it:

  The timetable has been altered again.

amend, emend

- To **amend** an error is to correct it; to **amend** a law, etc is to improve it.
- To **emend** a text is to correct the errors in it.

amiable, amicable

Both these adjectives mean 'friendly', but **amiable** is chiefly used about people, whereas **amicable** is used about dealings between people:

amiable companions;

an amiable smile;

I'm sure we can come to some amicable arrangement about parking.

angel, angle

- An **angel** (/ˈeɪndʒl/) is a heavenly being, a messenger from God:

  The angel Gabriel was sent from God to the city of Nazareth.

- An **angle** (/ˈaŋgəl/) is a corner or viewpoint:

  How many angles has an octagon?

  The Straits Times had a different angle on the matter.

annex, annexe

- An **annexe** (sometimes spelt **annex**), stressed on the first syllable, is an additional, often temporary building:

  We accommodate guests in the annexe when the hotel itself is full.

- **Annex**, stressed on the second syllable, is a verb: to **annex** somebody else's territory is to take possession of it:

  In 1871 Germany annexed Alsace-Lorrraine.

annual, annals

- **Annual** is an adjective: an **annual** event is one that happens once a year:

  the annual poetry festival

  Annual can also be a noun: an **annual** is a yearly publication:

  a television annual.

- **Annals** is a plural noun: the **annals** of a place, institution, etc, are its historical records, dealing with events year by year.

arc, ark

- An **arc** is a curved line, for example part of a circle, or a line of light leaping across a gap in an electrical circuit.
- An **ark** is a place of shelter or protection, for example the boat built by Noah to save the various species of animals.

artist, artiste

- An **artist** is a painter or sculptor, or a person accomplished in another of the fine arts. You are also an **artist** at something if you are good at it:

  She's an artist at constructing a plot.

- An **artiste** (/ɑːˈtiːst/) is a theatrical or circus performer, for example a dancer, singer or acrobat. This kind of performer can also be called an **artist**:

  a tightrope artiste (or artist)

ascent, assent

- The **ascent** of a mountain is the process of climbing it.
- You give your **assent** to a proposal when you agree to it.

  Assent is also a verb:

  He assented to the suggestion with enthusiasm.

ascetic, aesthetic see **aesthetic**

aural, oral

- **Aural** means relating to the ear or to listening:

  Every so often the children's aural comprehension is tested.

- Oral means relating to the mouth:

  oral contraception

  An **oral** exam is a spoken test as distinct from a written one.

averse, adverse see **adverse**

axis, axes

- The **axis** of the earth or other heavenly body is the line or pole around which it spins. The plural is **axes** (/ˈaksiːz/). The two **axes** of a graph are the vertical and horizontal lines along which measurements are marked.
- **Axes** (/ˈaksəz/) is the plural of **axe** (or American English **ax**).

bail, bale

- A prisoner on a criminal charge is released on **bail**, or **bailed** out, when money (**bail**) is paid to the court for his or her freedom until the trial.
- To **bale** out is to get rid of water from inside a boat, or to parachute from an aircraft in an emergency.

baited, bated

- A trap that is **baited** contains **bait** for attracting the intended prey.
- You listen or wait with **bated** breath when you hold your breath in excited anticipation.

ballet, ballot

- **Ballet** (/ˈbaleɪ/) is a specialized form of dance.
- A **ballot** (/ˈbalət/) is a secret vote taken to elect somebody, or decide something.

  Ballot is also a verb:

  We shall be balloting our members on this issue.

base, bass

- The **base** of something is the part or support on which it stands:

  The statue toppled off its base.

  An army **base** is its headquarters.

  Base is also a verb: somebody is **based** somewhere if that is where their centre of operations is:

  He's based in Northern Ireland.

- A **bass** (/beɪs/) singing voice is the deepest male voice, and a **bass** instrument is the lowest in the range:

  a bass guitar; a double bass; He sings bass.

bath, bathe

- In British English, to **bath** (/bɑːθ/) somebody, e.g. a baby, is to wash them in a **bath** or bathtub:

  She bathed (/bɑːθt/) the children and put them to bed.

- In British and American English, to **bathe** (/beɪð/) a wound or an injured part of the body is to wash it gently:

  His injured hand was bathed (/beɪðd/) and dressed.

- In British English you **bathe** (/beɪð/) when you go for a swim.
- In American English, you **bathe** (/beɪð/) when you take a bath, and **bathe** (/beɪð/) the children when you wash them in a bathtub.
- You can also say you are **bathed** (/beɪðd/) in sweat.

beach, beech

- A **beach** is a flat sandy or stony area beside the sea:

  We went down to the beach for a swim.

- A **beech** is a deciduous tree with a smooth pale bark.

beer, bier

- **Beer** is an alcoholic drink:

  a glass of beer

- A person's **bier** is the stand or support on which their coffin is placed.

birth, berth

- **Birth** is the process of being born:

  the birth of her first baby

- A **berth** on board a ship is a bed or bunk:

  a 2-berth cabin

  A ship's **berth** is its mooring place at a quay, etc.

  Berth can also be a verb:

  The steamer berthed in Portsmouth yesterday.

bite, bight, byte

- **Bite** is a verb or noun:

  Some dogs bite.

  He took a bite of his apple.

- A **bight** is a curve, especially an inward curve in a coastline:

  the Great Australian Bight

- A **byte** is a computing unit of eight **bits**:

  a 32-megabyte memory

bloc, block

- A **bloc** is a group of countries united by a common interest or ideology:

  the former Communist bloc.

- Use **block** for any other noun or verb sense:

  blocks of stone; a block of flats;

  a walk round the block; a road block;

  a mental block;

  Our way was blocked by fallen rock.

blond, blonde

These are originally French adjectives.

- **Blond** is masculine:

  He is blond.

- **Blonde** is used as a feminine noun or adjective:

  a glamorous blonde

  She's gone blonde since I saw her last.

  Notice that you can say:

  She has blonde (or blond) hair.

boar, boor, bore

- A **boar** is a male pig:

  the boar and sow

- A **boor** (/bʊə/) is a rude, ill-mannered person, especially a man.
- A person who is a **bore** is dull or uninteresting, or a nuisance.

  Bore is also a verb:

  Figures bore me.

born, borne

- **Borne** is the past participle of **bear**:

  He has borne his troubles with great fortitude.

  She had already borne her husband six children.

  The following points should be borne in mind.

  His assertion is not borne out by the facts.

  I found myself borne along by the crowd.

  The cost will be borne by the taxpayer.

- You use the passive verb **to be born** and the past participle **born** to refer to somebody's birth, or to the origin of something:

  a suspicion born of fear;

  He was born on New Year's Day.

  She was born of mixed Irish and Welsh parentage.

bough, bow

- The **boughs** (/baʊz/) of a tree are its branches:

  The boughs swayed in the wind.

- A ship's **bow** (/baʊ/) is its pointed front:

  I stood in the bow.

- A **bow** (/baʊ/) is also the gesture of bending the head and body forward in respect:

  The footman made a low bow.

  Bow is also a verb:

  He bowed politely as she passed.

  A **bow** (/boʊ/) is a two-looped knot, used for decoration, etc:

  He tied his shoelaces in a bow.

boy, buoy see buoy

brake, break

- A **brake** is a device for slowing or stopping a vehicle:

  Apply the brake gradually.

  Brake is also a verb:

  She braked suddenly.

- For other noun and verb senses the spelling is **break**:

  a coffee break; a break in the clouds;

  a break in continuity;

  You could break your leg doing that.

  Let's break for lunch now.

breach, breech

- A **breach** of something is the act of breaking it:

  a breach of promise;

  causing a breach of the peace;

  You are in breach of Clause 2 of the contract.

  A **breach** is also a break or gap:

  a breach in the fortifications;

  The inheritance issue had caused a breach between the sisters.

  Breach is also a verb:

  They have breached the agreement.

  The invaders had breached the city walls.

- The **breech** of a gun is the back part, where you load it.

  Breeches are trousers, especially the kind that are drawn in at the knee:

  riding breeches

breathe, breath

- **Breathe** (/briːð/) is a verb:

  Breathe deeply.

  He was breathing (/briːðɪŋ/) fast.

  Breathe in the fresh air.

- **Breath** (/breθ/) is the air you **breathe** in or out:

  His breath smelt of garlic.

  Take a deep breath.

bridal, bridle

- A horse's **bridle** is its harness.

  Bridle is also a verb meaning 'to respond or react angrily':

  She bridled at the criticism.

- **Bridal** is an adjective meaning 'relating to a bride':

  a bridal veil

broach, brooch

These words are both pronounced /broʊtʃ/.

- **Broach** is a verb: to **broach** a subject is to introduce it, or begin to talk about it; to **broach** a barrel of beer, etc, is to open it.

- A **brooch** is a piece of jewellery that you pin to clothing:

  She was wearing a diamond brooch.

buoy, boy

A **buoy**, pronounced in the same way as **boy**, is a large hollow floating ball anchored to the sea floor, used as a marker to guide shipping.

Buoy up is a phrasal verb, meaning 'to elate':

I was buoyed up by my success.

byte, bite, bight see **bite**

cache, cash

- A **cache** of something is a secret store of it:

  By chance I discovered his cache of chocolate bars.

- **Cash** is money, especially coins and notes:

  Have you any cash on you?

cannon, canon

- A **cannon** is a large field gun.

  A **cannon** can also be a shot in snooker or billiards.

  Cannon can also be a verb:
  He came rushing along the corridor and cannoned into me.

- A **canon** is any of the following: a senior clergyman; a musical composition in which voices or instruments come in with the same tune in overlapping succession; a set of recognized rules or principles; a set of books recognized as authoritative in a particular subject, etc.

canvas, canvass

- **Canvas** is a coarse woven material, used for example for making tents:

  We spent three nights under canvas.

  A **canvas** is a painting on **canvas**, or a frame covered with **canvas**, for painting on:

  her most recent canvases

- **Canvass** is a verb: to **canvass** voters is to try to get them to vote for a particular person or thing:

  I've been out canvassing for our local candidate.

carat, caret, carrot

- A **carat** is a unit of weight for precious stones, and of purity for gold:

  24-carat gold.

- A **caret** mark (^) is used to show where something is missing in a text.

- A **carrot** is a long narrow orange vegetable.

cartilage, cartridge

- **Cartilage** is firm elastic tissue in your body, forming parts of the skeleton.

- A **cartridge** is a container, for example for a bullet, or for a camera film, or for printing ink.

cash, cache see **cache**

caste, cast

- A **caste** is any of the classes into which some societies are divided:

  the Hindu caste system.

- **Cast** can mean a particular appearance:

  She had features of an unusual cast.

  The photos had come out with a bluish cast.

  The **cast** of a play is the group of actors who play the various roles.

censor, censure

- A **censor** is an official who checks books, films, etc before they are released to the public, and can order parts to be deleted, or forbid publicatio or release altogether:

  film censors

  Censor is also a verb:

  Parts of the film had been censored.

- **Censure** is disapproving criticism:

  He met with a lot of censure for not taking a firmer stand against corruption.

  Censure is also a verb:

  She was rightly censured for her part in the deception.

cheque, check

- In British English, a **cheque** is a slip of paper ordering money to be paid to somebody:

  I wrote him a cheque for £100.

  But in American English the spelling **check** is used instead of **cheque**, and can also mean a restaurant bill :

  Could we have the check, please?

- **Check** is a verb meaning 'make sure about something', or 'stop something':

  Could you check the time of the meeting?

  Check if the theatre still has seats.

  Steps were taken to check the spread of the infection.

  Check can also be a noun:

  Keep a check on expenditure.

choose, chose

- **Choose** is the base form and present tense of the verb:

  Give yourself time to choose.

  Choose a partner.

  I invariably choose chocolate gateau.

- **Chose** is the past tense of **choose**:

  The donor chose to remain anonymous.

chord, cord

- In music, a **chord** is a number of notes played together:

  the chord of A major

- **Cord** is a strong kind of string, or a ribbed fabric:

  cord trousers ; I need a length of cord for hanging this picture up.

  A **cord** in the body is a long, narrow, usually cylindrical structure:

  the umbilical cord; the spinal cord;

  the vocal cords

clash, crash

- A **clash** is the noise of heavy metal things striking together:

  the clash of swords

  A **clash** between people is an angry argument:

  Television viewers witnessed the clash between the Prime Minister and the Shadow Chancellor.

  Clash is also a verb:

  Swords clashed.

  The Prime Minister clashed with members of the Opposition today in Parliament.

  Appointments **clash** when they are scheduled for the same time. Colours, for example two different shades of red, **clash** if they look unpleasant together.

- A **crash** is the noise of something falling and breaking, or of things colliding:

  They heard a loud crash in the kitchen.

  A **crash** is also a vehicle accident:

  Several people were injured in the crash.

  Crash is also a verb:

  His car crashed into a wall.

  Her son has crashed her car.

close, closed

- **Close** is an adjective or adverb meaning 'near':

  a close relation; Stand close to me.

- **Closed** is the past tense and past participle of the verb **close**:

  The shop is closed.

clothes, cloths

- **Clothes** (/klouðz/) means clothing and is always plural:

  What clothes shall I put on today?

- **Cloths** (/klɒθs/) is the plural of **cloth**:

  Are there any cleaning cloths in the kitchen cupboard?

coarse, course

- **Coarse** materials are rough in texture or composition:

  coarse woollen cloth

  Coarse behaviour or language is rude or offensive.

- A **course** of lectures, or a study **course**, provides instruction through a series of teaching sessions.

  A **course** is also a fixed route:

  a race course

  Course can also be a verb meaning 'run':

  Tears coursed down his cheeks.

collage, college

- A **collage** (/kɒˈlɑːʒ/) is a picture made by sticking small pieces of cloth on to a large piece.

- A **college** (/ˈkɒlɪdʒ/), spelt with an **e**, is an educational insitution.

coma, comma

- A **coma** is a prolonged state of unconsciousness:

  The patient has been in a coma for two weeks.

- A **comma** is the punctuation mark (,):

  Do you put a comma before direct speech?

complacent, complaisant

These two adjectives are both pronounced /kəmˈpleɪsənt/

- **Complacent** people are too easily satisfied with themselves or their achievements:

  Don't be complacent — strive for something better!

- A **complaisant** person likes to keep other people happy and is inclined to fall in with their wishes:

  a complaisant wife

complement, compliment

- A **complement** is a part that **completes** or finishes something:

  In the sentences 'She became an actress', and 'I feel sick', the underlined words are complements.

  Complement is also a verb: one thing **complements** another if, by going well with it, it seems to complete it:

  Good wine complements a well-cooked meal.

- You pay somebody a **compliment** when you praise them.

  Compliment can also be a verb:

  She complimented him on his cooking.

complementary, complimentary

- Things that are **complementary** go well together or supply each other's lacks:

  complementary colours;

  They had complementary personalities.

- A **complimentary** remark is a flattering one; a **complimentary** ticket is one that is given to you free.

concert, consort

- A **concert** is a musical performance:

  We attended a concert in the Albert Hall.

  People do something in **concert** when they work together to achieve it.

  A **concerted** effort is a joint effort.

- A **consort** is a husband or wife, especially that of a reigning monarch.

  A group of musicians who perform together can also be called a **consort**.

Consort is also a verb: to **consort** with somebody is to be in their company a lot:

He began consorting with drug-pushers.

confident, confidant, confidante

- **Confident** is an adjective, meaning either 'self-assured' or 'quite convinced about something':

  a confident, outgoing personality;

  I'm perfectly confident that we shall succeed.

- **Confidant** (masculine) and **confidante** (feminine) are nouns, meaning 'a person to whom you confide your secrets':

  His younger sister was his chief confidante.

cord, chord see chord

corps, corpse, corpus

- A **corps** (/kɔː/) is a group of people engaged together on particular projects or duties:

  the diplomatic corps; a cadet corps; the corps de ballet.

  The plural is **corps** (/kɔːz/).

- A **corpse** (/kɔːps/) is a dead body:

  The corpses were thrown into a mass grave.

- A **corpus** (/ˈkɔːpəs/) is a large body of material, for example randomly assembled textual material used for language research; the plural is **corpora** (ˈkɔːpərə).

counsel, council

- **Counsel** is a formal word for 'advice':

  wise counsel

  A **counsel** is also a courtroom lawyer:

  the defending counsel

  Counsel is also a verb: to **counsel** somebody is to advise them, or to talk to them supportively:

  Those who have lost loved ones are receiving counselling.

- A **council** is a body of officials who are responsible for, for example, local government within a town or region, or for providing advice on something.

counsellor, councillor

The members of an administrative **council** are usually **councillors**, but the members of an advice-giving **council** may be called **counsellors**:

the Marriage Guidance Council

a marriage-guidance counsellor

course, coarse see coarse

courtesy, curtsy

- **Courtesy** is politeness:

  At least he had the courtesy to apologize.

- A **curtsy** is a respectful gesture performed by women, the equivalent of a man's bow, with a brief bending of the knees.

  Curtsy is also a noun:

  You'll all have to practise your curtsies before tomorrow's ceremony.

crash, clash see clash

crevasse, crevice

- A **crevasse** (/krəˈvas/) is a deep crack in a glacier or ice field, down which an unwary mountaineer might fall.

- A **crevice** (/ˈkrevɪs/) is a narrow split or crack in a surface:

  This plant flourishes anywhere, and can often be found growing in the crevices of a wall.

crochet, crotchet

- **Crochet** (/ˈkroʊʃeɪ/) is a craft similar to knitting, done with a single hooked needle.

  Crochet can also be a verb:

  a crocheted shawl

- A **crotchet** (/ˈkrɒtʃɪt/) is a musical note with the time value of two quavers or half a minim.

cue, queue see queue

curb, kerb

- A **curb** is something that restricts or restrains:

  economic measures which act as curbs on expenditure

  Curb is also a verb:

  Try to curb your spending.

- In British English, a **kerb** is the edge of a pavement:

  Don't step off the kerb till the road is clear.

  In American English the spelling **curb** is used for the edge of the sidewalk, rather than **kerb**.

currant, current

- A **currant** is either a small dried grape or a berry:

  currants and raisins; blackcurrants; redcurrants

- A **current** is a flow of water, air, or electricity, in a particular direction:

  The river is fast-flowing and full of dangerous currents.

  Current is also an adjective meaning 'belonging to the present time':

  current events

curtsy, courtesy see courtesy

dairy, diary see diary

decry, descry

- To **decry** something is to criticize it or disparage it:

  those who decry the Government's moves against the private motorist

- To **descry** something, especially a distant thing, is to spot it:

  We descried the French coastline on the horizon.

delusion, allusion, illusion see allusion

dependant, dependent

- In British English, your **dependants** are your children and other members of your family who **depend** on you financially.

  In American English the spelling **dependent** is used for this noun.

- **Dependent** is also an adjective:

  They are financially dependent on me.

desert, dessert

- A **desert** (/ˈdezət/) is a large, hot, dry, barren area, typically covered with sand.

  Desert (/dɪˈzɜːt/) is a verb, meaning 'to abandon somebody':

  He deserted his family.

- A **dessert** (/dɪˈzɜːt/) is the sweet course of a meal:

  We had pears and ice cream for dessert.

device, devise

- **Device** is a noun, meaning a tool or other contrivance for performing a task:

  a device for removing cherry stones.

- **Devise** is a verb:

  She devised a means of attaching her mobile phone to her handbag.

diary, dairy

- Your **diary** is the little book in which you write down your appointments: She made a note of the meeting in her diary.

- A **dairy** is a place where milk, cream, cheese, etc are processed or bought.

discomfort, discomfit

- **Discomfort** is a noun:

  Take painkillers if you experience any discomfort over the next few days.

- **Discomfit** is a verb meaning 'to embarrass or disconcert', usually used in the passive:

  He became very quiet, evidently discomfited at being criticized so publicly.

discreet, discrete

- **Discreet** is an adjective meaning wise, cautious, and careful not to say anything that might cause trouble or embarrassment:

  A private secretary must above all be discreet.

- **Discrete** is an adjective meaning 'separate and distinct':

  Certain organisms once classified together are now regarded as discrete species.

divers, diverse

- **Divers** is a formal, rather old adjective meaning 'several':

  He suffered from divers medical problems and frequently called on the services of his physician.

- **Diverse** is an adjective meaning 'different':

  widely diverse forms of animal life

dose, doze

- A **dose** (/dous/) of medicine is the amount you are given to take at one time.

  Dose is also a verb:

  He was dosed with brandy.

- A **doze** is a brief light sleep, especially during the day:

  She has a doze after meals.

  Doze is also a verb:

  He dozed off during the lecture.

draft, draught

- In British English, a first **draft** is a rough preliminary version, for example of a speech or paper:

  I submitted a draft of my paper to the committee.

  A **draft** of money is an order for its payment by a bank.

  In American English, the **draft** is the process of conscripting young men for statutory military service.

  Draft is also a verb:

  I sat down and drafted an introduction to the book.

  There were a number of dodges that young men resorted to, to avoid being drafted into the army.

- In British English, a **draught** is a current of air flowing through a room, etc:

  I found I was sitting in a draught.

  A **draught** is also an act of drinking:

  He took a long draught of ale.

  The **draught** of a ship is the minimum depth of water in which it will float.

  In American English the spelling **draft** is used for these three last senses, rather than **draught**.

  Draughts is a board game (called **checkers** in American English) for two participants, played with disc-shaped pieces.

dual, duel

- A **duel** is a fight between two people:

  It was the habit then to settle quarrels by fighting a duel.

- **Dual** is an adjective meaning 'double' or 'twofold':

  a dual carriageway; a dual-purpose tool

dying, dyeing

- **Dying** is the present participle of **die**:

  Those flowers appear to be dying.
- **Dyeing** is the present participle of **dye**:

  We watched them dyeing the sheep's wool.

eclipse, ellipse, ellipsis

- An **eclipse** of the sun or moon is its partial or total blocking or disappearance into shadow.
- In geometry, an **ellipse** is a regular oval figure.
- In speech or writing, an **ellipsis** is the omission of one or more words, or a set of three points (…) used to show that words have been omitted; the plural is **ellipses** (/ɪˈlɪpsiːz/).

edition, addition see addition

effect, affect see affect

elicit, illicit

- **Elicit** is a verb: to **elicit** information from somebody is to force them to give it to you.
- **Illicit** is an adjective meaning 'unlawful':

  illicit relations with an under-age girl

eligible, illegible

- **Eligible** (/ˈelɪdʒɪbəl/) means suitable or qualified for something:

  as soon as you are eligible for a pension
- **Illegible** (/ɪˈledʒɪbəl/) means 'not legible':

  illegible handwriting

elude, allude see allude

emend, amend see amend

emigrant, immigrant, migrant

- An **emigrant** is a person who is leaving their native country to settle in another country.
- An **immigrant** is somebody who has come from abroad to settle in the country under consideration:

  The government's present policy is to welcome immigrants.
- A **migrant** is a bird or animal that moves from one habitat to another with the change of season; a **migrant** worker is a person who travels from place to place in search of work.

  Notice also the nouns **emigration**, **immigration**, **migration**.

eminent, imminent

- An **eminent** person is somebody distinguished or important:

  an eminent surgeon
- An **imminent** event is one that is about to happen:

  their imminent departure for the States

emission, omission

- An **emission** of something is a release or discharge of it:

  an emission of radiation.
- The **omission** of something is the act of **omitting** it or leaving it out:

  He was offended by the omission of his title.

enquire, enquiry, inquire, inquiry

- The verb can be spelt **enquire** or **inquire** with no distinction of meaning.
- For the noun, the spelling **enquiry** often represents a simple question, whereas the spelling **inquiry** is often used for an investigation:

  the enquiry desk; a government inquiry

ensure, insure

- To **ensure** means 'to make sure':

  Please ensure that your seat belt is fastened and your table stowed.

- You **insure** somebody or something when you arrange for money to be paid in the event of their being harmed, lost, killed, etc:

  We insured the painting for £10,000.

entomologist, etymologist

- An **entomologist** studies insects.
- An **etymologist** studies the origin and development of words.

envelop, envelope

- **Envelop** (/In»vel´p/) is a verb, meaning to cover:

  The mountain was enveloped in mist.
- An **envelope** is a sealed cover for a letter:

  I addressed and stamped the envelope.

equable, equitable

- An **equable** person is calm, cheerful, and not easily upset.

  An **equable** climate is never extremely cold or extremely hot.
- An **equitable** arrangement between people is one that is fair to all parties.

especially, specially

- **Especially** means 'particularly':

  It's lonely here, especially in the winter.
- **Specially** means 'specifically and solely':

  I made this dessert specially for you because I know you like it.

exceed, accede see **accede**

except, accept see **accept**

excess, access see **access**

executioner, executor

- An **executioner** is an official whose job is to put to death people who have been sentenced to death.
- An **executor** (/ɪgˈzekjʊtə/) is a person appointed to carry out the instructions in another person's will, after their death.

exercise, exorcize

- People **exercise**, or **take exercise**, to get fit.
- To **exorcize** a ghost or demon is to get rid of it by prayer or other means.

expand, expend

- To **expand** is to become bigger, or to make something bigger:

  I fear my waistline is expanding.

  They have expanded their operations to include Internet selling.
- You **expend** money, energy, time, etc when you spend it:

  We shall expend no more of our valuable resources on something so unprofitable.

expiate, expatiate

- To **expiate** a sin is to do something that cancels out your guilt.
- To **expatiate** (/ɪkˈspeɪʃieɪt/) on a subject is to talk in detail about it.

extant, extinct

- Things that are **extant** exist at the present time:

  The original manuscript of the play is still extant.
- Things that are **extinct** have ceased to exist: **extinct** species have died out; an **extinct** volcano is no longer active.

fare, fair

- You pay a **fare** to travel on a bus, train, plane or ship:

  The return fare was £32.

- A **fair** is an event at which people gather to sell products, especially of a particular kind:

  an international book fair

  Fair is also an adjective meaning 'just':

  a fair criticism

farther, further

- **Farther** is used only with reference to distance:

  The summit was farther away than we thought.

- **Further** is used for the sense 'additional', and can also be used in reference to distance:

  Further instructions will be sent tomorrow. I can't go any further.

  Further is also a verb meaning 'to help or advance something':

  This unexpected publicity could further our chances of succeeding.

faun, fawn

- A **faun** is a mythical creature with a human head and body, and the horns and legs of a goat.
- A **fawn** is a baby deer.

  Fawn is also a light-brown or beige colour:

  a fawn scarf; You look nice in fawn.

ferment, foment see **foment**

fiancé, fiancée

- **Fiancé** is masculine: a girl's **fiancé** is the man she is engaged to:

  Lucy and her fiancé

- **Fiancée** is feminine: a man's **fiancée** is the girl he is engaged to:

  George's fiancée

final, finale

- **Final** is an adjective:

  in the final stages of the illness

  Final is also a noun: the **final** is the deciding match of a competition.

- The **finale** (/fɪˈnɑːli/) of a show, etc is the grand final scene or event:

  Everyone appears on stage for the finale.

fission, fissure

- **Fission** is the action of splitting:

  nuclear fission

- A **fissure** is a split or narrow opening in a surface:

  The lizard disappeared into a fissure in the rocks.

flagrant, fragrant

- **Flagrant** misbehaviour is behaviour that is very obviously outrageous:

  flagrant immorality

- **Fragrant** means sweet-smelling:

  fragrant herbs

flair, flare

- You have a **flair** for something if you have a natural talent for it:

  She has a flair for interior design.

- A **flare** is sudden flash of light or flame, or a device that produces a blaze of light, used for illumination.

flammable, inflammable, non-flammable

- **Flammable** and **inflammable** both mean 'readily burning or catching fire':

  inflammable fabrics;

  highly flammable substances

- **Non-flammable** means flame-resistant, or not burning easily:

  non-flammable paints

flaunt, flout

- To **flaunt** something is to show it off:

  flaunting her engagement ring

- To **flout** something such as the law, or a rule or convention, is to break it:

  openly flouting the school rules.

floe, flow

- A **floe** is a sheet of floating ice:

  the danger of colliding with an ice floe

- For other verb and noun senses the spelling is **flow**:

  a fast-flowing stream; a flow of air;

  the flow of ideas

foment, ferment

- To **foment** something such as dissidence or rebellion is to encourage it by stirring up resentment in people.

- Liquor **ferments** when sugar in it is converted to alcohol.

  Ferment is also sometimes used in the same sense as **foment**:

  He would try to ferment ill-feeling between the two friends.

forebear, forbear

- Your **forebears** are your ancestors. But note that the spelling **forbear** is also sometimes used.

- **Forbear** is a verb meaning to restrain yourself from doing something:

  I forbore to make any criticism.

foregone, forgo

- A **foregone** conclusion is an inevitable result that you can guess beforehand:

  The selection of Mike as captain was a foregone conclusion.

- To **forgo** something is to do without it:

  That's the second time this week I've had to forgo lunch.

font, fount

You can use both **font** and **fount** to mean a set of printing characters all in the same style.

foul, fowl

- **Foul** is an adjective meaning dirty, disgusting, detestable or offensive:

  a foul smell; foul language

  Foul is also a noun: to commit a **foul** in football, etc, is to break a rule of the game.

- A **fowl** is a bird, especially a domestic bird such as a chicken, turkey or duck.

found, founded

- **Founded** is the past tense and past participle of the verb **found**: to **found** something such as a institution or movement is to start it, or bring it into existence:

  King's College in Cambridge was founded by King Henry VI.

- **Found** is the past tense and past participle of find :

  I've found the missing cheque.

fragrant, flagrant see **flagrant**

funeral, funereal

- **Funeral** is a noun:

  I attended her funeral at the crematorium.

- **Funereal** is an adjective, meaning very slow, sad or sombre, reminding you of a funeral:

  The traffic was moving at a funereal pace.

further, farther see **farther**

gait, gate

- A person or animal's **gait** is the way they walk:

  the sailor's distinctive rolling gait

- A **gate** is a hinged barrier across an opening in a wall or fence:

  Close the gate after you.

gamble, gambol

- To **gamble** is to bet money on card games, races, etc:

  His gambling debts mounted to $4000.

- Young animals **gambol**, especially lambs:

  We watched the lambs gambolling in the field.

gaol, goal

- A **gaol** (/dʒeɪl/) is a prison; the normal American-English spelling is **jail**, which is often used in British English too:

  He had to spend a night in gaol (or jail).

  Gaol is also a verb:

  She was gaoled (or jailed) for the night.

- A **goal** (/goUl/) is what you score or defend in football and other games:

  We'll try Dave in goal.

gild, guild

These words are both pronounced /gɪld/.

- **Gild** is a verb: to **gild** something is to cover it with gold:

  We're sending the picture frames to be gilded.

- **Guild** is a noun: a **guild** is an association, especially of people working in a particular trade or craft.

gilt, guilt

These nouns are both pronounced /gɪlt/.

- **Gilt** is gold material used for gilding:

  The gilt is wearing off this picture frame.

- **Guilt** is the shame you feel after doing something wrong, or the fact of having done something wrong:

  Don't you feel any guilt?

  Her guilt was proved beyond doubt.

gorilla, guerrilla

These nouns are both pronounced /gəˈrɪlə/.

- A **gorilla** is a type of ape.

- A **guerrilla** is a member of an independent fighting force; you can also use the spelling **guerilla**:

  a party of guerrillas; guerrilla warfare

gourmand, gourmet

- A **gourmand** (/ˈgʊəmənd/) is a greedy person or glutton.

- A **gourmet** (/ˈgʊəmeɪ/) is a person who is an expert on good food, a food connoisseur. The plural is **gourmets** (/ˈgʊəmeɪz/).

grill, grille

- The **grill** in a stove or cooker is the part where food is cooked under direct heat.

  Grill is also a verb:

  grilled sausages

- A **grille** is a framework of metal bars, fitted for example across a window or an opening in adoor; it is sometimes spelt **grill**:

  She saw a pair of eyes observing her through the grille.

guild, gild see **gild**

guilt, gilt see **gilt**

hail, hale

- **Hail** is the name for the frozen raindrops that fall in the form of balls of ice, and is often used metaphorically:

  a hail of bullets; facing a hail of questions

  Hail is also a verb:

  Look, it's hailing outside.

  Hail also means to shout or call to somebody, e.g. a cab-driver:

  I hailed a cab.

The place you **hail** from is your native town or region.

- **Hale** is an adjective meaning healthy, literally 'whole'; you find it in the expression **hale and hearty**:

  His parents are both still hale and hearty.

hangar, hanger

- A **hangar** is a large shed housing aircraft.
- A **hanger**, also called a **coat-hanger**, is a metal, plastic or wooden device for hanging clothes on.

hanged, hung

- **Hung** is the usual past tense and past participle of **hang**:

  I hung my coat on a peg.

  Coloured lanterns were hung from the ceiling.

- **Hanged** is the past tense and past participle used with reference to dying by hanging:

  Judas hanged himself.

  People were hanged for stealing in the old days.

heroine, heroin

- A **heroine** is a female hero.
- The drug is spelt **heroin**.

hoard, horde

- A **hoard** of things is a secret store or stock of them:

  A hoard of coins was discovered under the floorboards.

- A **horde** of people is a great crowd or throng:

  Hordes of pilgrims visit the shrine every year.

human, humane

- **Humane** is an adjective meaning concerned to prevent or reduce suffering:

  the most humane method of slaughtering cattle

- **Human** is an adjective or a noun:

  human beings; Computers don't make analytical judgements like humans.

  It's human to make mistakes.

idea, ideal

- An **idea** is a thought, a notion, a suggestion or a plan:

  I've got a good idea!

  Let me have your ideas at our next session.

- Your **ideals** are the principles of behaviour that you respect and try to follow:

  It's impossible to live up to such high ideals.

  Ideal is also an adjective meaning 'perfect' or 'absolutely appropriate':

  The ideal solution would be to give him an opportunity to express his views publicly.

idle, idol

- **Idle** is an adjective meaning 'lazy' or 'unoccupied':

  idle workmen; during an idle moment;

  The machines were lying idle.

  Idle can also be a verb:

  The two boys were idling on a street corner.

- An **idol** is an image, or a person, that is worshipped:

  a golden idol; the pop singers who were the idols of our teenage years

illegible, eligible see **eligible**

illicit, elicit see **elicit**

illusion, allusion, delusion see **allusion**

immigrant, emigrant, migrant see **emigrant**

impractical, impracticable

- An **impractical** person lacks manual skills or common sense; an **impractical** idea or plan is one that is not sensible or realistic.
- A plan or idea that is **impracticable** cannot be carried out because there are too many difficulties:

  It's an attractive scheme, but quite impracticable.

ingenious, ingenuous

- **Ingenious** means very clever, especially in a surprising or original way:

  a new and ingenious method of preparing skin grafts

  The noun associated with **ingenious** is **ingenuity**:

  The ingenuity of some of the costumes was impressive.
- **Ingenuous** means any of the following: 'innocent, childlike, trusting, lacking suspicion, open and frank':

  ingenuous young girls

  The noun associated with **ingenuous** is **ingenuousness**.

inquire, enquire see **enquire**

insure, ensure see **ensure**

it's, its

- **It's** is short for **it is**:

  It's raining.
- **Its** is a possessive determiner:

  Rock-climbing has lost its appeal for me.

kerb, curb see **curb**

key, quay

- A **key** is a device for locking, or a button for pressing, or a musical scale:

  a bunch of keys; in the key of A minor
  Press the Home key.

  Key is also a verb:

  Key in your password.
- A quay (/kiː/) is a landing platform in a harbour or port, where ships can tie up:

  We left the yacht moored alongside the quay.

laid, lain

- **Laid** is the past tense and past participle of **lay**:

  He went to sleep as soon as he laid his head on the pillow.

  Have you laid the table?
- **Lain** is the past participle of **lie**:

  The letter had lain unopened on the doormat for a whole week.

lair, layer

- A wild animal's **lair** is its hole or den:

  The bear returned to its lair.
- A **layer** of something is a covering or thickness of it:

  alternate layers of pasta and cheese sauce

  The ground was covered with a thin layer of snow.

lama, llama

- A **lama** is a Buddhist monk or spiritual leader.
- A **llama** is a South-American animal related to the camel, with a soft woolly fleece.

latter, later

- The former and the **latter** are the first and second of two things or people just mentioned:

  I had to make a choice between waiting to be dismissed and resigning voluntarily, and I decided on the latter.

- **Later** is the comparative of **late**:

  I caught the later train.

  He shut up the shop later than usual.

lay, lie

- The verb **lay** is transitive; it takes an object: you **lay** something somewhere when you put it there:

  Ask the guests to lay their coats on the bed.

  To **lay** the table, or **lay** places, is to set out the cutlery required for those eating:

  Please lay four places.

  Lay is also the past tense of the intransitive verb **lie**:

  I lay down and went to sleep.

  The letter lay unopened on the doormat.

  He wondered what difficulties lay ahead.

- **Lie** is an intransitive verb and means to rest in a horizontal position, or be situated somewhere:

  I'll go and lie down on the sofa.

  The village lies just beyond the next range of hills.

  There is another intransitive verb **lie** meaning to say something that is untrue, with the past tense and past participle **lied**:

  It's simpler to tell the truth than to lie.

  He lied about his age.

layer, lair see lair

laying, lying

- **Laying** is the present participle of the transitive verb **lay**:

  'That's all for today,' she said, laying down the book.

- **Lying** is the present participle of both intransitive verbs **lie**:

  She's lying on the sofa.

  Was he lying or telling the truth?

lead, led

- **Lead** (/led/) is a metal:

  Most motor vehicles now use lead-free petrol.

  Lead (/liːd/) is a verb:

  I'll lead the way.

- **Led** is the past tense and past participle of **lead**:

  The guide led us through a series of tunnels.

lie, lay see lay

lightning, lightening

- **Lightning** is the electrical flash of light that accompanies thunder:

  A flash of lightning momentarily lit the landscape.

- **Lightening** is the present participle of **lighten**, meaning to make or become light or lighter:

  Find ways of lightening your work load.

  The sky was lightening in the east.

llama, lama see lama

loathe, loath, loth

- **Loathe** (/loʊð/) is a verb meaning to hate:

  I loathe shopping.

- **Loath** or **loth** (/loʊθ/) is an adjective meaning unwilling:

  I was loth (or *loath*) *to waste any more time searching.*

loose, lose

- **Loose** is an adjective:

  I'd better tighten this loose screw.

- **Lose** is a verb:

  Don't lose your ticket.

madam, madame

- **Madam** (/ˈmadəm/) is the English spelling, and is sometimes used as a polite form of address, for example by shop assistants or waiters:

  May I help you, madam?

  A female chairman is sometimes addressed as **Madam** Chairman.

- **Madame** (/ˈmadəm/ or /məˈdaːm/) is the French equivalent of **Mrs**, often shortened to **Mme**:

  Madame Matisse

marshal, martial

- A **marshal** is any of several different high officials, or a high-ranking military officer:

  a field-marshal

  Marshal is also a verb meaning to collect and organize something ready for action:

  Marshal your facts before the meeting.

- **Martial** is an adjective, meaning relating to war, soldiers, or military matters:

  martial music

marten, martin

- A **marten** is a small wild animal related to the weasel.
- A **martin** is a bird similar to a swallow.

mat, matt

- A **mat** is a rug for the floor, or a flat piece of material for resting something on :

  a mouse mat

- **Matt** is an adjective describing a non-glossy surface:

  Would you like the photos with a matt or glossy finish?

meat, meet, mete

- **Meat** is a noun:

  chicken and other kinds of white meat

- **Meet** is a verb:

  Let's meet for a chat.

  Meet is also an old adjective meaning 'suitable':

  topics meet for classroom discussion

- To **mete** out punishment is to impose it on wrongdoers:

  The department has the power to mete out severe fines to false claimants.

meridian, meridiem

- A **meridian** is a line of longitude:

  The Greenwich Meridian

- **Meridiem** is a Latin word meaning 'midday', found in the full forms of the abbreviations **a.m.** and **p.m.**, ***ante meridiem*** and ***post meridiem***, meaning 'before midday' or 'after midday'.

metal, mettle

- A **metal** is a substance such as gold, silver, steel or iron.
- Your **mettle** is your strength of character: you are on your **mettle** when you are poised ready to act with courage.

meter, metre

- A **metre** is a unit of measurement:

  three metres of cloth; a 30-centimetre ruler

  Metre is also the rhythm in poetry:

  metres used by Shakespeare

- A **meter** is an apparatus for measuring or timing:

  a water meter; a gas meter; a parking meter

In American English the spelling **meter** is used for both these words.

miner, minor

- A **miner** is a worker in a mine:

  coal-miners

- **Minor** is an adjective meaning 'lesser' or 'unimportant'

  some minor problems; minor roads;
  He had appeared in minor roles on television.

  A **minor** is a young person who is not yet legally an adult:

  Alcohol must not be sold to minors.

militate, mitigate

- Circumstances **militate** against something when they make it difficult or impossible:

Pressure on hospitals to free up beds militates against patients receiving the ideal amount of care before discharge.

- Circumstances **mitigate** something when they make it less bad:

  Her sentence was changed from the death penalty to life imprisonment because the cruelty she had suffered from her husband was seen as a mitigating circumstance.

moan, mourn

- To **moan** is to cry softly with grief or pain; **moan** also means 'to complain unnecessarily':

  Oh, do stop moaning.

  Moan is also a noun:

  She gave a moan of pain.

- To **mourn** somebody or something, or **mourn for** them, is to weep for their loss:

  They had hardly had time to mourn the victims of the first earthquake when the second struck.

  It's no good mourning for your lost youth.

momentary, momentous

- A **momentary** happening lasts only a moment:

  a momentary lapse of memory

- A **momentous** happening is an important event that makes history:

  momentous scientific discoveries

moral, morale

- **Morals** (/ˈmɒrəlz/) are principles of good behaviour by which people try to live.

  Moral is an adjective relating to these principles:

  moral standards

  The **moral** of a story is a principle of behaviour that you learn from it.

- Your **morale** (/məˈrɑːl/) is your state of confidence:

  The team's morale is high.

motif, motive

- A **motif** (/moʊˈtiːf/) is a pattern or design, such as a manufacturer's logo on clothing, etc; it can also be a recurring theme in a piece of music.

- A person's **motive** (/ˈmoʊtɪv/) for doing something is the need or desire that makes them do it:

  Which of the suspects had the most convincing motive for murder?

mystic, mystique

- **Mystic** is a synonym of **mystical**, and means mysterious or miraculous, especially in a spiritual or religious way:

  mystic rites; a mystic light

- **Mystique** (/mɪˈstiːk/) is a noun: the **mystique** associated with a profession or activity is the specialist knowledge and expertise that make it seem difficult to master:

  There's really no mystique about Chinese cuisine—it's quite straightforward.

naught, nought

Naught and **nought** both mean 'nothing' and are both pronounced /nɔːt/.

- **Naught** is hardly used now in British English except in the following expressions: a plan **comes to naught** when it fails or is frustrated; to **set something at naught** is to show contempt for it, or disregard it.

- A **nought** is a zero:

  Is this meant to be a letter O or a nought?

  In American English the spelling **naught** is used for zero.

naval, navel

- **Naval** is an adjective meaning 'relating to a navy or to warships':

  naval uniforms; a naval expedition

- A person's **navel** is the shallow hole in the front of their abdomen, where the cord attached them to their mother before birth.

net, nett

- **Net** is an open fabric, and a **net** is any of the many things made from it:

  net curtains; fishing nets;
  a badminton net; a mosquito net

- **Net** or **nett** is an adjective used to describe a final total after all deductions have been made:

  What were your net earnings for the financial year 1998-1999?

non-flammable, flammable, inflammable see **flammable**

nougat, nugget

- **Nougat** (/ˈnuːgɑː/ or /ˈnʌgət/) is a toffee-like white sweet containing fruit and nuts:

  a nougat bar

- A **nugget** (/ˈnʌgət/) of something, especially a precious metal, is a solid lump:

  gold nuggets; a useful nugget of information

o, oh

- **O** is an exclamation used in older poetry, often used for addressing a personor thing:

  O death, where is thy sting?

- **Oh** is now the usual form of the exclamation, and is often followed by a comma:

  Oh, what a pity! Oh, look out! Oh, thanks! Oh no! Oh yes! Oh, heavens!

official, officious

- Something that is **official** is backed by authority:

  This is an official order.

  An **official** is a person who holds a position of authority in an organization :

  I spoke to an official sitting at the desk.

- An **officious** person is somebody who is self-important and too inclined to use their position of authority to give other people orders, especially unnecessary ones.

omission, emission see **emission**

oral, aural see **oral**

paddle, pedal, peddle

- A **paddle** is a device like an oar for propelling a canoe through the water.

  Paddle is also a verb:

  We were paddling upstream.

- The **pedals** of a bicycle are the parts that you push round with your feet.

  Pedal is also a verb:

  I pedalled as fast as I could.

- **Peddle** is a verb: to **peddle** goods is to take them from place to place to sell, like a pedlar:

  She was suspected of peddling drugs.

passed, past

- **Passed** is the past tense and past participle of **pass**:

  He passed me in the street without recognizing me.

  Have we passed a petrol station yet?

  We passed the day in pleasant relaxation.

- **Past** is a preposition:

  She walked straight past me.

  Past is also an adverb:

  She walked past, looking straight ahead of her.

  The **past** is a noun referring to the time that has gone:

Forget about the past and concentrate on the future.

Past is also an adjective:

the past participle

We talked about past successes and failures.

pastel, pastille

- A **pastille** is a sweet, especially a medicated one:

  a tin of cough pastilles

- **Pastels** are chalks or crayons used by artists.

  Pastel is also an adjective describing pale colours:

  pastel shades of pink and blue

personnel, personal

- **Personnel** is a noun meaning the staff employed in a business, etc:

  Airline personnel have to be very carefully selected.

- **Personal** is an adjective, meaning relating to an individual person :

  your personal possessions;

  a personal matter;

  Will the princess make a personal appearance?

pidgin, pigeon

These nouns are both pronounced /ˈpɪdʒɪn/.

- A **pidgin** is a language developed from two or more languages, originally used in simple business communication in ports, etc.

- A **pigeon** is a large grey, white or brown bird that lives in cities.

plane, plain

- **Plane** is a noun with various meanings, for example, an aircraft; a kind of tool for smoothing wood; a flat surface in geometry; and a kind of tree:

  We just caught the plane.

  One plane dissects the other at right angles.

  Plane is also a verb meaning to glide through the air, or to move smoothly over water.

  Plane can also be an adjective:

  a plane surface; plane geometry

- **Plain** is an adjective with various meanings, for example, undecorated; simple; pure or unmixed; straightforward; clear; obvious:

  plain white walls;

  I'll just have a glass of plain water.

  Speak in plain English.

  It's plain that they're displeased.

  You describe a task as **plain sailing** if it is easily done.

poise, pose

- You **poise** (/pɔɪz/) yourself ready to jump or perform some other acrobatic feat:

  She poised herself on the diving board.

- You **pose** (/poʊz/) for a photograph:

  We posed in front of the fountain and Harry took a picture of us.

portion, potion

- A **portion** of food is a helping of it:

  I'll have a small portion of the chocolate cake.

- A **potion** is a drink containing medicine, poison, or a magic substance:

  The sorceress prepared a love potion for her.

practical, practicable, pragmatic

- **Practical** means concerned with action as distinct from theory:

  Put your ideas to practical use.

  A **practical** person has plenty of common

sense or is good at manual tasks.

- A **practicable** plan is one that can be carried out successfully.
- To be **pragmatic** is to decide on whatever course of action is possible and sensible in the present circumstances.

practice, practise

- **Practice** is a noun:

  recognized business practices;

  You need more practice.

  Let's put the idea into practice.

- **Practise** is a verb:

  I need to practise my English.

  We want to be free to practise our own religion.

In American English, **practice** is the spelling for both the noun and the verb.

pray, prey

- **Pray** is a verb:

  They prayed for rain.

- The animals or birds that are hunted by another, usually larger, animal, are its **prey**:

  Birds and mice are the typical prey of the cat.

  Prey is also a verb:

  The owl preys on small mammals.

precede, proceed

- To **precede** something or somebody is to come before them:

  Migraine is often preceded by visual disturbances.

  She preceded me on to the stage.

  You will find some useful emergency numbers on the preceding page.

- To **proceed** is to start some activity, or continue with it:

  The doctor proceeded to examine her.

  Please proceed with your work.

premier, premiere

- A **premier** is a prime minister:

  the British premier

- A **premiere** or **première** is the first performance of a play, film, opera, etc:

  The premiere was attended by a crowd of celebrities.

  Premiere or **première** is also a verb:

  The film will be premiered early in September.

principal, principle

- **Principal** is an adjective meaning 'main' or 'chief':

  Our principal aim is to prevent unnecessary expenditure.

  Principal is also a noun: the **principal** of a college or other institution is its head:

  The college has appointed a new principal.

- Your **principles** are the general rules of behaviour by which you live:

  Lying is against my principles.

  I object on principle to people smoking in public places.

  We agree in principle, but have to sort out the details.

  A scientific law can also be called a **principle**:

  the principle of gravity.

prise, prize

- **Prise** is a verb: you **prise** open a lid, or **prise** something off a surface, when you use something such as a knife as a lever to release it:

  I prised the shellfish off the rock.

- **Prize** is a noun:

  She was awarded first prize in the dancing contest.

  Prize is also a verb meaning to value or appreciate something highly:

  I prized his friendship and loyalty above everything.

This letter is my most prized possession.

In American English, **prize** is the usual spelling for the 'levering' verb, rather than **prise**.

proceed, precede see precede

program, programme

- The spelling **program** is normally used in computing contexts:

  Can you show me how to install this program?

  Program is also a verb:

  The machine is programmed to do a virus check whenever it is rebooted.

- Otherwise, in British English, the spelling **programme** is normal:

  I was watching a programme about early steam ships.

  Do you want to read the concert programme?

  Programme is also a verb:

  How shall we programme the evening's events?

  In American English, the spelling **program** is normal for all meanings:

  radio programs; a concert program

prophecy, prophesy

- **Prophecy** (/ˈprofɪsi/) is a noun:

  prophecies regarding the end of the world

- **Prophesy** (/ˈprofɪsaɪ/) is a verb:

  He prophesied that the world would end in the year 2000.

proof, prove

- **Proof** is a noun meaning 'conclusive evidence':

  Have you any proof that she's lying?

- **Prove** (/pruːv/) is a verb: to **prove** a theory is to provide conclusive evidence for its truth:

  Fingerprint evidence proved beyond doubt that she was responsible.

proved, proven

- **Proved** (/pruːvd/) is the regular past participle of **prove**:

  It was proved that she had been lying.

- **Proven** (/ˈproʊvən/) occurs in the Scots law verdict **not proven**, meaning that the evidence is insufficient for a conviction. Nowadays **proven** (/ˈpruːvən/ or/ˈproʊvən/) is often used instead of **proved** as the past participle of **prove**:

  a proven remedy

  The case against the drug has not been proven.

quash, squash see squash

queue, cue

These words are both pronounced /kjuː/.

- You stand in a **queue** to wait your turn for something:

  I joined the queue for tickets.

  Queue is also a verb:

  Hundreds of people were queuing for buses.

- A **cue** is a prompt, or a prompting device, for a speaker, reader or actor:

  reading the news from the autocue

  Cue is also a verb, meaning to bring in the next item, person, etc:

  Cue the balloons.

quiet, quite

- **Quiet** is an adjective meaning 'peaceful, calm':

  a quiet nap

  Quiet is also a noun:

  in the quiet of the evening

- **Quite** is an adverb meaning 'completely' or 'fairly':

  I've quite finished.

  It's quite good.

racket, racquet

- A tennis **racquet** (/ˈrakɪt/) can also be spelt **racket.**
- A **racket** is also, informally, a loud confused noise, or a commercial enterprise, especially an illegal one:

  Stop that racket at once, kids!

  He's been involved in a drugs racket.

raise, raze, rise

- To **raise** something is to lift it or make it higher; in American English, to **raise** children is to bring them up:

  He raised his hand and waved.

  We've decided to raise you salary.

  Don't raise your voice.

  I was raised in Indiana.

- To **raze** a building is to destroy it:

  His castle was razed to the ground.

- **Rise** is an irregular intransitive verb meaning to go upwards or higher:

  New buildings were rising up everywhere.

  He has risen fast in his career.

  Rise and **raise** are used respectively in British and American English as nouns meaning an increase in salary:

  They've promised me a rise (or, in American English, raise) in the new year.

rapt, rapped, wrapped

- **Rapt** is an adjective meaning wholly absorbed:

  For more than an hour he spoke to a rapt audience of young children.

- **Rapped** is the past tense and past participle of **rap**, meaning to strike:

  She rapped the table for silence.

- **Wrapped** is the past tense and past participle of **wrap**, meaning to put a covering round something:

  presents wrapped in coloured paper

read, red

- **Read** (/riːd/) is a verb; **read** (/red/) is its past tense and past participle:

  Read (/ri˘d/) this passage aloud.

  Mum read (/red/) to us every night when we were children.

- **Red** is a colour, used as an adjective or noun:

  red socks; You look nice in red.

reign, rein

- A monarch **reigns**:

  She reigned over the country for more than 60 years.

  Reign is also a noun:

  in the twelfh year of her reign

- A horse's **reins** are held by the rider, and form part of its harness.

  You keep a **rein** on something, for example expenditure, when you control it.

  Rein is also a verb meaning to check or restrain:

  Rein in your enthusiasm a bit.

respectful, respective

- **Respectful** words or gestures express **respect**:

  He made a respectful bow.

  Speak more respectfully.

- The **respective** jobs, possessions, etc of the people in a group are those specific to each one of them :

  They returned to their respective tasks.

  Respectively refers back to named individuals in the order in which they are mentioned:

  George and Michael were aged 10 and 8 respectively.

review, revue

- A **review** of something such as a book, play or film is a report that describes it and judges it, indicating its good and bad points:

I read your review of her book.

Review is also a verb:

The play was reviewed in the Straits Times.

- A **revue** is a theatrical entertainment consisting of a series of amusing acts and songs:

  She made her name in revue.

rhyme, rhythm, rime

- A **rhyme** is a poem or verse:

  nursery rhymes

- **Rime** is an old spelling of **rhyme**.

  Rime also means thick hard frost:

  trees covered with rime

- **Rhythm** is the beat in music, or the metre in poetry:

  a lively rhythm

role, roll

- A person's **role** or **rôle** in a play, film, or activity, is the part they play:

  His stage roles include Hamlet and King Lear.

  What was your role in the operation?

- You use the spelling **roll** for other noun and verb meanings:

  rolls of fabric; a bread roll;

  a roll of thunder; a roll of drums;

  The coin rolled across the floor.

  Roll the ball to me.

rout, route

- To **rout** (/raʊt/) the enemy in battle is to defeat them decisively and send them in headlong retreat:

  The invaders were routed.

  Rout is also a noun; A **rout** is a disastrous defeat.

- Your **route** (/ru:t/) to your destination is the way by which you arrive at it:

  My route took me along the ring road.

  Route is also a verb:

  The procession has been routed along the High Street and through Regent Square.

salvage, selvedge see **selvedge**

safe, save

- **Safe** is an adjective meaning unharmed:

  The child was found safe and well.

  Safe is also a noun: a **safe** is a secure metal container for money, jewels, etc:

  The wages were kept in a locked safe in the manager's office.

- **Save** is a verb: to **save** somebody is to rescue them from danger; to **save** money is to avoid spending it:

  We're saving up for a round-the-world cruise.

  Save is also a rather old and formal preposition meaning 'except':

  He forgot everything he had been taught save this one fact.

sceptic, septic

- **Sceptic** (/ˈskeptɪk/) is a noun: a **sceptic** is a person who doubts something that others believe, or who does not support something that others are enthusiastic about:

  The Euro-sceptics still form a strong lobby.

  The associated adjective is **sceptical**.

  In American English the spelling **skeptic** is used rather than **sceptic**.

- **Septic** (/septɪk/) is an adjective: a cut or wound goes **septic** when it becomes infected.

selvedge, salvage

- The **selvedges** or **selvages** of a piece of woven cloth are the firm edges that do not fray.
- To **salvage** property is to save it, for example from a wrecked ship or a fire-damaged building.

  salvage is also a noun:

  Salvage operations have commenced.

sensual, sensuous

These adjectives relate to the senses in different ways.

- **Sensual** means relating or appealing to the bodily appetites, especially the sexual appetite:

  a sensual and voluptuous woman;

  a sensual profile; sensual lips;

  people who give way too easily to their sensual desires
- **Sensuous** is traditionally a more neutral word, meaning appealing to the senses and perceptions rather than to the intellect: things such as a beautiful sunset, soft fabrics, colours, reflections in water, give us a **sensuous** thrill.

  Sensuous is the less frequent word, and is often now used interchangeably with **sensual**.

sew, sow

- To **sew** is to stitch with a needle and thread or a sewing machine:

  I should have sewn that button back on immediately.
- To **sow** is to put seeds into the earth:

  The wheat crop was sown very late this year.

specially, especially see **especially**

speciality, specialty

The subject you **specialize** in is your **speciality** in British English and your **specialty** in American English. But **specialty** is the normal word in both British and American English for the branch of medicine that a doctor specializes in.

squash, quash

- To **squash** something is to squeeze it flat:

  Who squashed my hat?

  Metaphorically, a person or their spirits can be **squashed**, for example by a sarcastic remark.
- To **quash** the verdict of a court is to declare it invalid; to **quash** a rumour is to deny it and stop it spreading; to **quash** a rebellion is to crush or suppress it.

stanch, staunch

- The verb **staunch** (/stɔːntʃ/ or /stɑːntʃ/), meaning to stop the flow of blood from a wound, is usually spelt **stanch** (/stɑːntʃ/ or /stɔːntʃ/) in American English:

  I tried to staunch the blood.
- The adjective **staunch** (/stɔːntʃ/), meaning faithful and true, is sometimes spelt **stanch** (/stɔːntʃ/ or /stɑːntʃ/) in American English:

  staunch friends; staunch supporters

stationary, stationery

- **Stationary** is an adjective meaning 'staying still, not moving':

  a row of stationary vehicles
- **Stationery** is a noun, meaning the equipment you need for writing, such as paper, pens, pencils, erasers, envelopes, etc:

  office stationery

stile, style

- A **stile** is a step built against a wall or fence to help you climb over it:

  The footpaths and stiles are kept in excellent condition.

- **Style** is fashion, elegance or chic, or the manner in which you dress or behave:

  She dresses with style.

storey, story

- A **storey** (plural **storeys**) of a building is any of its floors or levels:

  a twenty-storey block of flats

- A **story** (plural **stories**) is a tale, or the account of an event:

  The refugees had a distressing story to tell.

  In American English the **storey** of a house is sometimes spelt **story** (plural **stories**).

straight, strait

- **Straight** is an adjective and adverb:

  a straight line; a straight answer;
  Go straight home.

  Straight can also be a noun, meaning a straight part of a race track:

  The runners are in the final straight.

- A **strait** is a narrow channel between two larger expanses of water, and is usually used in the plural :

  the Straits of Gibraltar

  You say that somebody is **in dire straits** when they are in bad trouble, especially financially.

  Strait is also an old adjective meaning 'narrow, restricting', as in **straitjacket** and **straitlaced**.

straightened, straitened

- **Straightened** is the past tense and past participle of **straighten**, to make something straight:

  He straightened his tie.

- **Straitened** is an old adjective used in expressions such as **living in straitened circumstances**, meaning 'living in poverty'.

sty, stye

- A **sty** is the enclosure in which pigs are kept:

  a row of pigsties

- A **stye** is an inflamed swelling on the eyelid:

  I often used to get styes as a child.

  This swelling can also be spelt **sty** (plural **sties**).

style, stile see **stile**

swat, swot

These verbs are both pronounced /swɒt/.

- To **swat** an insect is to hit it, for example with a folded newspaper:

  I swatted the wasp with my concert programme.

- To **swot** is to study hard, especially before an exam:

  I spent every evening swotting.

  Swot can be a noun: a person who studies hard is sometimes rudely called a **swot**.

teeth, teethe

- **Teeth** (/tiːθ/) is a plural noun:

  How many teeth has the baby got now?

- **Teethe** (/tiːð/) is a verb, meaning to produce teeth:

  The baby is teething (/ˈtiːðɪŋ/).

tenor, tenure

- A **tenor** (/ˈtenə/) is a male singer with a high voice:

  We have too few tenors.
  Can you sing tenor?

  The **tenor** of something is its general course:

  Nothing disturbed the even tenor of their lives.

That was the tenor of her remarks.

- The **tenure** (/ˈtenjə/) of a position such as a teaching post, or the **tenure** of property, is the situation of holding or possessing it, especially on a long-term basis.

text, test

- A **text** is a written work, or a passage of writing; the **text** of a book is the printed words, as distinct from the illustrations:

  closely printed text;

  Students have three set texts per term to study.
- Teachers set students a **test** when they give them a number of questions to answer on what they have been studying:

  I failed the maths test.

their, there, they're

- **Their** is a possessive determiner:

  Show the guests to their rooms.
- **There** is an adverb of place, also used like a pronoun:

  Your desk is over there.

  There are a lot of problems, aren't there?
- **They're** is a contraction of **they are**:

  They're too young to stay out late.

then, than

- **Then** is an adverb of time, also used as a connecting word:

  What happened then?

  Then I'm sorry, I can't help you.
- **Than** is a conjunction or preposition of comparison:

  You're working harder than you need to.

  He's taller than me.

thrash, thresh

- To **thrash** somebody is to beat them hard, usually as a punishment, or to defeat them thoroughly:

  He was often thrashed as a child.

  We thrashed the other team.
- To **thresh** corn is to separate the seeds from the stalks by beating.

  People **thresh** about or **thrash** about, for example while lying down, when they toss about with violent movements of the arms and legs.

tire, tyre see **tyre**

ton, tonne

These units of weight are both pronounced /tʌn/.

- A **ton** is a British and American unit equal to 2240 pounds and 2000 pounds respectively.
- A **tonne** (also called a **metric ton**) is a metric unit equal to 1000 kilograms.

trail, trial

- A **trail** of things is what you leave behind you:

  a trail of clues; a trail of footprints;

  We're following a new trail.
- A **trial** is a test, or court case at which somebody is tried:

  The drug is undergoing a number of trials.

  He stood trial for murder.

troop, troupe

- A country's **troops** are its soldiers. A **troop** of soldiers or Scouts is a company of them. **Troops** of people means large numbers of them:

  Troops of tourists visit the shrine every day.

  Troop is also a verb, meaning to move in an orderly crowd:

  We trooped into the hall.
- A **troupe** is a performing company:

  a troupe of actors; a dancing troupe

tyre, tire

- In British English **tyre** is the usual spelling for the inflated rubber covering of a vehicle wheel :

  bicycle tyres; I had to change the tyre.

  In American English the spelling **tire** is regularly used instead of **tyre**.

- **Tire** is also a verb:

  Don't tire yourself out before tonight.

  She tires easily.

urban, urbane

- **Urban** is an adjective meaning relating to the city:

  urban scenery; an urban railway

- **Urbane** describes a person or their manner, and means cultivated, debonair and sophisticated.

venal, venial

- A **venal** person is inclined to accept bribes.

- A **venial** sin is one that is forgivable or pardonable.

veracity, voracity

- **Veracity** means truth:

  He is not known for the veracity of his pronouncements.

- **Voracity** means huge appetite:

  Sharks will feed with great voracity on most other inhabitants of the deep.

waive, wave

- To **waive** a claim, right, rule or charge is not to insist on it:

  The school waives the normal lunch charges for children without the means to pay.

- You use **wave** for other noun or verb senses:

  sound waves; a wave of hysteria;

  The waves broke over the deck.

  Wave goodbye to Daddy!

wander, wonder see **wonder**

want, wont see **wont**

wet, whet

These verbs are both pronounced /wet/.

- To **wet** something is to make it damp (note that if the dampening is deliberate, the past tense and past participle is **wetted**):

  Water splashed up from the gutter and wet my dress.

  I wetted a paper napkin and wiped the baby's face.

- To **whet** somebody's appetite is to make them keen:

  The course of lectures had whetted my appetite for travel.

whether, weather

- **Whether** is a conjunction:

  It's a good idea to get yourself insured, whether the trip you're planning is a long one or a short one.

- **Weather** is a noun or verb:

  fine weather; We shall weather the storm.

wit, whit

- **Wit** is humour:

  a writer of great wit.

- **Whit** is used in the expression **not a whit**, meaning not at all:

  He was not a whit embarrassed.

wonder, wander

- To **wonder** (/ˈwʌndə/) is to ask yourself something:

  He wondered whether he had offended her.

- To **wander** (/ˈwɒndə/) is to walk in various directions, but nowhere in particular:

  We wandered through the woods.

  Your mind wanders when you stop concentrating.

wont, want

- **Wont** (/woʊnt/) is an old noun, meaning habit:

  He got up earlier than was his wont.

- **Want** (/wɒnt/) is a verb and a noun :

  What does she want?

  We can supply all your wants.

wrapped, rapped, rapt see **rapt**

yolk, yoke

Both these words are pronounced /joʊk/.

- The **yolk** of an egg is the central yellow part.
- A **yoke** is fitted over the necks of two animals to make them move together, for example to pull a plough.

  Yoke is also a verb:

  The oxen were yoked together.

your, you're, yore

- **Your** is a possessive determiner:

  Take your partners for a waltz.

- **You're** is a contraction of **you are**:

  You're joking!

- **Yore** is an old word used in the expression **of yore**, meaning formerly:

  Home was not the happy place that it had been of yore.

DO IT YOURSELF

Select the correct word to fill the gaps in the following sentences.

1 The train remained __________ in the tunnel for several hours. (**stationary/stationery**)

2 The team's __________ has never been higher. (**moral/morale**)

3 Just __________ normally. (**breath/breathe**)

4 I must go and __________ a birthday card for Liz. (**choose/chose**)

5 The latest __________ to our collection of pets is a parrot. (**addition/edition**)

6 Dad was having a little __________ in his armchair. (**dose/doze**)

7 As a publisher she had a __________ for spotting a bestseller. (**flair/flare**)

8 Some children discovered a __________ of firearms in an empty house. (**hoard/horde**)

9 I've thought of an __________ solution to the problem. (**ingenious/ingenuous**)

10 Singapore has __________ attractions. (**its/it's**)

11 The straps are made of nylon __________. (**canvas/canvass**)

12 I've no idea how long I was __________ unconscious. (**laying/lying**)

13 I love going for walks, __________ in the mountains. (**especially/specially**)

14 She nodded her head in __________. (**ascent/assent**)

15 __________ not doing __________ best. (**you're, your**)

16 They __________ their business too rapidly, and lost money. (**expanded/expended**)

17 Those swindlers __________ on innocent, trusting people. (**pray/prey**)

18 She spent most of the week __________ her exam in the library. (**preceding/proceeding**)

19 The __________ reason for my return was to attend a job interview. (**principal/principle**)

20 You must keep a tighter __________ on your emotions. (**reign/rein**)

21 Put the key in your pocket in case you __________ it. (**loose/lose**)

22 A __________ of schoolchildren were going round the museum with their teacher. (**troop/troupe**)

23 He never __________ again to his adventure with the windsurfer. (**allude/elude**)

24 This recipe requires 200 grams of __________ . (**currents/currants**)

Irregular Verbs

BASE FORM	3RD PERSON SINGULAR	PRESENT PARTICIPLE	SIMPLE PAST	PAST PARTICIPLE
be	*is* (1st person *am*, other persons *are*)	*being*	*was, were*	*been*
beat	*beats*	*beating*	*beat*	*beaten*
become	*becomes*	*becoming*	*became*	*become*
begin	*begins*	*beginning*	*began*	*begun*
bend	*bends*	*bending*	*bent*	*bent*
bite	*bites*	*biting*	*bit*	*bitten*
bleed	*bleeds*	*bleeding*	*bled*	*bled*
blow	*blows*	*blowing*	*blew*	*blown*
break	*breaks*	*breaking*	*broke*	*broken*
bring	*brings*	*bringing*	*brought*	*brought*
buid	*builds*	*building*	*built*	*built*
burn	*burns*	*burning*	*burned,burnt*	*burned,burnt*
burst	*bursts*	*bursting*	*burst*	*burst*
buy	*buys*	*buying*	*bought*	*bought*
catch	*catches*	*catching*	*caught*	*caught*
choose	*chooses*	*choosing*	*chose*	*chosen*
come	*comes*	*coming*	*came*	*come*
cost	*costs*	*costing*	*cost*	*cost*
creep	*creeps*	*creeping*	*crept*	*crept*
cut	*cuts*	*cutting*	*cut*	*cut*
dig	*digs*	*digging*	*dug*	*dug*
do	*does*	*doing*	*did*	*done*
draw	*draws*	*drawing*	*drew*	*drawn*
dream	*dreams*	*dreaming*	*dreamed, dreamt*	*dreamed, dreamt*
drink	*drinks*	*drinking*	*drank*	*drunk*
drive	*drives*	*driving*	*drove*	*driven*
eat	*eats*	*eating*	*ate*	*eaten*
fall	*falls*	*falling*	*fell*	*fallen*
feed	*feeds*	*feeding*	*fed*	*fed*
feel	*feels*	*feeling*	*felt*	*felt*
fight	*fights*	*fighting*	*fought*	*fought*
find	*finds*	*finding*	*found*	*found*
flee	*flees*	*fleeing*	*fled*	*fled*
fly	*flies*	*flying*	*flew*	*flown*

BASE FORM	3RD PERSON SINGULAR	PRESENT PARTICIPLE	SIMPLE PAST	PAST PARTICIPLE
forget	*forgets*	*forgetting*	*forgot*	*forgotten*
forsake	*forsakes*	*forsaking*	*forsook*	*forsaken*
freeze	*freezes*	*freezing*	*froze*	*frozen*
get	*gets*	*getting*	*got*	*got, gotten*
give	*gives*	*giving*	*gave*	*given*
go	*goes*	*going*	*went*	*gone*
grow	*grows*	*growing*	*grew*	*grown*
hang	*hangs*	*hanging*	*hung*	*hung*
have	*has*	*having*	*had*	*had*
hear	*hears*	*hearing*	*heard*	*heard*
hide	*hides*	*hiding*	*hid*	*hidden*
hit	*hits*	*hitting*	*hit*	*hit*
hold	*holds*	*holding*	*held*	*held*
hurt	*hurts*	*hurting*	*hurt*	*hurt*
keep	*keeps*	*keeping*	*kept*	*kept*
kneel	*kneels*	*kneeling*	*knelt*	*knelt*
know	*knows*	*knowing*	*knew*	*known*
lay	*lays*	*laying*	*laid*	*laid*
lead	*leads*	*leading*	*led*	*led*
lean	*leans*	*leaning*	*leaned,leant*	*leaned,leant*
leap	*leaps*	*leaping*	*leaped, leapt*	*leaped,leapt*
learn	*learns*	*learning*	*learned,learnt*	*learned,learnt*
leave	*leaves*	*leaving*	*left*	*left*
lend	*lends*	*lending*	*lent*	*lent*
let	*lets*	*letting*	*let*	*let*
lie	*lies*	*lying*	*lay*	*lain*
light	*lights*	*lighting*	*lighted,lit*	*lighted,lit*
lose	*loses*	*losing*	*lost*	*lost*
make	*makes*	*making*	*made*	*made*
meet	*meets*	*meeting*	*met*	*met*
mistake	*mistakes*	*mistaking*	*mistook*	*mistaken*
pay	*pays*	*paying*	*paid*	*paid*
put	*puts*	*putting*	*put*	*put*
read	*reads*	*reading*	*read*	*read*
ride	*rides*	*riding*	*rode*	*ridden*
ring	*rings*	*ringing*	*rang*	*rung*
rise	*rises*	*rising*	*rose*	*risen*
run	*runs*	*running*	*ran*	*run*
say	*says*	*saying*	*said*	*said*
see	*sees*	*seeing*	*saw*	*seen*
seek	*seeks*	*seeking*	*sought*	*sought*

BASE FORM	3RD PERSON SINGULAR	PRESENT PARTICIPLE	SIMPLE PAST	PAST PARTICIPLE
sell	*sells*	*selling*	*sold*	*sold*
send	*sends*	*sending*	*sent*	*sent*
set	*sets*	*setting*	*set*	*set*
sew	*sews*	*sewing*	*sewed*	*sewn*
shake	*shakes*	*shaking*	*shook*	*shaken*
shine	*shines*	*shining*	*shone*	*shone*
shoot	*shoots*	*shooting*	*shot*	*shot*
show	*shows*	*showing*	*showed*	*shown*
shrink	*shrinks*	*shrinking*	*shrank*	*shrunk*
shut	*shuts*	*shutting*	*shut*	*shut*
sing	*sings*	*singing*	*sang*	*sung*
sink	*sinks*	*sinking*	*sank*	*sunk*
sit	*sits*	*sitting*	*sat*	*sat*
slay	*slays*	*slaying*	*slew*	*slain*
sleep	*sleeps*	*sleeping*	*slept*	*slept*
slide	*slides*	*sliding*	*slid*	*slid*
smell	*smells*	*smelling*	*smelled,smelt*	*smelled,smelt*
speak	*speaks*	*speaking*	*spoke*	*spoken*
spell	*spells*	*spelling*	*spelled,spelt*	*spelled,spelt*
spend	*spends*	*spending*	*spent*	*spent*
spill	*spills*	*spilling*	*spilled,spilt*	*spilled,spilt*
spin	*spins*	*spinning*	*spun*	*spun*
spit	*spits*	*spitting*	*spat*	*spat*
split	*splits*	*splitting*	*split*	*split*
spoil	*spoils*	*spoiling*	*spoiled,spoilt*	*spoiled,spoilt*
spring	*springs*	*springing*	*sprang*	*sprung*
steal	*steals*	*stealing*	*stole*	*stolen*
stick	*sticks*	*sticking*	*stuck*	*stuck*
sting	*stings*	*stinging*	*stung*	*stung*
stink	*stinks*	*stinking*	*stank*	*stunk*
strike	*strikes*	*striking*	*struck*	*struck*
swear	*swears*	*swearing*	*swore*	*sworn*
sweep	*sweeps*	*sweeping*	*swept*	*swept*
swell	*swells*	*swelling*	*swelled*	*swollen*
swim	*swims*	*swimming*	*swam*	*swum*
swing	*swings*	*swinging*	*swung*	*swung*
take	*takes*	*taking*	*took*	*taken*
teach	*teaches*	*teaching*	*taught*	*taught*
tear	*tears*	*tearing*	*tore*	*torn*
tell	*tells*	*telling*	*told*	*told*

BASE FORM	3RD PERSON SINGULAR	PRESENT PARTICIPLE	SIMPLE PAST	PAST PARTICIPLE
think	*thinks*	*thinking*	*thought*	*thought*
throw	*throws*	*throwing*	*threw*	*thrown*
tread	*treads*	*treading*	*trod*	*trodden*
understand	*understands*	*understanding*	*understood*	*understood*
undo	*undoes*	*undoing*	*undid*	*undone*
upset	*upsets*	*upsetting*	*upset*	*upset*
wake	*wakes*	*waking*	*woke*	*woken*
wear	*wears*	*wearing*	*wore*	*worn*
weave	*weaves*	*weaving*	*wove*	*woven*
weep	*weeps*	*weeping*	*wept*	*wept*
wet	*wets*	*wetting*	*wet, wetted*	*wet, wetted*
win	*wins*	*winning*	*won*	*won*
wind	*winds*	*winding*	*wound*	*wound*
write	*writes*	*writing*	*wrote*	*written*

Appendix 2

ANSWERS

Page 25

1 defying
2 committing
3 slimming
4 recurring
5 focusing
6 rescuing
7 differing
8 cleansing
9 whingeing
10 enrolling
11 labelling
12 facing, tackling
13 seeing, believing
14 preferring
15 queuing
16 living, dying
17 sharing, halving
18 mimicking

Page 30

1 visited
2 spent
3 fried
4 skied
5 paid, left
6 queued, bought
7 conveyed
8 learnt (*or* learned), remembered
9 felt, satisfied
10 cancelled, postponed
11 keyed, spelt (*or* spelled)
12 denied, judged, freed
13 laid, served
14 stepped, hurried
15 agreed, deferred, known
16 leapt (*or* leaped), galloped
17 slowed, trotted
18 regretted, refused, offered

Page 33

1 relies
2 woos
3 relaxes
4 teaches
5 specifies
6 employs
7 radioes
8 worries
9 skis
10 travels

Page 40

1 campuses
2 cries
3 crises
4 bookshelves
5 casinos
6 loaves
7 tattoos
8 housewives
9 kidneys
10 skis
11 genera, species
12 handfuls
13 reefs
14 hundred, reindeer
15 volcanoes
16 comedies
17 beliefs
18 appendices
19 alibis
20 allies
21 jockeys
22 dashes, parentheses

Page 45

1 slimmer
2 stupidest
3 earlier
4 better
5 further
6 staler
7 more hopeful
8 humbler
9 most elderly, liveliest
10 heavier
11 saddest
12 sunniest
13 commonest
14 worse
15 cleverer
16 bigger

Page 49

1 pathetically
2 duly
3 gravely
4 funnily
5 shyly, politely
6 monthly
7 economically, pricily
8 nimbly
9 luckily, amazingly, quickly
10 simply, expensively
11 publicly, privately
12 wholly
13 idly, cruelly
14 wryly, finally
15 militarily, strategically
16 momentarily
17 solely
18 tactfully, hastily
19 equally, best
20 normally, orally

Page 54

1 regrettable, avoidable
2 pitiable
3 arguable

4 referable
5 chargeable, payable
6 enviable
7 advisable, unpronounceable
8 disposable
9 comparable
10 doable
11 unforgettable
12 indescribable
13 diggable
14 unmanageable
15 datable
16 transferable
17 unjustifiable
18 adorable

Page 68

A
1 deafening
2 maddening
3 worsening
4 loosening
5 freshening
6 softening
7 ripening
8 fattening

B
1 blackened
2 quickened
3 toughened
4 stiffened
5 saddened
6 widened
7 reddened
8 livened

Page 74

1 perpetrator
2 distillers
3 landowners, picnickers
4 chronicler
5 surveyor
6 demonstrators
7 doers, facilitators
8 tumble-dryer
9 pacifier
10 skier
11 narrator
12 governor
13 controller
14 burglar

Page 77

1 forceful
2 skilfully
3 unlawful
4 woefully
5 earful
6 delightfully, peaceful
7 plentiful
8 tablespoonful
9 awfully
10 wilfully
11 mercifully
12 gracefully
13 fanciful
14 disgracefully, disrespectful

Page 90

A
1 baseless
2 soulless
3 mercilessly
4 guileless
5 noiselessly
6 clueless

B
1 abridgement (*or* abridgment)
2 attachment
3 instalment
4 involvement
5 advancement
6 accompaniment.

C
1 boniness, oiliness
2 aloneness
3 shyness
4 unevenness
5 miserliness
6 naughtiness

Page 94

1 glamorous
2 generosity
3 vigorous
4 humorous
5 favourable
6 curiosity
7 honourable
8 impetuosity
9 callousness
10 rigorous
11 clamorous
12 luminosity
13 pomposity
14 monstrosity

Page 100

1 garlicky
2 frayey
3 painty
4 lacy
5 catty
6 gravelly
7 purply
8 carroty
9 spiky
10 cottony
11 gossipy
12 icy
13 snowy
14 boggy

Page 112

1 misunderstood
2 unplugged
3 rebuilt, redeveloped
4 undone
5 retold
6 rewound, replayed
7 misspelt (*or* misspelled)
8 disqualified
9 untying
10 rewritten, resubmitted
11 unwrapping
12 resurfacing
13 unbuttoning
14 miscast

Page 127

A
1 it's
2 wasn't
3 hadn't

4 oughtn't
5 couldn't you
6 we've
7 Jean's
8 shan't
9 how's
10 mustn't

B 1 have not
2 we had
3 where is
4 do not
5 it will
6 you would, you had
7 we shall (*or* we will)
8 there has
9 need not
10 will you not
11 does he not, he has
12 let us

Page 130

1 hostess's
2 Williams's
3 police's
4 weeks'
5 boys', ladies', children's, misses'
6 Frances's
7 people's
8 month's
9 actresses'
10 babies'

Page 137

A 1 sister-in-law
2 never-to-be-forgotten
3 status-conscious
4 splendidly dressed
5 twelve-month-old
6 six- or seven-week
7 out of date
8 pre-Christmas
9 brick-red
10 odd-looking
11 waist-high
12 self-conscious

B reck|on,
com|edy,
traf|fic
tra|dition *or*
tradi|tion,
mal|ice,
acknowl|edgement *or*
acknowledge|ment,
col|lege, gra|cious,
pas|sage

Page 142

1 fossilized
2 crystallize
3 perilous
4 modelling
5 distillery
6 tranquillizers
7 signalled
8 medallists
9 fulfilled
10 stillness
11 finalists
12 scandalous
13 pencilled
14 symbolizes

Page 200

1 stationary
2 morale
3 breathe
4 choose
5 addition
6 doze
7 flair
8 horde
9 ingenious
10 its
11 canvas
12 lying
13 especially
14 assent
15 you're, your
16 expanded
17 prey
18 preceding
19 principal
20 rein
21 lose
22 troop
23 alluded
24 currants